FIVE BIG MOUNTAINS

MERCER
UNIVERSITY PRESS

Endowed by
Tom Watson Brown
and
The Watson-Brown Foundation, Inc.

FIVE BIG MOUNTAINS

A Regular Guy's Guide to Climbing
Orizaba, Elbrus, Kilimanjaro,
Aconcagua, and Vinson

David N. Schaeffer

Mercer University Press
Macon, Georgia

MUP/H809

© 2010 Mercer University Press
1400 Coleman Avenue
Macon, Georgia 31207
All rights reserved

First Edition.

Books published by Mercer University Press are printed on acid free paper
that meets the requirements of American National Standard for Information
Sciences—Permanence of Paper for Printed Library Materials.

Mercer University Press is a member of Green Press initiative
(greenpressinitiative.org), a nonprofit organization working to help publishers
and printers increase their use of recycled paper and decrease their use of fiber
derived from endangered forests. This book is printed on recycled paper.

Cataloging-in-Publication Data is available from the Library of Congress

Schaeffer, David N., 1956-
Five big mountains : a regular guy's guide to climbing Elbrus, Orizaba,
Kilimanjaro, Aconcagua, and Vinson / David N. Schaeffer. -- 1st ed.
p. cm.
Includes bibliographical references and index.
ISBN-13: 978-0-88146-210-4 (hardcover : alk. paper)
ISBN-10: 0-88146-210-1 (hardcover : alk. paper)
1. Mountaineering. 2. Schaeffer, David N., 1956---Travel. I. Title.
GV200.S33 2009
796.52'2--dc22
2010025353

CONTENTS

This book is dedicated to my wife, Kim, and my children, Daniel and Lora, who have allowed me to fulfill my dreams with only minimal protestation, okay, in Kim's case, considerably loud protestations! And these stories are written in fond memory of Alexandr "Sasha" Venger, our Russian guide on Mt. Elbrus, who tragiccally died while rock-climbing in the Crimea in 2005, less than a year after he took me and two friends to the top of Europe.

ORIZABA

"Thank God For Duct Tape"

D avid, you've got to turn back," my brother yelled through the bitter wind.

"No, I've got some duct tape on my ice axe. All I have to do is wrap it around my boot and crampon so it won't come off again," I hollered back.

"You're crazy," he said. "It won't hold. It's too cold."

My fingers were quickly freezing in the sub-zero temperatures. Scratching the edge of the duct tape wrapped around my ice axe, I managed to pry a section loose. Normally pliable, the grey duct tape felt stiff and fragile as it peeled off the axe.

Perched on the forty degree slope of the Jamapa Glacier on the highest mountain in Mexico, I dared not look down at the rocks below. Careful not to lose my balance, I reached down to my right Solomon Super Mountain 8 boot and stuck the tape across the toe and around the jagged metal spikes below the steel plated sole of the boot. All the while, I stiffened my left leg which was anchored into the glacier surface by the crampon attached to my left boot. One slip and I knew I would slide 1500 feet down the steep ice and snow into the black rocks below.

With the first piece of tape securely wrapped, I returned my fingernails to the ice axe and began to work another piece of duct tape free.

"It's not going to hold," my brother warned again.

Ignoring him, I continued to pull on the tape with one hand, while steadying myself on the ice axe with the other. As my gloveless hand became numb in the cold wind, I panted for breath in the thin air. At 17,000 feet, even a slight increase in my exertion level used up most of the oxygen reaching my lungs.

After a few more minutes, I had successfully wrapped four pieces of duct tape around the front of my right boot and crampon and they felt reasonably secure. Hopefully the crampon would not slip off again. I had felt shivers down my spine both times the crampon had come loose minutes before. Had I slipped without traction, I would have been another victim on this mountain's history of casualties.

"If it comes off again, I'll turn back," I shouted to my brother. "But we've come this far and I'm not giving up yet."

He shrugged and turned his back, slowly moving away and up the slope at an angle.

Leaning onto my ice axe, I pressed my cold hand into my double-lined Gore-Tex gloves, adjusted my hand around the pick end of the axe, and then took six steps up the icy incline. The tape held for now, but my eyes remained locked on the toe of my right boot.

If only one of the other climber's guides hadn't mentioned that twelve climbers had slid to their deaths the year before on this very mountain, Pico de Orizaba.

People always ask me what got me into climbing. I tell them that this somewhat crazy, regular guy started climbing as a child.

At age 5, Mt. Pisgah, near Asheville, North Carolina, was my Mt. Everest, its radio tower rocketing skywards from its forested peak. But we really climbed it to pick the luscious blueberries at the top, not to feel the rush of making it to the summit. Then at age 8, on a trip to Italy, my family climbed Mt. Vesuvius, the famous volcano that erupted and destroyed the city of Pompeii below. I just remember it was really hot, dusty and brown. I don't recall making it to the top, but it sure was fun throwing lava rocks at my brothers on the way up.

In 1978, after graduating from Duke University (I played varsity soccer, not lacrosse), I headed out west with one of my best high school friends, Steve. There we climbed up to some frozen lakes on the high slopes of the Tetons, hiked up towards the glaciers above Lake Louise in the Canadian Rockies, got lost on some modest mountains in Olympic National Forest in Washington, and climbed to the top of Upper Yosemite Falls in a terrible rainstorm. All in Sears work boots, cut-offs and no rain gear. Fun, but stupid. I had never heard of REI and couldn't afford decent gear back then anyway.

Years later, after getting married and having two children, I soloed to the top of Alta Peak in Sequoia National Park, hiking from 6000 feet to almost 12,000 feet in one afternoon. Geez, I used to be in really good shape!

But that was it—nothing extraordinary, nothing difficult. Just fun stuff with no expense and no equipment.

Then, about eight years ago, two of my brothers, Brent and Eric, who live overseas had overlapping home leaves for the first time in about a decade. So I hatched the idea of a brothers' bonding trip to climb Mt. Whitney, which at 14,494 feet is the highest peak in the continental United States. I'm not sure why I picked Whitney, but I have always tried to push my limits and figured we were still young enough to handle the challenge. I was forty-four and my oldest brother was 51 at the time.

My other brother, Mike, the soccer coach from North Carolina, joined us for the trip. I planned to do it leisurely, not sure of everyone's fitness level. To be on the safe side, I procured a two-night back country camping permit to pitch our tents at the high camp at 12,000 feet. At that time, one had to get the permit through a mindless lottery/call-in system six months ahead of the actual climb. It took me eleven days in February to get the permit for two nights in August.

Ultimately, we struggled to make it to the high camp with full backpacks on the first day, as we had not built in time to acclimatize. After pitching our tents, we were all deliriously light-headed. The next morning, we slogged our way up the ninety-seven switchbacks and then plodded up the long stretch to the summit in record slow time, watching Boy Scout troops, middle-aged women, and a few octogenarians pass us on the way to the top. Two of my brothers were too nauseated to eat the picnic we had planned for the summit. But there were almost too many people up there to find a good place to sit anyway. When we signed the book at the little stone house at the summit, we were successful climbers #'s 125, 126, 127, and 128 that day, and it was just noon.

Let's just say that my euphoria over reaching the top was somewhat diminished by the commonness of it all. Maybe too many regular guys and gals, old and young, were able to conquer that peak. Perhaps I felt like I had not been challenged sufficiently to garner a full sense of accomplishment. Whatever it was, this regular guy decided to look for more extraordinary climbs and a stiffer challenge. I needed to find a beginner's high altitude mountain. Little did I know at the time that my search would ultimately lead me to mountains on every continent on the globe.

I never knew that the third highest mountain in North America was in Mexico. I had always assumed that Alaska, with Mt. McKinley leading the way, had all the highest peaks. But the second highest in North America is Mt. Logan in Canada, and in third place is Pico de Orizaba, south of the border.

Mt. McKinley, or Denali as it is sometimes called, was out of the question. At over 20,000 feet and so far north, that climb was fraught with life-threatening dangers. I had heard horror stories about expeditions caught in week long snowstorms with disastrous consequences on that mountain. My own two day hike in Denali National Park several summers earlier, during which I never was able to see any of the upper half of the mountain, reinforced my feeling that safety considerations ruled out an attempt to scale that peak.

So I pulled out my World Atlas and searched on the Internet for alternatives. To my surprise, I learned that Mexico boasts four or five volcanos, each higher than Whitney and all supposedly "walk-up" mountains, meaning reachable with nothing more than crampons and ice axes and no technical rock or ice climbing. My attention quickly gravitated to the largest and highest of the lot, Pico de Orizaba, with a summit at 18,851 feet − or 18,401 or 18,700 feet—depending on the particular source of the information.

Within days, I had amassed at least twenty website articles about climbing Orizaba, also known by its native name, Citlaltepetl—don't ask how that is pronounced. All the articles described the mountain as an excellent beginning step for high altitude climbers. The climb sounded so easy. No crevasses to worry about, No technical challenges, just a steady climb to the top. According to the web information, anyone in decent shape who owns an ice axe and crampons can do it. I actually believed this, and the fact that I had never worn crampons or held an ice axe before did not deter my interest in the least.

The next step was to find a trusted and equally adventuresome companion to go along for the hike. Hiking alone can be very dangerous, and climbing high peaks with someone who is not reliable, inexperienced, or is out of shape can be even more risky. My three brothers who climbed Whitney with me seemed to be reasonable candidates. However, two of them had some level of high altitude sickness—nausea and headaches—at 14,000 feet on Whitney, and they were not too thrilled about going higher. My oldest brother, Brent, who had done well on Whitney, had home leave only on alternating summers. Given that Orizaba must be climbed between November and March when the glacier is solid and avalanche risks are minimal, his participation was unlikely. So I looked outside the family.

Unfortunately, the second hardest part of climbing high altitude mountains is getting spousal permission. Several friends who normally love to hike and climb and are otherwise adventurous and in good shape sheepishly declined my invitations after speaking with their wives. The typical reaction from the fairer sex is, "You want to do what? You have small children, you know!" This is a powerful guilt trip which discourages most husbands and fathers from making climbs of a lifetime.

A simple piece of advice: if you want to climb the high mountains of the world, do it before you get married, if you can afford it. After marriage and kids, it's too easy to feel guilty about leaving your family for a few weeks at a time or risking one's life and leaving the kids fatherless. Of course, if one waits until the kids are grown, one is too old and decrepit to make it up the slope. The best alternative is to marry a wonderful woman like my wife, who may not like it, but does not stand in the way of my adventurous spirit. And then make sure you prepare, prepare, and prepare again, so as to minimize unnecessary risks, something which took several trips for me to fully understand.

In the end, Brent, then living in Cairo, came through. A well timed conference in Washington D.C. enabled him to travel back to the United

States and extend the trip long enough to climb Mexican volcanos. The trip was scheduled for December, 2001, and in July, I mapped out a careful four month training schedule to physically prepare for the climb. This consisted of dietary changes to lose weight, strenuous hill work on the steep neighborhood street on weekday evenings, and six and seven mile runs twice on the weekends. The intensity of the workouts steadily increased as I approached the trip.

Unfortunately, the events of September 11, 2001, played havoc with the schedule. My brother's conference in D.C. was postponed and a medical emergency in his family rendered the original timetable impossible. The climb was re-scheduled for the last week of January 2002.

This was not a big problem, except that, mentally, I had focused on completing the climb before Christmas, and physically, I was reaching my peak condition at the end of November, hoping to ease up on the training just a bit before embarking. I had lost 18 pounds and my cardiovascular training was completed. Now I had to extend all the training and my diet through the holidays and for another six weeks. Worse yet, I had gone without cokes, candy bars, cookies, cake, french fries, chocolate, ice cream, and all my favorite junk food for four months and I was ready to binge! Trying to avoid such temptations through Christmas is almost impossible.

Over the holidays, despite my efforts to strictly adhere to my regimen, I quickly gained five pounds back. Fortunately, I had three weeks to salvage my condition. I intensified my workouts once again through the chilly evenings in January. I knew that on summit day, I would need every bit of leg strength and endurance I could muster. I had to have a strong base on which to draw when the going got tough. Meanwhile, my neighbors thought I was truly crazy, running up and down the steep street in the freezing cold in the middle of the dark winter nights.

The flight from Mexico City to Puebla, Mexico took less than an hour, but the scenery was breathtaking. As we left the runway in Mexico City, the nearby snow covered peaks of two volcanos, familiarly known as Popo and Ixta, dominated the skyline to the east. Popo, at over 17,000 feet, was still smouldering from a recent eruption that closed that mountain to all climbers indefinitely. Due to the heat of the eruption, most of the snow on that peak had disappeared. Ixta, pronounced "Ista", is also over 17,000 feet and resembles a woman laying on her back, covered from head to toe in snow and glaciers. Many climbers use Ixta as a preliminary acclimatization trek before tackling Orizaba. However, my brother and I opted to acclimatize on another volcano close to Puebla called La Malinche.

As we approached Puebla, La Malinche loomed over the airport like a sentinel, its long lower slopes covered in evergreens and its sharp central peak glistening in the late afternoon sun. We had been told that there would be very little snow on La Malinche, but even from the airport tarmac, the entire peak looked snow-capped. Apparently, our 14,600 foot "tune up" might pose a bigger challenge than we had anticipated. Yet our driver assured us that we would not need crampons to climb the mountain. "Everyone climbs it in sneakers."

At 6:00 A.M., after a restless night in a little cabin at a State Park at the base of the mountain (altitude 10,000 feet), we started up a 3 mile paved road to the trail head for La Malinche in our sneakers. The forest was somewhat eerie in the dark and the temperature was well below freezing. I noticed the perspiration in my hair was frosting over. However, by the time we reached the trail head, or what we thought was the trail head, the sun was rising and the temperature was slowly climbing. This also described our movements as we adjusted to the altitude—slowly climbing.

The trail led us up through a thick forest, with patches of snow scattered among the trees. As we ascended, the snow patches multiplied and soon we were working our way around the snow and crossing short sections of ice. Then, without warning, the trail disappeared and we were instantly lost. Several unsuccessful efforts to locate a trail ensued. But we could see the central peak through the trees above us and decided to just keep climbing up through the snow and pines, struggling over fallen trees and erosion ditches and trying not to fall on the slippery ice patches.

"Just keep going," I said to myself. "This is just the tune-up, for crying out loud."

A half hour later, we heard human voices ahead of us, and quickly found ourselves following three Mexican youth who seemed to know their way up the mountain. Miraculously, the trail once again appeared and soon we came to a large grassy clearing with a large stream flowing down the right side fed by the snow fields above.

"Holy shit," I said out loud as I looked at the peak in front of us. The entire central volcanic peak loomed 2000 feet above us, covered from east to west in snow.

I looked down at my Nike Air sneakers, which had served me well so far, but which now seemed a tad inadequate for the rest of the climb. I assured my brother that I was told we would not need anything more than sneakers to climb this mountain, but my words were not delivered with much confidence. However, I looked at the footwear of the Mexican climbers gathered in the field next to us and no one had anything much more gripping than a pair of tattered Keds.

Gazing up at the mountain, I focused on a thin brown line that snaked through the snowy slopes up to a "shoulder" on the right side of the peak at what was probably about 14,000 feet. As I stared upwards, I began to see dark specks slowly moving up the brown line—30 or 40 specks in all. Obviously, we were not the first climbers that day.

Minutes later, Brent and I were well on our way towards the bottom of the brown line, which turned out to be a narrow, steep trail of loose scree through the snow fields on the side of the mountain.

After a mere three steps into the scree, I was gasping for breath. Like climbing sand dunes, it was two steps forward and one slip back. The dark brown sand and small black volcanic rocks provided no solid footing. Our exertion level immediately tripled, and suddenly, the altitude, now at approximately 12,500 feet, began taking its toll.

There was nothing we could do but slog up and up. Rest whenever necessary. Watch helplessly as the young Mexican lads push ahead, seemingly oblivious to the altitude. They were leaving us literally in the dust. But upward we marched, one step at a time, dragging our tired legs up the unstable slope as it got steeper and steeper. As my brother started to lag behind, I found myself taking longer and longer rests to keep contact with him. We were going to make it to the top together, or not at all.

"How ya doin', Brent?" I yelled down to him after reaching a convenient, large rock on which to sit almost two-thirds up the brown streak.

"Okay," he gasped back. "Slow and steady. I'm seven years older than you, you know."

"Yeah, but you look older than that today," I teased him. "How are the legs?"

"Tired, but I think I can make it up to the shoulder. We'll take a long rest there."

"Agreed." I needed a break too, and I was relieved that my brother was still optimistic about pushing on up the mountain.

As I slowly worked my way up the final section of scree, my thighs and calves burned with each step. I flashed back to an exercise video I once watched in which the instructor, a beefed up stud with an European accent, constantly encouraged his viewers to "feel the burn." I'd like him to "feel the burn" of the La Malinche scree torture.

Plodding step by agonizing step, I finally reached the "shoulder" and looked to my left across the thirty-five degree snow slope. Beyond it on the horizon, I could see the faint outline of Pico de Orizaba, almost eighty miles away, its Jamapa Glacier at the top majestically gleaming in the morning sunlight, I couldn't help but stop and stare at the sight of the huge volcanic shape. A photograph did not do it justice, but I snapped a shot or two to document the view and began wondering how in the hell we were going to climb that monster.

The "shoulder" was not as flat as it looked from below. In reality, it was a steep slope of hard grey ash and crushed rock leading up to an even steeper boulder field filled with large rocks and snow. Though the sun was now glaring down on us, the "shoulder" was totally unprotected and the wind whipped across the ridge. I had stripped down as I worked my way up the scree, but now I quickly covered up with every layer I had and then pulled out my Gore-Tex shell, gloves and a woolen hat. It was also time for us to enjoy a few bites of candy bar and meat sticks to replenish our energy.

However, rather than a taking the luxury of a long rest, we quickly realized that we would freeze if we didn't keep moving. Soon we were crawling on all fours straight up from one boulder to the other, trying to avoid the ice and snow nestled in between the cracks. We watched several Latinos slide precariously as they moved too quickly. Fortunately, we were in no hurry, so we took our time negotiating the terrain, making sure we had good hand and foot grips before hoisting ourselves up the rocks. I felt like a spider climbing a wall.

Soon we saw the climbers ahead of us disappear from view. The summit looked close now—just ahead—maybe 200 feet above us. All my tiredness dissolved as I felt the anticipation of reaching the top. I pressed forward, pulling up with my arms and breathing hard until I stood on a level patch of rocks at the top of the boulder filled ridge. The summit— yes, the <u>lower</u> summit!

Beyond the ridge across another boulder field and up an angled stretch of very steep snow was the true summit.

"Shit," I said to myself as my brother scrambled up behind me.

"Are you kidding me?" he said as he realized we had reached a false summit.

"Well, it's not that much further, " I said, "but no way am I gonna cross that snow in my sneakers."

Just then I saw several climbers working their way up along some rocks bordering the left side of the steep snow section.

"This way Brent," I said, as I headed in that direction.

But my brother walked ahead, aiming directly for the naked snow slope.

"Brent, it's safer this way, " I warned, pointing towards the rocks on the left. But my brother, his judgment perhaps affected by the altitude or fatigue, continued straight ahead.

I stopped, frozen in place, as Brent stepped slowly onto the 45 degree snow slope. If he slipped, there was nothing to stop him from sliding down and over a cliff into the rocks several hundred feet below. He had no ice axe or hiking pole to dig in or act as an anchor.

He carefully placed each step into the shoe marks of previous climbers and worked his way across, pausing several times to adjust his balance. I held my breath nervously until he reached the other side, then I hurriedly scrambled up the rocks on the "safe" route to join him just below the summit.

"No problem," he said nonchalantly.

"You're a dumb ass!" I responded.

Moments later, we scrambled up a fifteen to twenty foot high section of rock and pulled ourselves up onto the real summit.

What a glorious sight! A perfectly day—a crystal clear sky—and amazingly not a hint of wind. The sun warmed our sore muscles as we gave each other congratulatory hugs. We exchanged high fives with the locals who had made the summit minutes before and were already enjoying a light lunch.

To the south we could now see Orizaba clearly, its peak poking out from a stretch of lower clouds. To the west, Popo and Ixta rose across the horizon in front of the murky smog of Mexico City. We were standing at 14,600 feet, slightly more than 100 feet above Whitney, and at that time, the highest altitude I had ever achieved.

Despite the fact that it was still below freezing, we felt warm and fuzzy. Somehow in our euphoria, we forgot about our aching legs and weary lungs. We simply enjoyed the moment.

It is hard to explain the peaceful feeling which comes when a summit is reached. The sense of accomplishment and relief is overwhelming. The beauty of looking down on everything around and holding one's arms up to the sky is unsurpassed by almost any other experience. Intelligent design becomes a reality. Either that or one simply is so exhausted that the whole scene becomes surreal. Whatever it is, there is no feeling quite like it in the world.

But then reality returns. It took us five and one half hours to make it to the top and we had only three hours to make it back down to catch our ride to Tlachichuca, the little town next to Pico de Orizaba. But first we needed to replenish our energy with a delicious lunch of chocolate chip Granola bars and a few handfuls of gorp, a blend of Chex mix, peanuts, M&M's and raisins. Delicious!

Of course, more climbers are injured coming down mountains than going up. Fatigue and carelessness are the primary factors. With that in mind, Brent and I slowly worked our way down through the snowy boulder field, which seemed considerably slicker on the way down. Several times I found myself involuntarily sliding down to the next boulder, but I managed to keep my balance and control.

Once off the "shoulder" and onto the scree, we quickly realized that short careful steps on the brown dust took too much energy. Gravity was pulling us down, and soon we were sliding ten and twelve feet at time, our shoes filling with dust and sediment. We really didn't care. We just wanted to get off the steep slope and hit solid ground again. Soon my thighs were burning like a downhill skier trying to hold his tuck. But I hung in there to the bottom.

Back at the large clearing, we were surprised to see hundreds of parents and children picnicking and kicking soccer balls in the bumpy grass. All of them must have climbed hours to get there. The clearing was at least five miles from the State Park, and they had carried baskets, food and paraphernalia for their Sunday afternoon picnics. Some of them had carried babies. What for us was a strenuous and exhausting mountain hiking "tune up" was a weekend tradition for the people of Puebla—a Sunday afternoon walk halfway up the local volcano.

It was an amazing scene, but we couldn't dawdle. We dragged our tired legs over the ridge and pressed down through the forest. Breathing became easier with every step as we descended. We knew we would make it once we saw the paved road below. Exactly nine hours after we headed up the road that morning, we collapsed in the parking lot of the State Park and awaited the arrival of our ride to Orizaba. I don't think we could have walked one step further.

Sipping light beers at an outdoor café on the town square in Tlachichuca that evening, Brent and I could not keep our eyes off the stunning peak filling the horizon just to the left of the church bell tower at the other end of the square. Orizaba soared into the sky and looked incredibly imposing as clouds crossed well below the peak. We could just imagine the cold as we saw gusts of wind sweep across the Jamapa Glacier. We began to pray for good weather.

One block from the square, the Reyes family compound was surrounded by high walls topped by barbed wire, as if there was something very valuable inside. However, once inside, we saw only a few well-traveled Land Rovers, a truck that looked like a paddy wagon, and a lot of used automobile parts and tires scattered across a small grassy enclosure. To the right was a long house with a bed of pretty red flowers soaking up the sun in front. To the rear on the left was a smaller building, which housed all of the bathroom and showers for the complex.

Inside the long building was surprising cool. The first room contained multiple flags from hikers all over the world and some comfortable couches and chairs around a cold pot-bellied stove. Hiking and climbing books and magazines were strewn everywhere—on tables, shelves, chairs and window sills. Beyond the first room was a chamber full of hiking gear, duffle bags, and camping equipment. All of our gear had to be stored in this room 24/7 while at the compound. Up some narrow steps in the middle of the building, we were led to the dormitory, a large room filled with some of the narrowest bunk beds we had ever seen. Up to thirty-six climbers, both male and female, could sleep in this room at a time. But if one needed to urinate in the middle of the night, one had to creep across the creaky floor, down the stairs, across the long room, through the grassy courtyard, and into the small latrine building on the other side.

The remainder of the large building contained an impressive kitchen, filled with the aroma of freshly baked bread, a spacious dining area with three long tables and a dusty "movie" room which looked like it was never used.

The Reyes family has been facilitating climbing groups on Orizaba for several generations. We had been ferried from Puebla by one of the younger generation, who clearly exuded an air of superiority among the hired help and other members of the family at the compound. He was bilingual, but most of the other family members, cooks and drivers did not seem to speak a word of English. The Reyes family is not a mountain guide service. Rather they provide accommodations and transport to the base hut at about 13,500 feet on Orizaba, commonly referred to as Piedra Grande. Then climbers are on their own unless they have brought private guides with them.

We, of course, had no guides and planned to climb this "beginner," high altitude mountain alone. It seemed like a good idea at the time.

Some of our gear did not make it to Puebla airport by the time we had left for La Malinche, so I had to travel back to Puebla to retrieve the gear the day after we arrived in Tlachichuca. We had been warned about unexpected losses of baggage and the need to include several days of surplus time in our itinerary. As it turned out, my legs were so sore from the climb up La Malinche, a day relaxing in the soft seat of a taxi was not a bad thing. However, by the time I returned to the Reyes compound that night, my legs were so stiff I could hardly walk. Fortunately, the following day, despite what appeared to be a pretty sunny day in the town, we were told the weather did not look good and were advised to rest one more day before moving onto the mountain.

I sat out in the sun that day, warming and rubbing my legs for hours, just trying to relax the muscles and relieve some of the pain. A few Tylenol tablets gave me some relief, but I feared I would not be able to hike again for days. My brother's legs were also sore, but he seemed to be able to at least move around without groaning.

That evening a large contingent arrived back from the mountain and, over dinner, shared their experiences. One man and his private guide had made it to the top without too much difficulty, though the guide said he had to attach ropes to the climber near the top when he got a bit nauseous and unsteady. One large group with some female guides had very mixed results. One guy in the group had made it up to the crater rim, but not to the summit. Two others had turned back halfway up the Jamapa Glacier, and one female climber had vomited and stopped at the bottom of the glacier. That whole group appeared to be in such questionable shape that I wondered why they tried the ascent in the first place. Another young couple had made it to the top and did not look too worse for the wear, but the young lady confessed that most of her fingers and both of her feet were completely numb. She had climbed in regular hiking boots and had inadequate gloves. Another young stud had lost his sunglasses and had climbed without eye covering. He was now snow-blind, almost unable to see, and in a great deal of pain. Fortunately, by the next morning his condition had improved considerably. Needless to say, proper equipment and clothing is critical to successful and safe climbing.

The professional guide queried us about our high altitude experience and training with crampons and ice axes. We sheepishly told him that we had climbed only 14,000ers and that we would be using crampons for the first time. He frowned with a look of disgust which had "beginners" written all over it. Then, he asked if we knew that twelve climbers had slid to their deaths on the Jamapa Glacier the prior January. Brent and I glanced nervously at each other and did not respond.

"Be careful and if it gets to hairy, don't be stupid," the guide advised, then excused himself, apparently having already sized us up as idiots.

I went to bed that night with far too many thoughts and concerns to fall asleep. The two foot wide bunk bed combined with the entire dog population of the damned town barking all night did nothing to help my restlessness.

Somehow, through it all, I must have dozed for several hours, because in the morning, I felt rejuvenated and my legs miraculously felt brand new. The pain in my thighs and calves had disappeared. The sun was out and Orizaba looked magnificently clear. There were no clouds in sight and by 8:00 A.M. the Jamapa Glacier was gleaming in the sun-light. Regardless of the warnings, it was time to go for it.

We packed up our gear, with full backpacks, camping and cooking gear. The first night would be in a hut, but we planned to hike up into a valley just below the glacier on the second day and sleep in a tent at a high camp before making our assault on the summit. Some climbers choose to hike all the way to the top from the base hut, but we felt that would be too demanding and that another night acclimatizing was the safer course.

The ride to the base hut was not what we had expected. First we drove along flat dirt roads next to plowed fields, stopping several times to take photos. But soon the road got very steep. Then it completely disappeared. We were "off road" in the paddy wagon looking vehicle, which obviously had four-wheel drive but had no padding on the seats lining the back cab. As the truck hit rocks and muddy ditches and narrowly missed trees, we were thrown up and down and against the sides of the truck while trying to avoid hitting our heads on the ceiling or cracking our spines on the metal supports along the back of the seats. Uncomfortable hardly describes the experience.

After what seemed like five hours, but which was really only slightly over three, we cleared the forested areas and sped across a well worn road on a long rise towards the base hut at "Piedra Grande." At 2:00 P.M., the sun was beating down on the hut and the rocks were warm to sit on. As we unloaded our gear and grabbed a bit of lunch, we scanned the steep section of rocks, scree and long strips of snow directly above the base hut.

One by one, hikers appeared from the snowy valley above, removed their crampons, and worked their way down the rock and scree. A couple of braver climbers kept their crampons on, stayed on the steep snow patches, and quickly descended to the rocky path leading to the base hut. As they arrived, we learned that some of them had made it to the top that day, some did not. However, all of the climbers had to be back at the base hut by 3:00 P.M. to catch their return ride to Tlachichuca in the miserable paddy wagon in which we had ridden up.

Three o'clock passed and there were still two climbers unaccount-ed for. Concerned looks heightened on the faces of the hikers that had made it down. However, the driver and one of the Reyes crew with a radio did not seem worried. They hummed or sang Mexican tunes, interrupted only by their cutting up of orange slices, chewing and spitting out seeds.

Finally, the last two climbers appeared at the top of the scree and waved to let their friends know they were okay. The slow pace of their descent indicated complete exhaustion, and, when they reached the base hut, they collapsed on some rocks, swearing that they would never do this again. Brent and I looked at each other. I could tell he and I were thinking the same thing. All of the guys who had just come down were at least fifteen years younger than us and appeared to be in excellent physical condition. This was going to be tougher than we thought. I wondered if we were too old to successfully climb this peak.

After the paddy wagon headed down the mountain, I decided to scout around the area above the hut. We had been told that thieves regularly frequented the area and that we would need to leave nothing in the hut while we climbed. Any extra gear would need to stowed in a padlocked duffle bag and hidden in the rocks. As I searched for an appropriate hiding place, I suddenly realized that I had walked into a memorial rock garden of sorts. Metal crosses and painted epitaphs were scattered among twelve to fifteen large rocks. Each rock had the name of a climber and the date he had died on this mountain. A significant number of them were from just the year before—not a reminder that I needed at that particular moment.

I quickly retreated out of the area. This was now no longer a fun and carefree adventure on a beginner's mountain. Real people had died on the slopes above—lots of them and recently. I had never worn crampons before or climbed with an ice axe, and suddenly I was looking at grave markers.

That evening Brent and I cooked some freeze-dried stew on our tiny Whisperlite camping stove and silently ate our meal in the hut. There was very little to say, but the tension was clear from the looks in our eyes.

Some Austrians showed up in the early evening, and we watched as they hiked furiously up the steep scree and rock section as if it was flat. These guys were in unbelievable shape. When they returned, we were surprised to learn that they were just doing some trekking and would not be going to the top.

After dinner that night, we noticed a tent had been erected in the rocks above the hut and learned that two more climbers had been up to the glacier that day just for acclimatization. They told us they would be going up with their tent to the high camp the next day and planned to go for the summit the following morning. This was exactly our plan and it felt good to know that we would not be alone up on the mountain when it counted.

When asked why they weren't staying in the hut, they laughed and said the hut was infested with rats. They preferred their tent. Brent and I glanced once more at each other. Rats, thieves, and a mountain full of memorials is not exactly what I had bargained for when I signed up for this trip.

There were three levels of plywood bed racks in the base hut and Brent and I chose the second floor accommodations. With a bedroll and a sleeping bag, it was comfortable enough. Even a mild headache and the scratching of the rats below, I quickly fell asleep and, according to my brother's account the next morning, I was soon snoring up a storm. However, it was not a storm that woke us up at about 3:00 A.M., but a small earthquake.

"What the hell is that?" I asked as I sat straight up and felt the entire hut shaking.

"Have you never been in an earthquake before?" Brent queried.

"Hell no, where do you think I'm from, California?" I responded.

For about thirty seconds the whole world around us shook and swayed back and forth. It was a minor tremor, but scary enough to keep us up the rest of the night.

In the morning, we checked outside the hut and there was no sign of damage. The weather was beautiful and the sun was already starting to warm up the rocks. It was as if nothing had happened. We decided to ignore the quake and hope for the best.

After a good breakfast, we carefully packed the necessary gear into the backpacks, and stowed all extra clothing, books and equipment in a padlocked duffle bag. Just dragging the bag for two or three minutes to the hiding place I had picked was an effort. By the time I returned to the hut, I was completely breathless. Yet we had to climb up the steep rock and scree wall in front of us for at least two hours with full, sixty pound backpacks, then three more hours up a sloping valley of snow.

That is the problem with training to climb very high mountains. One can never actually train at the height to be achieved. Atlanta is under 1000 feet in altitude, so I wondered whether my faithful hill work would hold up under real climbing conditions. It was time to find out.

Soon after working our way up the rocky trail, we wished we had gotten up earlier, before the sun was a factor. Even though we were at almost 14,000 feet, the temperature soared as we climbed into the late morning. By 11:00 A.M., we were able to progress only fifty feet at a time before having to rest and take water breaks. The day before, watching the Austrians zoom up this section (without backpacks), it seemed so easy. But in real time, we began to understand why some climbers skip the high camp just to avoid having to climb with heavy backpacks up the scree. It seemed like we were crawling by the time we reached the top of the rocks. As we collapsed at the top, we could see the long valley of snow before us. Thankfully, the rest of the day would be a gradual climb.

After a short lunch, it was time to break out the crampons. Brent had a traditional strap-on pair that he had rented from the Reyes family compound. I had purchased a "state of the art" pair of step-in crampons which had a metal bar across the toe that fit snugly like a ski binding onto a compatible set of mountain boots. The heel snapped on tightly and there was a built-in rubber strap around the heel. I had pre-adjusted the settings back in Atlanta, and the crampons felt well-secured.

We kept a fairly leisurely pace on the afternoon hike up to the high camp. The only difficult part was keeping our breathing steady as the air got thinner and trying to avoid "postholing" into the snow where it was starting to melt in the sun. One step down to my thigh in the deep snow quadrupled my heart rate and exertion level. As a result, whenever possible, we kept to the shadowy sections of snow which were still firm.

Despite the sun overhead, it was cooler here in the valley, and the scenery was beautiful. We felt like special visitors to an amazing winter wonderland. The sun glistened against the ridges of rocks to our left and the Jamapa Glacier shone like a huge, slanted ice rink above us, until it dipped behind the imposing wall of rock and snow at the end of the valley as we reached the high camp.

Or what we thought was the high camp. Actually, it was a nice area for a camp, but the designated, sheltered area with rock walls for the tents was hidden behind an escarpment just beyond where we stopped. Of course, we discovered that too late the next day.

In any case, we scraped a clear area of fine scree on which to erect our tent, with only a few rocks to interrupt the soft powder under our tent floor. At almost 16,000 feet, we felt fortunate to be able to camp on ground rather than snow or ice, so we were pleased with our effort. And an effort it was. Just working with the tent poles and pounding a few stakes into the ground exhausted us and left us gasping for air.

By 5:00 P.M., the sun started to descend below the high rocks on our right and the temperature dropped precipitously in a matter of minutes. We promptly added clothing and prepared a quick dinner of soup and gorp. By the time the meal was over, we had no option but to sip down some hot chocolate with the remaining boiled water and call it a night, as the cold and wind was rapidly descending on us. Soon I was huddled inside my twenty below mummy bag in two layers of thermal fleece, gloves and a woolen hat. Still I was shivering down to my bones. The one rock on my side of the tent seemed to be placed just in the wrong spot and poked into my lower ribs, making sleep almost impossible. By 9:00 P.M., I had pulled on every layer I had brought. It was still freezing cold, but I was able to maintain a manageable body temperature inside my sleeping bag. Somehow I fell asleep, dreaming of a glorious summit the next day. The alarms on our watches were set for 3:00 A.M., with the goal of beginning our summit push before four o'clock.

I woke up, stiff and frozen, with my back aching from the rock pushing up into my sleeping bag. All was quiet except for the gentle breathing from my brother's side of the tent. The wind had subsided, but it was horribly cold. I looked at my watch and struggled to find the button to light the digital time display. It was 2:52 A.M., just about time to get up. For a moment, I thought about turning over and going back to sleep and forgetting about the climb ahead.

"Why don't we just stay here and then go down in the afternoon and say we made it to the top?" I asked myself. No one would ever know. "Just say the camera didn't work, but the view from the top was amazing."

Then I figured I hadn't come all this way to turn back now. I searched for my flashlight, contact case and water bottle. The water bottle had partially iced over, but a few drips came out—just enough to rinse my contacts and get them into my eyes. They felt goopy, but after a few blinks seemed okay.

By now, Brent was stirring and moaning just like I had a few minutes before.

"Ready or not," I announced. "Want some granola bars and Vienna sausages for breakfast before we head out?"

Brent groaned and turned back over.

I decided to check out the weather and see what we were in for. I was already almost fully dressed for the climb and just had to pull on my boots to crawl outside. The zipper on the front of the tent was frosted over, but after a few attempts it slid up and around the flap and I was able to slide out.

What I saw was incredible. The sky, completely clear of clouds, was absolutely filled with stars from east to west and south to north. The moon was full, shining like a beacon. The entire landscape and snow leading up to the glacier was fully lit up. We would not need any headlamps on this climb. I marveled at the sight for a few minutes, until I realized that I was getting really cold again.

"Brent, it's amazing out there. Perfect. You should see the stars. And the wind is completely gone. Let's get going!" I could not hide my excitement.

"Alright, alright," he said, wriggling out of his sleeping bag.

Thirty minutes later, I zipped close the tent flap and headed up the mountain with nothing but water, a first aid kit, a rope, a few candy bars, gorp mix, meat sticks, and an extra fleece inside my day pack. I wanted to be as light as possible, because from here on, we were going straight up.

As we scaled the steep section leading up to the glacier, we quickly realized why crampons and ice axes were essential on this climb. At twenty five degrees, the slopes were steep enough to slide a long way without good traction. But the crampons eliminated any slippage, the ice axe poked into the snow provided a secure anchor. I found myself moving quickly up and up, my progress slowed only by the difficulty breathing and the need to keep together with my brother.

After an hour of climbing, I had fallen into a steady and monotonous pace, resting on rocks as needed and drinking plenty of water. Brent kept close behind, but I had time to admire God's handiwork. The stars now looked so close that I almost felt I could just reach up and pluck them right out of the dark sky. Looking down was just as clear. The lights of Tlachichuca were twinkling on the plain below and I wondered if the dogs were already barking to announce the approach of dawn.

By 6:00 A.M., we climbed over a crest and the Jamapa Glacier rose before us in all its glory. Just imagine a triangular, snow-covered ice rink almost 3000 feet high and 4000 feet wide at the base angled upwards at thirty to forty-five degree angle with the slope increasing in steepness all the way to the narrow top. The glacier formed almost a perfect cone covering the entire peak of the volcano. Other than a large outcropping of rocks directly to our right, the glacier and snow appeared entirely smooth, with no rocks exposed anywhere. While this was a beautiful sight, it also meant that there was nowhere to sit and rest—anywhere.

We kept moving, following a set of wands which marked the route at an angle heading slightly towards the right side of the glacier. We stayed clear of icy patches and drifts of snow where possible and tried to climb only on areas of hard packed snow that had formed a certain firmness from hours of melting during the day and re-freezing at night.

By seven o'clock, we had climbed maybe a quarter of the glacier and we began to see a glimmer of orange-pink light on the horizon to our right. The moon was descending in the sky to our left. As dawn approached, the light emanating from the sun below the horizon and the moonbeams collided, creating a prism-like merger of light resembling a shadowy mountain in mid-air. I stopped to take a photo of this amazing phenomenon, nearly losing my balance as I tried to steady the camera for the shot.

"Okay, no more photos until the top," I said to myself cautiously.

Moments later, I felt a loss of traction on my right foot. Looking down, I realized that my right crampon had released from the toe clip and was dragging behind my foot, attached only by the gray plastic strap around my ankle.

"Shit! When did that happen?"

"Hold on Brent, I've got a problem," I yelled across the glacier to my brother.

We stopped and without too much difficulty, I was able to reattach the crampon until it felt snug.

"Okay, let's get going again," I said as I took a few steps up the slope.

I didn't get fifty feet before I looked down again and the damned crampon was dragging behind me again.

The expletive I uttered at that time is unprintable, but needless to say, I was a bit upset. How was I supposed to climb this glacier without two fully secure crampons?

Fortunately, I had the cure-all. Duct tape. And lots of it!

As I began to feel comfortable with my patchwork duct-tape bindings, I kept an eye on the two climbers who appeared to be about an hour ahead of us. They were specks on the right side of the glacier and seemed not to be moving much, if at all. My brother also seemed to be slowing down as the slope got steeper and steeper. The gradual 25-degree slope had increased to 30-35 degrees and the tip of my ice axe was going into the snow and ice at a level higher than my knees ahead of me. Worse yet, the slope clearly looked like it got steeper and steeper the higher we got. My brother started veering to the right to try to attack the slope at a lower angle. But the glacier was conical and whether going straight up or at an angle made little difference. I continued climbing directly up the wand line and tried not to look down behind me.

At approximately 17,500 feet, my brother started angling back towards me.

"David," he yelled, "I'm not going any further. It's getting too steep for my comfort level."

"What? You've got to be kidding me!" I shot back. We had agreed that we would go to the top together and would not split up. I could not believe that I had come this far and, just when I was starting to get near the top, I might have to turn around. I felt fine physically, and though the mountain was somewhat steeper than I had anticipated, I had not lost my nerve yet. I'm sure the frustration showed clearly on my face.

"Look, if you are comfortable with it, go on up. Don't mind me. I can dig out a seat in the snow and enjoy the view," he said to me.

"Are you sure you don't want me to turn around and just come down with you? We agreed to stay together."

"David, I'm not going to hold you back. Go for it if you want to. I'll wait here for you on the way back down."

"No, you should at least go back down to the bottom of the glacier and get off this slope."

"I feel better staying right here where I can see your progress, and I might go over there to get a better look at that rock outcropping," he said, pointing to the right.

"Okay...be careful. I better get going. I will see you right back here as soon as I can get up to the top and back down."

I knew I was taking a risk by going up solo. Everyone always says that you should never climb alone. I justified it to myself by knowing that two climbers were ahead of me and by thinking that it was only about an hour up to the top from where I left Brent.

But after another hour, it still looked just as far to the top. I knew I was making progress as I watched snowdrifts or creases in the snow, which were actually tiny crevasses, go by me and disappear below me. But every time I looked up, the crater rim, or what I thought was the crater rim, looked just as far away.

Just when I had gotten used to a steady, repetitive rhythm of ten steps up and dig in and rest, the ground in front of me was suddenly wide open. I could see fifty feet down into an icy green crevasse about one foot wide at the top, but quickly widening to five or six feet just below the surface.

"Shit," I said out loud as I came to an immediate halt. They had told us there were no crevasses. I quickly wondered whether the ice on which I was standing would hold me. I glanced to my left and to my right and the crevasse went as far as I could see in either direction. Without thinking, I took a deep breath and leaped upwards across the opening, landing in a crouch and digging in hard with both crampons and my ice axe. A stupid, senseless move, but nevertheless the crevasse was behind me.

I quickly climbed ten more steps and stopped to catch my breath and to regain my senses.

Nothing is going to stop me now.

The slope was now forty-five degrees and I could stand almost straight up and touch the snow in front of me with my hands at chest height without even stretching out my arm. My water bottles were frozen at the top and only a trickle of water was available to quench my thirst as I struggled to climb up and up. My ten step rhythm decreased to eight, then seven, then five, and soon I was only able to take three steps up before resting for a good 20-30 seconds.

But I felt fine. My legs did not ache. I had no headache. I had no sense of time or danger. I was alone on the mountain with only my own breathing and the crunch of my crampons to keep me company. I just kept going—up and up—oblivious to anything around me.

My isolated thoughts were interrupted by noise from my right.

"Hey, guy, are you okay...the summit is around that way...to the right," I heard someone say.

I looked up and saw that the two climbers who had been ahead of us were coming back down.

"Did you make it?" I asked. "How much further?"

"It's not that far now—probably another forty-five minutes. But you need to head up to the right to get to the summit," one of them responded.

"I'm going straight up to the crater rim and then go around at the top," I responded, repeating the advice one of the guides had given us down at the village.

"Okay, good luck. Be safe and we'll see you back at the hut," the other said as they resumed their descent.

A few minutes later I reached a small ridge of rocks which I had thought for hours was the crater rim. But on arrival, I looked up and realized that my eyes had been playing tricks on me. Now I could see the clear line of the crater rim—another 500 feet above me.

Tears formed in my eyes as I vacillated on whether to continue. I had no climbers above me as a safeguard, I had no rope, no safety cushion, no one with whom to share the summit. My right crampon was still holding together by the incredible duct tape, but it looked like it might give away anytime.

Give it up, David. You've made it higher than ever before. The summit is not that important. Just let it go.

"NO!" I said out loud.

I'm almost there. Don't you dare stop now you wimp.

I took a swig from a new bottle of water, adjusted my day pack and sunglasses and resolved to go on.

With renewed vigor following my indecisive rest, I pushed back up to eight steps at a time, resolving not to decrease the pattern until I reached the crater rim where I knew I could sit down.

Now I knew what it took for the other climbers we had met at the Reyes compound to have felt good about making the crater rim, even if they did not make the summit. I wondered how I would feel when I reached the rim.

A half hour later, I collapsed on the bare dirty ground of the crater rim just beyond the jagged edge of the top of the glacier. Ten feet beyond the glacier edge, the ground dropped off steeply into the crater of the volcano. It was an almost perfectly preserved upside down cone, but the rim to my left was much lower than the rim to my right. As I looked over towards where I thought the summit should be, I saw a tall rocky peak with a razor sharp top to it.

"No way I'm going up that," I said to myself, thinking it was the summit peak.

I sat down, disgusted that I had come this far and now the summit seemed out of reach again.

But then I remembered that the summit photos I had seen had an old rusty cross at the top and there was no sign of any cross on the peak to my right.

Where the hell is the summit?

I started towards that sharp peak. When I neared it, I saw boot prints in the glacial snow around it to the right. Back on the top of the glacier, I followed the trail around the peak, and lo and behold, on a ridge another 200 yards ahead of me, the old cross lay diagonally on the ground, the top and left side of it clearly visible from my vantage point. *The summit!*

Suddenly, I felt like I was on a cloud. I do not remember crossing the last 200 yards. The sun was warm, my legs were fresh, my spirits were revived. Moments later I stood next to the cross with my arms thrust up towards the sky. Everything was perfect again.

"YES!" I shouted.

Once again I found myself wiping tears away from my eyes. I looked at my watch. It was 10:15 A.M. I had been climbing upwards non-stop for well over 6 hours.

I looked around. Everything was now below me. The peak that I thought was the summit was a little notch on the crater rim. It looked like nothing. Across the way, I could easily see La Malinche, over 4000 feet below. Further beyond, barely visible on the horizon, Popo and Ixta gleamed through the hazy air towards Mexico City.

Standing alone on top of Pico de Orizaba, higher than anyone in North America that day, I wanted someone with whom to share my euphoria. But I was there by myself, with no one even to take my photo.

Making sure the cross was behind me, I held my camera out in front of me, stretching my arm as far as it would go before snapping a few shots. It looked stupid, but no one was there to make fun. I just hoped the photo would show me with part of the cross behind me to prove I had made it to the top.

The descent was treacherous to say the least. Before I stepped back onto the glacier, I found a roll of white athletic tape in my pack and carefully wrapped my entire right boot and crampon until it was firmly and irreversibly secure. If my crampon came off on the way down the forth-five degree slope, I would be a goner. I was taking no chances now.

Rather than returning to where I first reached the crater rim, I followed the steps, presumably of the two climbers who had reached the top before me, which led diagonally across the top of the glacier. Here the surface was ribbed in sharp vertical sheets of ice, but the tops of the sheets were softer and served almost as steps leading away from the rim. The other climbers had obviously gone down this way and I followed their steps until the surface became smoother.

With the steepness, it was almost impossible to go straight down, so I began working my way to the right for about fifty feet and then turned and went left and down sideways for another fifty feet, constantly digging in my ice axe in the slope above me for balance. The downward switchbacks took some of the pressure off of my thighs, which rapidly began to ache from the exertion of keeping my upper body close to the slope and not tipping outwards.

On occasion, I stopped to rest and marvel at the mountain below me. The bottom of the glacier, which was 25-30 degrees in steepness looked almost flat from above. I still could not see Brent or the other climbers. I figured Brent was probably in the area obscured by the steep slope below me and the other climbers were likely already off the glacier.

I kept working my way down, zigzagging along for what seemed like hours. Slowly the slope eased and there was Brent, standing with his arms wrapped across his body for warmth.

"I made it," I shouted when I saw him.

"It's about time. I'm starting to get cold," he replied, smiling.

"Well let's get the hell out of here, then. We have to get back down to the hut by 3 o'clock," I said happily.

It was 1:15 P.M. by the time we finally reached our high camp at just under 16,000 feet. We collapsed inside the tent, intending to rest just for five minutes. Fifteen short minutes later, I woke up and shook Brent.

"We've got to go. I'm not staying on this mountain another night."

We hastily packed our gear and jammed the tent into its case. Our backpacks were not very organized, but everything was stuffed or tied on for the slog back down the snow valley.

As we reached the bottom of the valley and the top of the scree section at 2:45 P.M., both of us were almost too exhausted to stand. But the time was too short to slowly work our way down the scree, so we did what we had seen others do two days before. We went straight down the steep tongues of snow that divided the scree. Much faster, but clearly the more difficult choice. After about 15 minutes of severe damage to our thigh muscles, we reached the bottom of the snow, leaving only a few hundred yards of rocky trail to the hut.

We could see the paddy wagon already at the hut. I recognized the two climbers from the colors of their jackets and the drivers from the Reyes family compound waiting for us to arrive. I waved at them, knowing that our trek was over and we had made it back just in time. More importantly, we had made it back safely.

In retrospect, it is hard to believe all the mistakes and risks I took on the Mexico trip. First, though I thought I did a good job of researching the mountain, I obviously did not do so sufficiently to learn what dangers were in store. Second, I never considered hiring a guide because internet trip reports (which, as I have learned, are rarely accurate) recounted multiple unguided ascents to the top without complications. Third, though I purchased great boots and what was supposed to be "state of the art" crampons, I did not try them out on any safer, small mountain before heading for Mexico. Fourth, even after my crampons failed and my brother turned back, I kept going with duct-taped spikes tenuously attached to my right boot. Finally, with no rope, no crevasse training, and no intelligence at all, I hurdled a potentially dangerous crevasse uphill at forty degrees with no one there to save me if I stumbled or fell in.

Orizaba is the last high altitude mountain I have climbed without an experienced guide.

ELBRUS

"If At First You Don't Succeed..."

D o you vant to go on?" our Russian guide, Sasha, yelled from a foot in front of my face.

I could barely hear him above the roar of the sixty mile an hour wind and deluge of frozen sleet and hail slamming against my face and glacier glasses.

"What?" I shouted back, still not focusing on the issue to be decided.

I looked around and could see nothing. We were in a "whiteout," a dense snowstorm at an altitude of 17,875 feet on Mt. Elbrus, the highest mountain in Europe.

Sitting slumped in the snow beside me was an overweight English policeman, a member of our team who had somehow made it to the "saddle" between the two volcanic peaks of Elbrus. The Brit was now almost incoherent.

I looked at my brother, Brent, his beard and moustache caked in ice and his jacket coated thick with frosty snow particles. He uttered no words, his mind and body apparently numb from relentless uphill climbing since we had left the base hut six hours hence. My friend Jim from Atlanta, standing next to Brent, looked like he could keep climbing, but he appeared less than confident about going higher in this storm.

The fifth member of our team, a small, but gnarly climber from Canada decked out in yellow North Face gear from head to toe, appeared ready to go for the summit, no matter the conditions.

"Do you think ve should turn back, Dah-bid?" Sasha asked again, this time only inches from my face.

"It's pretty bad," I shouted into the wind. "I can't see anything. The Brit looks wiped out. Brent is exhausted. What do you think?"

"Ve can go up if you vant. I have compass and altimeter to guide us," Sasha offered.

Are you crazy? We can't see ten feet in front of us. What good would it be to go to the top in this blizzard and not be able to see anything anyway? We might never get down.

The blitzkrieg of wind and snow blasting across the "saddle" pelted us even harder as I tried to make sense of our situation. There was nowhere to get away from it – no rocks to hide behind – no shelter to use as a refuge. My Julbo glacier glasses were coating over with about a quarter inch of solid ice, making vision through the lenses impossible. I nudged them down a notch on my nose so I could look out above them, only to get an eyeful of sleet. My hands were frozen and my face was whipped.

Two days of travel across the world to this remote area not far from Chechnya, five days of acclimatization under nearly perfectly clear blue skies, and now 700 vertical feet from the summit, suddenly I was faced with the ultimate mountain climbing decision. Should I go forward and risk not making it back, or turn around and miss the opportunity to bag my first of the Seven Summits, maybe never to return? Five months of intensive training and sacrifice were rapidly going down the drain.

"Damn it, this sucks!" I yelled at the top of my lungs.

"Let's go to the top. Don't be woosies!" the English bloke jeered deliriously as he tried to get up from his sitting position. He stumbled as he managed to rise up to his full height, then covered his face with his arms as the snow blasted him. "I'm ready to go."

He looked anything but ready.

"Sasha, is it safe to go up – yes or no?" I screamed at our guide through the wind.

"Sure..." he responded, a reply I had already learned meant anything but "sure." Sasha regularly replied "sure" when he didn't understand the question or if he didn't want to concern us.

"Ve must rope up – too many crevasses – can't see – don't vant to lose anyone," Sasha added, his gold-capped tooth sparkling as he grinned against the elements.

Great! We can't see anything. Crevasses all around us. Wind and a brutal snowstorm knocking us off our feet. A crazy Brit to drag us down. And an indecisive Russian guide.

My head was telling me to turn around.

Don't be crazy. Kim and the kids want you to come back.

But my heart was telling me I'll never get another chance. How many times does an Atlantan get to travel to Caucasus mountain range in Southern Russia, halfway between the Black Sea and the Caspian Sea. *It's just another 700 feet.*

The Canadian in the yellow North Face gear drew near. "David, whatever you decide is okay with me," he yelled in my ear. Then he added, "I'd like to go to the top, but it's not worth risking our lives. Your call, one way or the other. I'll support your decision."

Brent and Jim looked at me, shrugging their shoulders, as if to say it was up to me. I had organized the trip, however I was not really prepared to make this decision alone. Nevertheless, I knew everyone was looking at me to make the call. Why was I hesitating?

Finally Jim broke the silence. "I'd rather come back when we can see the view from the top."

"Me too, " I replied, instantly latching onto the logical solution offered by my friend. "Let's turn around," I announced to the group.

"You're climbing Everest?" my neighbor asked as I rested from yet another trip up the steep hill above my house during one of my training sessions.

"No, not Everest. I'm not that crazy. I'm going to climb Mt. Elbrus—E-L-B-R-U-S – in Russia. It's the highest mountain in Europe."

"I thought the Matterhorn and Mount Blanc were the tallest mountains in Europe."

"Mont Blanc is the tallest in the Alps. But the Caucasus mountains in Russia are much bigger and higher. Elbrus is over 3000 feet higher than anything in the Alps."

"Oh – never heard of it."

"That's alright. Neither had I until about a year ago."

In fact, I first heard of Mt. Elbrus after I returned from climbing Pico de Orizaba in Mexico and ran into another climber who had also successfully reached the summit of Orizaba. He asked me what was my next mountain. When I hesitated, he immediately suggested Elbrus, one of the Seven Summits. He described it as a "walk-up," meaning not technical.

I started reading up on Elbrus and explored the internet for information and guide groups. I quickly learned that Elbrus is in a fairly remote region of Southern Russia near the Black Sea. Technically, it is not part of the Caucasus mountain range, but sits 10 kilometers away like a huge watchtower overlooking the jagged range of snow-capped peaks covering almost 700 miles. A two-peaked volcano, Elbrus is covered in snow and glaciers from about 12,000 feet up to its summit of 18,618 feet.

Most of the major mountain climbing outfitters have fifteen day Elbrus trips which include several days of sightseeing in St. Petersburg and Moscow at the beginning or end of the trip. Since I had already spent time in both of those cities with my wife, I searched further. Finally, I found a guide group with a ten day trip with no frills or side trips. EWP was the name of the outfit. Centered in Wales, it specialized in guide trips to European and Russian mountains, especially Elbrus and a few others in Russia and eastern Europe. It also organized trips to Kilimanjaro.

Lucy at EWP quickly became my email pen pal as I gathered information and organized the trip. She was an expert on getting Russian visas, a ridiculously complicated task which defies all intelligent reasoning. Why they needed to know every subject I took in college was a mystery, but merely putting one's major area of study on the application would assure its immediate rejection. I later learned that Russia was merely copying the United States' enhanced visa requirements following 9/11, tit for tat.

Getting my group together for Elbrus was easier than expected. My brother Brent, who had moved from Moscow to Cairo with his job for USAID, was more than happy to return to Russia for a mountain climb. My friend, Jim, a classmate from University of Virginia Law School and fellow attorney in Atlanta, also jumped at the chance. Jim had traveled to Russia several times for work as a patent lawyer and had more than his fair share of vodka party stories. As naval airship navigator, he had also studied Russian aircraft and generally was far more into Russian culture and history than I will ever to be. Jim had done some high altitude climbing, including an ill-fated attempt to climb Popocatepetl in Mexico a number of years ago before its eruption. That climb had been cut short when Jim's group turned back to help rescue a fallen climber from another expedition who needed to be carried off the mountain on a stretcher. Jim was excited about the opportunity to climb a major mountain to its summit, especially one in Russia.

Elbrus, as I learned, is a few hundred feet lower than Orizaba, but involves a larger mountain, large enough to create its own weather patterns. The climb involves a long trek through crevasse fields on the southern side of the mountain, making an experienced guide essential. After Orizaba, I had vowed never again to climb a big mountain without a guide. EWP promised the "most experienced" guide at Elbrus, one who had led successful groups to the top of Elbrus over 100 times. Sasha was his name and climbing Elbrus was his game.

To prepare physically for the trip, this time I set up a five month training schedule, one month longer than I had trained for Orizaba. I added length to my weekend runs and planned a hill running schedule up my street which would culminate at thirty-five hills in a row.

Unfortunately, in my zeal to be in peak condition, I overdid it. My left knee becoming painfully swollen only two months into my schedule. After staying off it for a week, I resumed my hill work and instantly my knee swelled up to twice the size as before. This was not good. *How can I climb Elbrus if I cannot even make two hours of hills on my street without my knee blowing up like a grapefruit?*

There was nothing I could do but stay off my leg. So I switched over to daily sit-ups and pushups for two weeks, followed by a slow pace on the exercise bike using mostly my right leg. Slowly but surely my left knee recovered and, after a month's absence, I resumed my hill training.

But I had lost precious time and had to start slowly again, working my way back up to fifteen hills and only running three times a week instead of five. Fortunately, the Atlanta weather began to heat up significantly as we approached the July trip. Though I was short on my hills, I was able to lose more weight with less training due to the heat and extreme sweat generated by any exertion during the hot Georgia evenings. As my weight dropped, so did the stress on my left knee. Soon I was able to catch up on my training schedule.

Jim and I started meeting for breakfast at a local bagel place on Saturday mornings every other week to check on each other's progress and conditioning, as well as to discuss plans and equipment lists. Jim was training by running up office steps in his building – twenty-one floors worth—several times a week. He was adding pounds to his backpack to make the step training even more challenging. He was primarily working on leg strength and not weight loss as he was 6' 4" and at least thirty pounds less than me already. "Skin and bones" is how I would describe it, but the muscle and sinews that were in there were tough. I had seen Jim compete in a triathlon one time down at Callaway Gardens and I knew he had the determination and endurance to take on a challenge like Elbrus.

The flight from Atlanta to New York was uneventful. Delta was not yet flying directly to Moscow, so our trip to Mother Russia was split between two flights. Our bags were checked through to Moscow and the transfer at Kennedy Airport was smooth.

Nine hours after taking off from New York, we approached the largest of Moscow's four airports with a name I could not begin to pronounce. It sounded like a Russian female tennis player. As we descended, the green rolling hills outside Moscow appeared quite different from most Westerners' impressions of a grey, snowy Russian landscape. For decades, almost every photo or television picture of Russia seen by Americans were in black and white or greys as if nothing in Russia had any color to it. My experience in Russia was quite different, at least in Moscow and St. Petersburg, both of which are very colorful, vibrant cities with a lot of bustle and verve.

After landing, we breezed through customs and approached the exit where hundreds of people were lined up, many holding placards with passenger names on them.

A young Russia woman with very pointed, stiletto shoes and a cell phone in her ear held up a card that said EWP. Soon we were following her out into the warm morning sun through a jammed parking area immediately outside the terminal. She moved quickly, constantly chattering into the cell phone in Russian. I struggled to keep up, pulling my luggage and climbing gear on rollers, and balancing my backpack on one shoulder. Jim fell behind quickly, as he had brought all of his gear in two enormous black duffel bags, neither of which had any wheels. He would definitely regret that mistake at our next airport stop in Mineralnevody the next day.

Soon we were fighting traffic as we made our way into the central district of Moscow. Our itinerary included one night at the famous Rossia Hotel, near Red Square and the Kremlin in the very center of the city. As we worked our way towards the inner city, I noticed hundreds of billboards advertising the latest products, most of them imports. I struggled to decipher the Russian letters. It is not easy. In Russian, a "c" is an "s", a "p" is an "r" and an "h" is an "n". Thus, the word on the window of a café is "pectopah", pronounced "res-to-ran", and means restaurant!

As we came across a wide bridge, the gold onion domes and green tiled roofs of the brick watch towers at the Kremlin came into view. Beside the largest of the Kremlin towers, the one with the enormous clock, sat St. Basil's Cathedral, the wonderfully colorful, multi-onion domed chapel at the end of Red Square. Our van turned off the bridge, made a sharp u-turn and swung into one of the entrances to the Rossia Hotel.

Constructed in the Stalin era, the Rossia was the largest hotel in the world at the time, and certainly one of the ugliest. A square block of aging steel and glass with virtually no ornamentation, the hotel be-smirched the surrounding area of small medieval churches and historical buildings. The only redeeming value in the place was its proximity to Red Square and a tall tower on one side of the building which provided stunning views of the city. The Rossia was the Rockefeller Center of its time, but in 2003, it was a dilapidated mess, its carpeting worn and its tiny rooms and submarine-like bathrooms obsolete.

Equally as obsolete was its communistic approach to security. Our passports were immediately confiscated in the front lobby by a young but frigid looking hostess wearing a light blue dress that looked like it had been borrowed from a nearby mental ward. We were told to pick the passports back up in two hours. I hated to give up my passport in any foreign country, especially Russia, but we were given no option. Next, after an interminably long registration process, we were assigned rooms and given elevator tickets to get to our floor. When we asked for our keys to the room, we were told we would be given them when we arrived at our floor. As we entered the elevator area, a pale, unhappy peon in a hotel jacket scrutinized us suspiciously, checked each of our elevator tickets, and then motioned us to the elevator opening to our right. At our floor, we were greeted by a sour older woman who apparently was the constable for our floor, as well as the guard of all room keys. She also had the only key to the water and soda machine in the corner. After a long look at our elevator tickets and registration slip, she passed over the room key without speaking a word.

When we asked which way it was to the room, she frowned as if to ask why we were trying to talk to her in English, but she did point down the hall to our right.

"Spasibah", I mumbled in very poor Russian and headed down the four hundred yard long hallway which was not more than three feet wide.

About two hundred yards down on the left was our room. But the key, attached to a wooden ball slightly bigger than a golfball with the room number faintly painted on it, did not work. It fit perfectly in the lock, but no matter how we turned it, the door would not open. I tried, Jim tried, then we tried together. The door remained locked. Finally, Jim leaned hard into the door with his shoulder, turned the key, and the door lurched open.

"Frickin' commie doors; just takes some force and the proper leverage to get them to move," Jim said triumphantly.

Once inside, I retired the tiny room looked like a ship cabin. Two single beds about two feet wide almost touched each other and a chair was crammed between the far bed and the window. A bathroom was squeezed in immediately to the left of the door with hardware that also looked like it came out of a merchant sea vessel. The dresser and cabinets were functional and narrow. The 12 inch black and white TV did not work.

"Nice," I said sarcastically.

"Typical Stalinistic design," added Jim.

"And a bathroom from hell," I responded, holding up the toilet paper, a grey-brown roll of narrow cardboard-like crepe paper apparently designed to scrape one's tush, rather than to wipe. Obviously, comfort was not high on the priority of Russian toilet paper manufacturers.

We quickly decided that, despite the lack of sleep on the plane and jet lag, we would rather be outside the hotel than inside. We locked our gear in the room, returned our key to the Gestapo lady at the elevators, re-secured our elevator pass, and descended to the lobby. It was time for some quick sightseeing.

As we escaped from the elevator area with a quick wave of our tickets, we ran into Brent, just arriving at the front desk. He had an old beat up suitcase and an enormous cardboard box, which turned out to be a container for his backpack. Apparently the Cairo airport does not allow backpacks to be checked without being encased in a huge box.

Brent quickly passed on joining us for the sightseeing tour as he had lived in Moscow for five years and there was very little he had not already seen.

"Enjoy the rooms," I said as we left. "They are NICE!"

We had only two hours before we had to meet our climbing "mates" from England and Canada and get briefed on the following day's trip to Southern Russia, so Jim and I made a quick beeline to Red Square through an underpass that came up right next to St. Basil's Cathedral. I had seen it four years before on an overcast day, but the colors of the onion domes looked even more spectacular in the summer sun. The shadows from each dome accentuated the different patterns and nodules on each tower. Several towers were encased in scaffolding and green plastic sheets, but we were told that they would be coming down for a Paul McCartney concert in the next few weeks. Apparently, what McCartney wants, he gets. Meanwhile, our photos of the church would have some scaffolding in them no matter from which angle we snapped our shots.

Next, we entered the G.U.M., a huge shopping mall housed in a large palace-like building on the side of Red Square across from the Kremlin walls. The G.U.M. boasts hundreds of posh stores, including many well-known western world labels. The shops are spread across three long concourses, two stories high. Small souvenir vendors are scattered throughout the mall, selling brightly-colored carved, wooden figures and babushka dolls by the dozens.

At the other end of the G.U.M., we exited next to a large, dark red, multi-towered building which houses the Russian History Museum and a very nice souvenir shop on the side. The History Museum acts as a bookend to Red Square on one end, with St. Basil's being the bookend at the other end. Red Square is the size of about ten football fields and is paved with cobblestone throughout. Looking back towards St. Basil's, halfway on the right, is the brown marble tomb of Lenin, a large mausoleum guarded by soldiers 24/7. The block letters LEHNH are carved in the marble facing Red Square. I remembered that "h's" are "n's" and "n''s" are "i's" in Russian. My wife and I had been able to go inside and actually see Lenin laying in a glass casket in the middle of the mausoleum when we had visited Moscow a few years before. I remember well the guards making sure that no one stopped as we walked around the handrail, never being able to get closer than twenty feet to the casket. Jim would have liked to have seen it, but on this day it was closed.

Instead, we walked back out of Red Square, along the outside walls of the Kremlin, and past the Russian version of the eternal flame, which was guarded by two young soldiers. Soon we were at the draw-bridge entrance to the Kremlin. To our right were fountains, beautiful flower gardens and yellow-painted, grandly decorated buildings – not exactly how most people envision Moscow.

The interior of the Kremlin was even more magnificent. For twenty bucks, Jim and I hired an English-speaking guide to give us an hour tour of what we had always been led to believe was the central fortress of the "axis of evil." Interestingly, the Kremlin's most visible structures are five incredible churches, all with gold onion domes and ornate mosaic interiors with gorgeous icon-filled altar walls. Each one seemed more ornate than the next. One has a huge bell tower which stands above everything else, casting a long shadow across the Kremlin walls and down to the river below. Near it stands the largest cast iron bell ever made, which ironically was never used because a section broke off of it before it could be placed into use. Further back, and not on the tour, were the yellow-painted government/parliament buildings and presidential residence. Very off limits and very well guarded. In the center of the complex was a garish performing arts center built by Stalin and resembling the Rossia Hotel, with its drab sixties-style metal and glass exterior. It looked completely out of place.

Jim snapped photos of everything in sight, much like I had on my first trip to the Kremlin a few years earlier. His prize photo, however, was a natural wonder—a Russian babe clad in a pair of cargo pants which fit her well-shaped derriere quite tightly. Women's lib had come to Russia in full force.

With time running short, we hurried back to the hotel to meet our climbing team at an early dinner. The meal was served in a very tacky restaurant at the end of one of the four hundred yard hallways of the Rossia, complete with a parakeet cage with annoying birds constantly chirping. Brent joined us and we sat down for a light meal, Russian style. That almost always means bread and butter, a cucumber and tomato salad, and a mystery meat soup with God knows what in it.

I'm a regular guy and generally am not too hard to please when it comes to food. I would rather eat a good meatloaf at home and watch TV until I fall asleep than to go out to some high-priced gourmet restaurant where I'm forced to search for an ounce of meat under all the vertical piles of seaweed and other roughage. But that Russian broth with unrecognizable lumps was tough to stomach. Washing it down with a lukewarm Coke seemed to help.

Halfway through our meal, in walked the British policeman and the Canadian who were to join our climbing team. I immediately noticed the Brit was considerably overweight and was already wearing his red mountain jacket and high altitude climbing boots. Upon our inquiry, he informed us that he had decided to "pack light" and had failed to bring any other shoes. Apparently, he had brought no other clothes either as he wore the same black Gore-Tex pants, red shell jacket, and hiking boots the entire trip. The Canadian fellow seemed much more prepared. We quickly learned that he was the most experienced climber in the group, having already climbed Denali (Mt. McKinley) in Alaska, the highest mountain in North America, and Kilimanjaro, the tallest mountain in Africa. Elbrus would be his third of the Seven Summits.

It would be our first.

Getting to Elbrus the next day was an adventure in itself. From the Rossia, we took a van through heavy traffic to another one of the four airports in Moscow. The Russian EWP woman with the stiletto shoes guided us through a maze of ticket lines and window over to where we had to pay for overweight bags. Finally we boarded a beat-up Aeroflot plane with a glass-covered front nose. Jim, the former naval aeronautical expert, quickly informed us of the make and model of the plane. He described it as the workhorse of the Aeroflot fleet, adding that it was one of the safest aircraft in the world. Despite his assurances, I wondered if the crate would hold together for the two-hour flight south.

One thing the plane obviously lacked was air-conditioning. Within minutes we were sweating in our seats wondering if anyone on the entire plane had used deodorant. The only bright spot was the stewardesses, who unlike most American flight attendants, were still young and strangely attractive in sort of Bolshevik way. But talk about no non-sense. It was as if they would be fired if they cracked even the slightest smile or exhibited any personality whatsoever.

Jim quickly dubbed them the "ice bitches," but I noticed that he kept ogling them as they walked up and down the aisle. As did I.

The airport at Mineralnevody (meaning "mineral water"), looked much more impressive from the air than after we disem-barked from the plane. A short walk across the hot tarmac led us into the "terminal and baggage claim area." The small aluminum structure with a cracked concrete floor filled with what appeared to be Armenian men, each vying to provide transport to God knows where. They were all Russians, of course, but I quickly realized that Southern Russia is much closer to Turkey than Moscow and the men's complexions reflected the region.

We pressed our way through a narrow gauntlet between the noisy taxi-drivers, keeping a close hand on our wallets. Finally, we saw the EWP sign once again, this time held by a salt and pepper haired, slender man in black jeans and a T-shirt. He looked to be in his early forties. He waved and smiled, a gold-capped tooth glistening in our direction.

It was our guide, Sasha, and he greeted us as if we were long lost friends. He spoke English "not so good," but well enough to show us where our baggage would arrive—in an adjacent smaller room, reachable through a very narrow opening in the wall.

After about a fifteen minute wait, Sasha ushered us through the wall slit. Before us sat two large trailers of bags and suitcases. No baggage carousels here—just a mad dash into the piles to uncover and drag away the bags and backpacks, only to be log-jammed at another narrow opening in the front wall of the enclosure. There, every passenger crushed forward to have their bag labels checked against their luggage receipts by a Mafia-like "bouncer." We wisely hung back and waited for the mob to disperse through the narrow slot. Finally it was our turn, and Sasha led us by the huge luggage checker, through the opening, and into the open air.

Inside the tin structure it had been cool. But once outside, I quickly felt the heat of the hot sun. The air was dry an dusty, and I instantly needed a drink of water, but none was available.

The parking lot was about a quarter mile away to our left. To get there we had to pass numerous beggars looking for handouts of any sort. Sasha motioned not to stop and led the way to the dusty parking lot. Jim struggled to carry both of his enormous black duffel bags and soon was surrounded by beggar women in long dresses and sandals. He would have to fend for himself. I arrived at the van first and was immediately confronted by a gypsy-like woman carrying a small baby and moaning constantly. She reached out repeatedly for a coin, and in a moment of weakness, I gave her a quarter. This turned out to be a major mistake. Within seconds I was surrounded by at least twenty identical women carrying babies, all asking for the same treatment and pawing me to death.

Mercifully, Sasha intervened and quickly ushered me into the van. Jim finally arrived, pushing his way through the horde of gypsies, managing to stow his duffel bags and jumping in the side door without giving up a dime. We drove off to the wild fistful gestures of the women, angry at not coming away with more money.

As we pulled out of the parking lot, we watched the women descend on the next group of travelers, pawing them and working them for more coins.

The van ride to Cheget, the little village near the base of Elbrus, took four hours. The trip was interrupted several times by Russian police officers wielding black and white striped "pajousta" sticks/batons motioning the van over to the side of the road randomly, followed by an exchange of paper and lots of incoherent Russian jibberish between the driver and the police. It sounded like they were angry at each other and we fully expected to be arrested at any moment, but each time, after a few minutes, they let us proceed.

Soon we were flying by endless acres of sunflower fields, shining in the afternoon sun. The land was very flat and I wondered how we could be that close to some of the largest mountains in the world. Slowly but surely, we worked our way through the plains and began to drive into the hills leading towards the Caucasus mountains. Eventually we turned right at a large roundabout and soon we were cruising down the road along a rushing river along a narrow valley between two moderately high mountain ranges. The driver seemed to pick up speed and appeared oblivious to the poorly paved road, which was filled with potholes and strewn with small boulders.

Periodically, the driver would swerve to avoid either boulders or cows congregating on the road, usually just around corners. Southern Russia cattle farms have no fences, and, on more than one occasion, I was sure we were going to have fresh steak for dinner, that is if the van survived a collision with the bovines. Despite the danger, the driver never once slowed down for any creature in the road, narrowly missing the cows by two or three inches at least a dozen times.

We stopped at what appeared to be a deserted old mining town for a final inspection of our passports and travel papers. This gave us an opportunity to stretch our legs for a few minutes. As we walked up the sidewalk near the van, we saw a garden with a large bust of Stalin in the middle. It seems that during his era, he was revered everywhere. But now the bust was rusted and the garden unkempt, a historical remnant of its time. Jim took a picture "just for posterity."

For the rest of the trip to Cheget, our necks were craned up towards the sky as the mountains to our left and right became more jagged, higher and finally snow-capped. The air was cooling and I could feel a sense of nervousness in my stomach, knowing that I was approaching the largest mountain I had ever attempted to climb.

Finally, we turned left at a minimally marked road, crossed a river filled with churning grey, ashy glacier water, and pulled up in front of a huge concrete "chalet" with basketball courts in front of it. This was the Hotel Cheget, a monstrous building that typically housed young Russian athletes in training—mostly wrestlers, cross-country skiers, and basketball players. To the left of the structure was a large, unfinished wing of open concrete, which looked like it had been abandoned decades ago. In front of and below the basketball courts was a large gravel area maybe two acres in size, surrounded by more recent structures, including several new hotels with red or green roofs. Vendors' booths were scattered on both sides of the gravel area and café tables were seen to the left and right. This was the new, capitalistic growth in the Cheget community, a stark contrast to the heavy, dark bunker design of the older Hotel Cheget.

To the right was a ski lift, with single chairs swinging upwards on the very steep slope of Mount Cheget, one of the foothills to Mt. El-brus. In the winter, the entire mountain is covered in snow and people can ski from the top all the way to their hotels at the bottom. That day, however, there was no snow in sight. Sasha informed us that Cheget would be our first acclimatization trek the next day. But we would not be taking the chair lift.

Straight across, the clouds lifted momentarily to reveal a spectacular jagged peak called Donguzaran, with glaciers hanging from its summit and cascading down its face in the form of the number seven. It looked impossible to climb, but Sasha boasted he had climbed it five times.

After stowing our gear in what turned out to be decent rooms, complete with faux Zebra skin covered chairs, we strolled down to the gravel area to check out the cafes and vendors. As we turned around to look back at the Hotel Cheget, we realized that Elbrus filled the sky behind it, looming across the entire horizon. It was covered in clouds and we only got glimpses of the slopes headed toward its twin peaks. Nevertheless, it was enough to get our hearts pumping.

That night we had cucumber and tomato salad, bread and mystery soup once again. In the morning, we had cucumber and tomatos, bread, and oatmeal (which I skipped), but at least they gave us some cheese and tasty jams to go with the bread. The same basic meal was served at the Hotel Cheget, morning, noon and night.

Delicious.

Five minutes into our first acclimatization hike the next morning, I was already sweating profusely. My legs felt like they were about to collapse and I could not catch my breath. We were working our way up the first steep slope to the left of the chair lift, and my body was just not working. I had bundled up in way too many layers of clothing, the steepness of the slope was about three times that of the hill on my street, and we were now hiking at about 8000 feet in altitude. I sucked it up until we reached a level spot about ten minutes up the hill, then begged for time to discard layers and to take a water break. Sasha turned and smiled.

"Sure..., " he said, but I could tell that he already felt he was ushering greenhorns up the mountain.

Sasha kept a steady pace no matter how much we were struggling, but soon I fell into a rhythm and was able to keep up. Barely.

Jim, Brent, and the Canadian seemed to be having no problem at all, but within a half hour the British cop was starting to fall seriously behind. Sasha told us to go ahead; he would reel in the Brit when we stopped for water breaks.

The steepness of the slope rarely let up. Soon my thighs and calves were burning as we just kept climbing up and up. Twice early on, we were treated to incredible views of Elbrus in all its glory about ten miles away with no clouds to obscure its peaks. Sasha explained that the mountain was almost always clear in the morning, but by the afternoon, clouds and storms would come in and cover the peaks for the rest of the day. I snapped about a dozen photos of it while it was clear, being careful to get some purple flowers in the foreground.

By the time we reached the first chair lift stop, the Brit was about fifteen minutes behind. We rested there and enjoyed another spectacular view of Elbrus. When the Brit finally arrived, Sasha bought him a ticket to the second chair lift stop and told him to meet us there.

On the second section, Sasha's pace quickened, as if to test us. We struggled to keep up. At about 9500 feet and climbing fast, I was dying for air. But Sasha did not let up much, maintaining a steady pace just below our breaking point. We barely had time to glance at the magnificent sight of Dongurazan to our left and the steep banks of multi-colored wild flowers on the hills to our right. Almost an hour later, the Brit smiled like a Cheshire cat as we limped into the next chair lift stop about 750 feet further up the trail. *That SOB!*

The final section of Mt. Cheget involved climbing across a large snowfield on a steep slope, then up a stretch of boulders with no trail. By now the sun was in full glory, and despite the altitude and snow beneath us, I was sweating bullets. The Brit quickly fell behind again, and Sasha stayed back to make sure he did not get lost. Jim, Brent and the Canadian seemed to already be acclimatized and bounded from one boulder to another working their way up towards the top. I struggled across the snowfield and then followed them up the boulders, but at a slower pace. I saw no reason to rush since Sasha and the Brit were considerably behind me.

I reached the top of the boulders about ten minutes after the others and was treated to a great view. But I noticed we were still not at the top of the mountain. To our left was a rise with a large wall of snow, leading to the summit. At the edge of the snow was a cornice which hung out over about a thousand foot drop off.

In a moment of bravado, we decided not to wait for Sasha and the Brit. We worked our way up through a gap in the snow wall and then scrambled up a section of dark black rocks, which were still dripping from the melted snow. We climbed through the rocks, being careful to stay away from the edge of the cornice. Within minutes, we were sitting at the top of Mt. Cheget, having successfully reached the 11,000 foot summit of a small foothill of the Caucasus range. I was exhausted, but was more than happy to bask in the glorious sun and look across the valley at the early afternoon clouds streaming across Elbrus' peaks over 7500 feet above us.

"Today ve go to Diesel Hut and maybe up a bit higher to acclimatize, yes?" Sasha said at breakfast the next morning. "Be ready at nine o'clock vith all your gear for the mountain. Ve are not coming back until ve have summited—four, maybe five days."

The Diesel Hut is the base hut for the Elbrus climb. Situated about a thousand feet above the top of two sets of gondolas and a chair lift at the bottom of the mountain, the hut is still approximately 5000 feet below the summit. Sasha was wasting no time getting us to the base camp, but our summit attempt would still be several days away.

The van took us about ten miles to the bottom of the gondola system. Behind the gondola station, the local vendors were already setting up their tables and wares. I couldn't resist buying a few plastic bags of hazelnuts and almonds, which one lady was selling for a dollar a bag. The rest of the market items would have to wait until we came back down. I was already carrying as much as I could handle in my faithful grey backpack that had served me well for over twenty years, including my trips up Whitney and Orizaba.

The first gondola took us up to the bottom level of the glaciers and snow. The car was filled with climbers and local snow-boarders who were up for the day. The lower slopes of Elbrus are well-used as a ski resort. At least one internet site I had surfed back home referred to Elbrus as the Chamonix of Russia.

Soon we were on the second gondola section, flying over a snowy set of jagged black rocks. A few skiers were skiing down between the rocks, but the main slopes were still above us.

At the top of the second gondola section, we struggled to gather our gear over to the chair lift station. The trick here was to send all the gear up on separate chairs so that we could all hold boxes of food and other provisions when we went up on the chairs. The cook and Sasha's assistant went up first so that they could remove the gear as it arrived at the top of the chair lift. Sasha and several other men, whom we didn't recognize, masterfully loaded backpacks and other gear onto the individual chairs so that they would not fall off on the way up. Finally, we were told to stand in place holding a box of bread or vegetables, just in time for the next chair to swoop us up.

The chairs waited for no one and the timing was critical. Once on the chair, I had to maneuver the small bar in front of me to hang on. There were no locks or hand grips, just a bar on a hinge to hold onto with one hand while holding the box with the other. This was not too difficult until the chair got to the main cable support towers where it jumped up and down as it crossed the support. Each time, I hung onto the box and the chair for dear life. As I looked down to the snow and rocks below, I saw crashed cardboard boxes of provisions or backpacks which had not survived other long trips up the chair lift. Fortunately, our group had no mishaps and all our gear and provisions made it safely to the next stop.

At the top of the chair lift are the Barrel Huts. These shelters, about eight of them in a row, look like large round tin cans with a door in front and resemble small military barracks. Each of them is lined on the left and right with bunk beds with very little headroom. At one end of the row is another small structure that houses a kitchen and a few picnic like tables. Across the way are some nasty latrines/outhouses with no seats, just a hole in the floor over which to squat. Fortunately, I needed to go only #1 at that time.

After a twenty minute pause to organize the boxes and provisions for transport up to the Diesel Hut on a "Snow-Cat", Sasha informed us that it was time to do a bit of climbing.

"It's maybe one hour up to Diesel Hut," he said, smiling. "No crampons. Zee snow, it is soft and not so steep here. Use ski pole and good boots only."

I wondered about his estimate of time, as the literature I had indicated that the Diesel Hut was at least 1500 feet above the Barrel Huts. However, I did as I was told. I strapped on my backpack, adjusted my gloves and ski pole, and fell into line behind Sasha, our fearless leader.

This time Sasha started out at a very slow pace, digging in with his toes in the soft snow and establishing footprints to follow. We all mimicked his movements and soon we were advancing up the hill, leaving one clear trail of footprints behind us.

"No need to rush today," Sasha said. "Today ve go easy—get use to snow—acclimatize. Then rest—yes?"

"Sounds good," I responded, then concentrated solely on putting one foot after another in the prints in front of me.

Over an hour later, I was sweating profusely, again overdressed for the climb. I stripped off two layers and ditched my woolen hat.

Shortly thereafter, we caught our first glimpse of the Diesel Hut. Sitting atop a steep hill on the left side of the passable portion of the mountain, its silver roof glistening in the afternoon sun. Beyond it, there was a wide section of snow surrounded on both sides by straight lines of rock ridges or moraines which led up to the Pashtukova Rocks, which were maybe 2000 feet above the Diesel Hut. Above that was a wide expanse of snow leading up to the East Peak of Elbrus. If we squinted just right, we could see tiny dots slowly moving diagonally down the snowy expanse from the top left where a "saddle" formed between the two peaks.

"Climbers coming down from the top," Sasha noted. "Today is beautiful. Perfect weather for summit."

I could only hope that it would be the same the day we were ready to climb to the top.

The final push up to the Diesel Hut seemed to take hours. The slope increased significantly just below the hut and Sasha led us diagonally away from the hut to lessen the grade as we approached it. My legs felt like slush as we moved up the incline. At the top of the hill, we turned sharply to our left. Soon we were crossing the slope easily, level to the hut. We had been hiking for less than two hours, but I was ready for a rest.

I had been told by Lucy at EWP that our group would have its own room on the main floor of the hut, so I was anxious to lay down. Alas, whatever arrangements that had been made had not been passed onto the current occupants of the hut. No room was presently available. Sasha told us to leave our gear in the stowage area in the center of the hut and wait for lunch to be prepared.

"After lunch, ve hike up the hill a little bit—yes?" Sasha asked, but he was not looking for approval.

While waiting for lunch, I took the opportunity to explore the environs of the Diesel Hut. Immediately inside the narrow front door to the right were two tables for eating. Beyond that on the rear of the hut was a corner devoted to cooking, with heavy iron stoves and large water containers against the wall. All the water was carried from a spring beyond the hut and then boiled before drinking. To the left was the open stowage area for organizing gear and another picnic table where a bunch of grizzled guys were reading and chatting up a storm. Beyond that were three doors, presumably into bunk rooms or storage closets. Near the front door were narrow wooden stairs to the second level. I did not go up there, but periodically, more climbers would appear from upstairs, looking for water or stepping outside to go to the bathroom.

The latrines, I was told, were in the rear of the hut—outside of course. Circling the hut counterclockwise from the front porch, I passed a few female climbers laying on some planks of wood in the after-noon sun, then stepped through some narrow gaps between the rocks to encounter the famous double-door outhouses of the Diesel Hut. The right door was wider, because that side was a two-holer. The left side had just one hole and I chose it for my first Elbrus dump. I had a fresh roll of Russian crepe paper toilet paper with me. Once again, like the latrine at the Barrel Huts, there was no seat, just a hole with two short two-by-fours nailed next to it on which to squat. Below the hole about thirty or forty feet was the frozen accumulation of decades of human waste forming brown stalagmites below. I had no problem performing the usual functions until I went to wipe myself. The wind was rather cold coming up through the hole, but I did not fully appreciate how strong the updraft was until I dropped the wiped toilet paper through the hole and it flew back up in the air beside my face!

Automatic TP return feature! Cool.

After a few tries, I got the hang of dropping the toilet paper near the edge of the hole so that it hit the bottom of the boards and then dropped out of the wind current. I felt pleased to have mastered something on this mountain.

Things got a bit more serious after lunch. The slope above the Diesel Hut was steeper, and though some locals climbed without crampons, Sasha had each of us attach our crampons to our boots. Since it was afternoon and the snow conditions would be soft, he also advised us to wear Gore-Tex pants with gaiters.

Once moving, we quickly passed a burned out hut just above the Diesel Hut. That shelter had been destroyed in a fire a few years earlier and now served as a windbreak for tent campers who liked the fresh (and much colder) outside air.

The hiking regimen was much like on the trip up to the Diesel Hut—Sasha setting the pace and kicking in the footprints in front and the five of us following close behind, trying to match his prints. This time, however, he seemed to be testing us again, with the pace a bit brisker than in the morning climb from the Barrel Huts. At first the snow was a bit slushy in the afternoon sun, but as we moved up the mountain, the wind increased and the snow got crunchier under foot.

After twenty minutes, we were gasping for air. We were now at almost 14,000 feet and the altitude was making a difference. We stopped for some water, and I looked back towards the breathtaking Caucasus mountain range. As far as we could see, from right to left, were snow-capped, jagged peaks in the distance, some still higher than where we were standing. I scanned the foothills to try to find Mt. Cheget, where we had been the day before, but could not pick it out. There were just too many peaks. The view was so magnificent I just wanted to sit and watch it.

"Must push on. Ve learn to breathe up here—yes?" Sasha said after a five minute break.

We immediately fell in behind him again. I found myself simply matching Sasha's breathing and footsteps automatically. I kept an eye on prominent rocks ahead of us on the ridge to our right and felt a sense of accomplishment every time I reached the same level as the rocks I had picked out. Each time I reached my target rock, I felt like I needed to take a break, but Sasha kept moving up and up, never slowing the pace. At some point, my steps became robotic, and despite the fatigue, my mind starting wandering. I envisioned myself working my way up towards the South Col of Everest like in the Imax movie, almost forgetting that I was a continent away on an entirely different mountain.

Just as my legs were about to fall off, Sasha stopped.

"That's far enough today. Ve climb up, then sleep down. Tomorrow ve go to the Rocks," he said. "Must acclimatize or ve get sick."

"I still feel good, man," Jim piped up. "Mind if I go on up to the Rocks today?"

Sasha shrugged. "Sure...if you vant. But if you feel tired, turn around. Ve vill all go tomorrow and then the next day higher. Three days acclimatize before try for summit."

"Jim, you're crazy. Let's stay together. There's no need to push it," I advised.

"No, I feel good. I want to see the Rocks today. There's plenty of light left. I'm going for it."

"Okay, your choice. I'm going to take it easy and rest down at the hut."

I looked up at the Pashtukova Rocks above us. They looked fairly close, but I knew from prior experience that distances can be deceiving on large mountains.

A few minutes later, Jim headed up the mountain by himself. His arms were folded behind him, resting on his buttocks and lower back. Like a long distance ice skater, his long legs strode confidently up the slope.

The rest of us turned and headed down. This time, no one followed Sasha, and we enjoyed a leisurely jaunt back to the hut, sliding much of the way due to the wet snow. My thighs began to burn a bit before we got there, but nothing too bad.

Back at the hut, we relaxed on some boards out in the sun. Every half hour or so, another group returned from the summit and we tried to listen in on their stories. Unfortunately, many of the climbers were not English-speaking and we only got a bit of the adventures. However, clearly it had been a perfect day to go to the top. Everyone had made it all the way and had a wonderful time.

Late afternoon came and went, yet there was no sign of Jim. I checked inside the hut to make sure I hadn't missed him when I was snoozing in the sun. I asked our cook if she had seen him, but she was not sure which climber Jim was at that point and was of no help.

As the sun started to get low on the horizon, Sasha came out and announced that our room was ready. Apparently, a group that had reached the summit that day had already packed up and headed off the mountain, leaving one of the main floors bedrooms open. We grabbed our gear and followed Sasha to the room on the back left of the Diesel Hut.

The room was not exactly what I expected. Pie-shaped and wedged into a corner of the hut, the room was very cramped. The door opened just far enough for us to get through the doorway and crawl up onto a fan-shaped, plywood platform about ten feet wide. All five of us would sleep side by side with our feet towards the door and our heads up next to the outer wall. There was one small window, more like a porthole on the back left wall, but it did not open. Its sole purpose was to let a little light into the room. The room was dank and hot and did not look like a place in which I wanted to spend much time.

After spreading out our mats and sleeping bags, the whole platform was fully covered and the mats overlapped at our feet. Almost all of our gear had to be stowed under the platform. Access to the storage area below was limited to one climber at a time, as the floor space in front of the door was about two feet wide.

Just as it was getting dark, Jim finally returned from the Pashtukova Rocks. He looked whipped. I resisted the urge to throw in a "told you so" comment, but one glance from him let me know that he already knew it.

"It was a little further than I thought," Jim finally told us over supper. "Cold up there also. The wind was incredible."

I noticed that Jim's nose and upper lip were red and a bit swollen. Obviously the weather had changed further up the mountain while we were relaxing at the hut. Jim was unusually quiet most of the evening. I interpreted this to mean that the serious stuff was still ahead of us.

The next two days were devoted to more acclimatization.

The first morning involved a climb to the Pashtukova Rocks. We left the hut about 10:00 A.M. and followed the same path as the previous afternoon. In the morning the snow was much harder and crunchier. The footing seemed more secure. This time, the prominent rocks I had picked out the day before seemed to fly by. We quickly passed the spot where we had stopped the prior afternoon, which turned out to be about one-third of the way to the Rocks. One day of acclimatization had already made a huge difference in our ability to breathe and climb at this height.

Way up the mountain on the traverse to the saddle, we saw clouds sweeping across the mountain, obscuring the slopes above the Rocks.

We pressed on, this time at a very deliberate and steady pace from Sasha. We were in no hurry. We had all day to get up to the Rocks and back.

"Ve pace ourselves today," he said. "It gets a bit steep before the Rocks."

Indeed, the Rocks looked like they were right above us. I fully expected to get there anytime. However, just when I thought we were close, we came to the top of a steep section and realized that we were still at least thirty minutes away. The Rocks, a scattered accumulation of sharp black boulders spanning the approximately sixty yard width of the section between the two vertical rock ridges, was still a good way ahead of us, perched on what looked to be the steepest section of snow yet. Above the Rocks, clouds continued to sweep across the mountain. Occasionally the clouds cleared, revealing tiny dots starting to come down from the saddle.

As we approached the Rocks, Sasha started veering right and left, moving us into slight switchbacks, rather than going straight up. It was definitively getting steeper, but was still manageable. At the end, the last fifty feet of the slope below the Rocks was steep enough that I found myself opening my feet and essentially duck-waddling up to the top, my crampons digging in sideways to avoid sliding down the mountain. The exertion of the last few feet caused me to collapse in the snow on my side next to a collection of black rocks.

"Made it," I gasped triumphantly, while reaching for water.

Of course, at the Rocks, we were barely above 15,000 feet, only a quarter of the way to the summit from the Diesel Hut. Still, it felt like a big accomplishment at the time.

Jim, Brent and the Canadian had made it to the top just before me and looked to be in pretty good condition. The British guy had fallen behind again on the last slope. We all watched him struggle up the final steep section, his red jacket standing out among the climbers below and his two ski-pole, swinging arm technique slowly pushing him up the hill.

I had envisioned making it to the Rocks and enjoying a nice, casual meal of nuts, gorp, meat sticks and candy bars which I had snuck into my day pack. However, the combination of being extremely tired and the stiff wind whipping across the Rocks from the west, guaranteed that this would not be a pleasant picnic. There were a few tents nearby behind rocks that looked like they were about to fly away.

Within minutes, we were pulling on several addition layers, our Gore-Tex shells, gloves and woolen hats, just to stay warm. The temperature felt like it had dropped twenty degrees.

Jim assured us that this was nothing compared to how it was the afternoon before, when he had soloed to the Rocks. I could only wonder, if it was this bad at the Rocks, how bad would the wind be at the top?

Needless to say, we spent a lot less time than anticipated at the Rocks. After about ten minutes in the freezing wind, we had zoomed back down to the Diesel Hut for another afternoon of basking in the sun.

This time, as the groups from the summit arrived back at the hut, they seemed a bit more haggard than the climbers the day before. Most had serious wind burn on their cheeks, and none of them were very talkative. They looked exhausted and numb from the experience. Still almost all of the climbers had made it to the top and several commented on the awesome view from the summit.

I couldn't help but notice that the arrival times of the returning groups were later in the afternoon as compared to the day before. This time, most of the climbers arrived too late in the afternoon to head down to the lifts to go off the mountain that evening. It had been a much tougher day on the mountain and the hut was very crowded that night.

Our dinner of cucumber and tomato salad, soup, bread with cheese, and hot chocolate seemed especially delicious that evening. My appetite was voracious. I began to realize that I was using up all my calories climbing at these altitudes and that I could not eat too much. Somehow, I sensed the comradery of our group growing stronger as we all began to anticipate summit day, only about thirty-six hours away.

After a fitful night listening to all four of my climbing team snore most of the night, we got up at dawn, grabbed some breakfast, and headed out for our final acclimatization hike before dawn. Sasha was trying to move our schedule closer to summit day conditions.

At 6 A.M., the snow was completely packed hard from the sub-zero night. As a result, our footing was firm and the climbing was easier. What took us an hour and a half to go up the slope the first warm afternoon on the mountain, took us about one half hour in the cold, brisk temperatures of our third day on the mountain. Breathing the thin air was much easier, and I could tell that acclimatization was working well.

By 8 A.M., we were scrambling up the last slope to the Rocks. The Brit was at least twenty minutes behind again, but we could see him in his red jacket, gradually working his way up, his arms pumping with both ski poles.

The wind at the Rocks was twice as hard as the prior day, almost knocking us off our feet. Damn it was cold. I could feel the wind go right through my shell, through three layers of fleece and into my bones. Sasha immediately told us that we would just catch our breath and keep going up. I sipped some hot tea from a large thermos Sasha had stowed in his much larger pack and munched down a Granola bar. Then, as soon as the Brit caught up with us, we fell in behind Sasha to go into new territory.

Most of the section above the Rocks was shrouded in clouds as we started up again. Every once in a while the sky cleared and we were treated to views of the two peaks. We could see a few small dots moving up near the saddle, still going up. But in a split second, the view disappeared and we were back in a completely white hazy cloud cover with, at most, several hundred yards of visibility.

As we had become accustomed, we moved single file, following in the footprints of Sasha. In the section above the Rocks, the slope was about thirty degrees and I could really feel it in my legs. Sasha made subtle changes of direction to simulate some sense of switchbacks, but there did not seem to be any direction which improved the slope or made it any easier.

Sasha never told us how far up we were going that day—just that we would be practicing some rope technique and self-arrests, to get us ready for the summit day.

All I know is that every step got tougher. It was getting steeper and the altitude was getting higher, a vicious combination.

Sasha seemed to vary the pace at times, always checking to see how we reacted. This time, we waited when the Brit fell behind, making sure the team stayed together. It was unsaid but apparent that Sasha treated the mountain above the Rocks differently than below them. It was like a dividing line between casual day-hiking and serious, life-threatening climbing. Not far above us were the crevasse fields. We would have to climb through them on our way to the summit the next day.

My altimeter read 16,000 feet when Sasha announced that we would go just a bit further, then practice our self arrests. I was ready to stop, but we pushed on another 300-400 vertical feet before stopping.

"This starts the traverse," Sasha said, pointing up and to the left. "Must be careful now—many crevasses from here up. Tomorrow ve go all the vay. Today ve practice safety—yes?"

Sasha then demonstrated the proper self-arrest technique three times, his ice axe thrusting into the snow beneath his chest, causing him to immediately stop sliding down the slope. He then demonstrated improper technique and quickly slid thirty feet below us before he turned and thrust the ice axe in properly, coming to an abrupt halt.

"If you do it wrong, you end up in crevasse," he said. "Now, let's see vat you can do."

For the next half hour, each of us took turns falling backwards, turning over onto our stomachs and jamming our ice axes into the snow. Each time Sasha gave us pointers to help us hone our technique. The position of our hands on the ice axe was a key. The placement of the spike end of the ice axe in our lower hand outside our bodies was another key. The angle of the axe shaft was yet another. There would be no self arresting by swinging the ice axe into snow above our heads and hanging on to the strap for dear life like in the silly movies.

After we all mastered the technique to Sasha's satisfaction, we lined up and held our carabiners out for Sasha to connect us all with a rope. Sasha explained that he would always lead the rope team. The strongest climbers would be immediately behind him. On summit day, Sasha's assistant, whom we had not yet seen, would be at the end of the rope. Once attached to the line, we practiced moving up and down the slope and then across on a level, making sure to keep the right distance between climbers at all times. Whenever someone went too fast or too slow so that too much of the rope was dragging on the ground, Sasha scolded us. This was my first time being roped up and it was somewhat awkward at first. But, after a few missteps, I got the hang of being part of the team. Soon, we succeeded in keeping spaced just right. With the rope in place, I instantly felt more secure on the slope.

While I was concentrating on the rope, I did not notice that the clouds had become more dense. Visibility had been reduced to about fifty feet. I looked down towards the Rocks and could see nothing but white clouds below us. It was lighter above us, but there was no break in the clouds. It was like we were in our own little world of snow on the side of the mountain.

"Follow me," Sasha said after unhooking us and carefully packing the rope back in his large pack. "Ve go straight down to the Rocks and then back to the hut. Stay close, I don't vant to lose you."

Surprisingly, Sasha then bolted down the slope at a very brisk pace. We scrambled down to keep him in sight. Several times he almost disappeared in the clouds below us as we struggled to keep up. Obviously, he was testing us again.

Sasha did not let up again until we could actually see the Rocks below us through the clouds.

"You must be able to get down off the mountain quickly if veather gets bad—yes?" he said to the group. "You can go down from here by yourselves. I must go quickly—get things ready for summit tomorrow."

Before we could say anything, Sasha literally took off, almost skiing down the slope. We saw him dip down beyond the Rocks and out of sight within minutes. We turned and followed him at a considerably slower pace.

An hour later, when we arrived at the hut, Sasha was nowhere to be found.

This time, it was a bit too windy and cool to lay out in the sun outside the hut. We had enjoyed a late lunch as we didn't get back to the hut until after 2:00 P.M. There was no view of the two peaks that afternoon and the clouds continued to obscure the traverse, making it impossible to see the usual dots coming back from the summit. Three o'clock passed. Four o'clock passed. Still no one had made it back down from the top. Finally, about 4:15 P.M., a group of lean young men well-clad in expensive mountain gear arrived, chatting excitedly about the sixty mile per hour winds that nearly blew them off the mountain at the top. They talked about several groups that had turned back. One of them said that they had stayed at the summit only for two minutes and barely could get any photos. They got no good views from the top, but they had reached the summit and returned safely. They seemed both satisfied and disappointed at the same time.

"I hope everyone makes it back today," said the last fellow as he stepped into the hut, pulling off his hat and goggles to reveal a very bad case of wind burn.

That afternoon, I could feel my stomach tighten and my nervous energy build as, one by one, groups returned from the upper mountain. About a half of them had made it to the top—barely. The other half had turned back due to the winds and the lack of visibility. All of them looked like whipped puppies, whimpering back to the safety of the doghouse—in this case, the Diesel Hut.

Climbers continued to dribble in as the sun set and darkness started to descend. Eventually, all climbers were accounted for and a collective sigh of relief could be heard across the room.

Finally, just as the light outside disappeared, Sasha arrived with a backpack full of additional provisions, along with a short, cigarette-smoking comrade whom he quickly introduced as Igor, his assistant guide for the summit attempt. Sasha had gone all the way down and off the mountain for more provisions and to pick up Igor. They had just hiked up from the Barrel Huts in thirty minutes, according to Sasha.

"Ve leave for the summit tonight. Eat dinner, then sleep. Vake up at one-thirty and be ready to go at two, two-thirty," Sasha announced.

Then, turning to the Brit, Sasha added, "Igor will go vith you on two o'clock Snow-Cat to Rocks and ve catch up vith you at the saddle."

This was a command, not a question. The Brit was given no opportunity to protest. The decision had been made that he would not be allowed to hold the team back. Instead, he would be given an artificial "headstart" on the Snow-Cat, saving him two hours of climbing.

Jim and I looked at each other with raised eyebrows. Our five man team was down to four, which might be good, but the weather seemed to be deteriorating and Sasha's assistant was not too impressive.

How in the hell can a guy climb and chain-smoke at the same time at this altitude?

One-thirty A.M. came awfully early the next morning—if you can call it morning. I had gotten very little sleep, too nervous to settle in deeply.

"Time to go, gentlemen," I said as the others stirred quietly in their sleeping bags.

We tried to dress without making a sound, but it was impossible. Outside our room, another team was getting ready as well, joking and laughing without regard to others sleeping nearby. This is a ritual practiced night after night at the Diesel Hut. Those going to the summit that morning get up in the wee hours, excited and noisy. Those still acclimatizing try to get some serious zzzz's to rest up for the later summit attempt. It is a clash of interests and usually results in no one getting any good sleep.

Our cook, a rather plain woman with a nice smile and constant good humor, was already preparing a quick soup and oatmeal breakfast for us. She had also filled our bottles with boiling water and placed them out to cool. They would be ice cold in no time.

We ate breakfast silently, using our headlamps for lights. Then, without delay, we dressed and finished packing our gear for the summit attempt. The last chore was to put our gaiters and crampons on outside on the bench on the front porch of the hut.

Brent and I sat together silently as we strapped on our crampons. Outside, we could see the moon above us, lighting the snow quite brightly.

"We may not even need headlamps this morning," I said.

"Yeah, I hope it stays clear, but I don't see any stars further up towards the peaks," Brent warned. "At least we won't be slowed down. Our friend from the U.K. left on the Snow-Cat about ten minutes ago."

Five minutes later, we were climbing, four in a row behind Sasha. We followed the exact same line as the prior three days. The pace was moderately fast, but seemed manageable. Each time we had headed up the mountain, it had gotten easier. Now we were ready.

As we climbed, several Snow-Cats zipped past us carrying climbers from other groups. Some guides figure that if the climbers have been up to the Rocks several times already, it is acceptable mountaineering etiquette to start anew at the Rocks with fresh legs and summit from there. We felt that was cheating, so we still included the two hours from the hut to the Rocks at the beginning of our summit day.

Amazingly, we reached the Rocks in an hour and forty-five minutes under moonlit skies. Sasha had kept his headlamp on, but had told us to turn ours off, since the moon was providing ample light.

However, just as we reached the Rocks, the moon disappeared behind the clouds and the wind swept in, making us button up and switch on our headlamps.

Once up at the Rocks, the wind blasted across the mountain, making any lengthy stop impossible. We briefly sipped some hot tea, munched on a few almonds, and then kept going.

Above the Rocks, we quickly fell in behind Sasha as he started his subtle switchbacks. The wind did not abate and soon we could see only about fifty feet in front of us. I could feel my hands getting cold and I found myself wiggling my toes inside my boots to stave off tingling down there. When we stopped briefly for a water break about a half hour above the Rocks, I noticed that my water bottle spout was half covered in a thin glaze of ice. I had no idea how cold it was, but clearly we were at temperatures not previously experienced on our acclima-tization days.

Sasha would not let us tarry. It was too cold to stop long. We needed to move quickly if we were to make it up and back that day.

An hour later, we reached the point where the traverse across to the left up to the saddle began. Visibility was down to about thirty-five feet, just enough to see the next wand marking the safe part of the "trail" through the crevasses. The crevasses were marked with two wands forming an "X" in the snow, twenty or thirty feet to our left and right.

The wind had not let up and there was no sign of the clouds clearing. It had to be well below zero, as several of my fingers were now decidedly numb and tingling. At this point, wiggling my toes inside my boots did not seem to be doing much good.

We caught up to a large group of about twelve climbers and three guides. They had taken Snow-Cats up to the Rocks but now were already discussing whether to go on or to turn back. I thought I heard the lead guide from the other team tell Sasha that it doesn't look good above, but Sasha seemed to discount the warning and quickly told us that we needed to move on.

The next three hours was like a slow moving black and white movie. Everything was white, except occasional scattered black rocks in the snow. The only color was our clothes and the pale straw colored wands. We steadily climbed, working left, then right, following our leader. The slope kept getting steeper and soon we were resting at each of the wands that were stuck in the snow about fifty feet apart.

Brent and I started repeatedly falling about ten feet behind the others and struggled to catch up while the others rested at the next wand. And so it went, one wand after another. I stopped worrying about my fingers and toes and just concentrated on making it up to the next wand, resting my forehead on the top of my ski pole at each rest until my breathing recovered for the next push up the mountain.

I also began to notice that the visibility was getting worse. Soon, we could not see the next wand until we were almost halfway there. Fortunately, prior groups had left solid tracks to follow and the footing was secure. Sasha seemed to know every rock and crevasse on the side of the mountain and confidently led us up and up and up through the winter dreamland.

"Come on Brent," I said as I waited for him to catch up. "We have to be getting close to the saddle."

"We better," he replied. "I don't know how much longer I can keep going up like this."

"How much longer to the saddle?" I yelled up to Sasha.

"Not long now," he said. "Only about one more hour."

Jesus. I closed my eyes and said a prayer. Then I raised one tired leg after another, joining Sasha, Jim and the Canadian at the next wand. I hardly noticed a team coming down the mountain toward us.

"It's pretty nasty ahead. Snow, sleet, lots of wind!" a female guide yelled in Sasha's direction. She was physically supporting an older gentleman (probably no older than us) by his arm and leading him down the mountain. He looked like hell with snow caked on his moustache and his shoulders slumped as if he had no energy left.

"Are there others up at the saddle?" Sasha asked her.

"Yes, but you may not see them. It's really stormy up there."

"Okay...sure. Good luck," Sasha replied. Then he waved us forward and up beyond the guide and her ward.

"Ve are almost to saddle. Could be bad veather up there, but ve can't tell until ve get there," Sasha said. "Get some vater now and candy bar. Ve may not have time to stop at saddle. Ve push straight to the top."

Jim, the Canadian, Brent and I all looked at each other, saying nothing. We were following the leader, doing as we were told. There was still no sign of the Brit. He had to be already up at the saddle as we had not passed him or seen him or Igor coming down.

"It's on to the saddle, then," I said cheerfully after downing a Snickers, squelching the rumbling of my nervous stomach.

After five hours of steady uphill climbing, we crested the traverse and moved onto the relatively flat section of the saddle between the two peaks of Elbrus. Of course, that day, we could not see either peak or anything else more than twenty-five feet around us. We could have been on the moon for all we knew.

As we reached the flatter portion of the snowy wasteland of the saddle, we picked up the pace, and soon I was feeling almost giddy. A forty-mile an hour wind was behind us and pushing us forward to the center of the saddle. At the same time, frozen precipitation – a cross between sleet and hail – began to blast us from all sides.

I assumed wrongly that the saddle would have some rocks or shelter or something that we could hide behind to escape from the storm. But we appeared to be in the middle of a vast space with no barriers anywhere. The wind was practically knocking us off our feet.

Towards what I can only guess was the middle of the saddle, we literally ran into the Brit and Igor, sitting in the snow, huddled together against the wind. The Brit looked wasted and out of it. Igor stood when he saw Sasha. Somehow he had managed to light a cigarette and the wind was stoking the red ash as he inhaled. They whispered to one another while we checked on our chubby friend from the U.K. He was not doing well, unable to coherently respond to any of our questions.

I looked around in the direction from which we had come. This turned out to be a mistake, as the wind and frozen sleet was coming from that direction. Instantly my glacier glasses glazed over with thick film of ice.

Just then, the storm ratcheted up another notch, blasting us unmercifully. Ice and snow was gripping onto our jackets, gloves and pants like magnets. We were inside a giant sandblaster, except instead of sand, it was sleet and hail pounding us right and left.

I looked over to Brent and saw that his beard and moustache were completely frosted thick with ice. His jacket, which had started a deep burgundy, was now almost completely white. I could only see ten feet in front of me. Soon we were all huddled together around the Brit, who remained seated on the ground covering his head with his arms.

I could envision the storm slowly closing in and carrying us off to heaven in one great white light, but that would be too easy.

"Do you vant to go on?" Sasha yelled from about a foot in front of my face...

After we made the difficult decision to turn back, Sasha roped us up. Sasha took the lead position, followed by the Canadian and Jim, then me and Brent, followed by the Brit and Igor pulling up the rear. We had seven in our rope team, including one near the back who could barely get up, let alone walk.

"Ve must get out of this vind," Sasha yelled. "Follow me."

Sasha started out directly down the center of the saddle rather than retracing our steps.

"Shouldn't we go back the way we came?" I yelled as hard as I could through the storm. Sasha either didn't hear me or ignored me. It was impossible to tell. Either way, he kept going the way he started.

Now, off the path worn down by prior climbers and in virgin snow, our feet were sinking in at least six to eight inches with each step. This made walking twice as difficult—like walking in sand dunes.

Fortunately, the rope was tight and with seven men moving together and the rope doing its work, we started to move smartly across the windswept saddle, still being pounded by the snow and hail.

Just as I was beginning to gain confidence, the ground below me collapsed.

"WOAH!" I screamed at the top of my lungs, as my body crashed downwards. I shot my arms out, grabbing the rope with one hand, and closing my eyes as my body smashed down and jerked to a stop. I couldn't breathe. I couldn't feel anything. I couldn't think.

To my right was one rather impressive crevasse, the green ice just inviting me to drop on in. I had fallen in up to my shoulders, but luckily landed on a narrow ledge of ice. Somehow, I remained calm.

The rope is holding you. You are not going to fall. Catch your breath. Don't panic. No one moved in front of me or behind me. If they moved, the rope would loosen and drop me further down.

Just climb out idiot. Use your crampons.

I instantly scrambled up onto solid ground and knelt until I could regain my composure. The whole collapse and climbing out of the crevasse had taken only a few seconds, but it seemed like an eternity—almost like in slow motion.

"You okay?" I heard Brent say behind me.

"Yeah. Just give me a minute to regroup," I replied. But before I could rest any more, I heard Sasha yell "Go," and the rope pulled me to my feet. We were moving again as if nothing had happened.

The storm did not let up once we got below the saddle. If anything it got worse. At this point, my glacier glasses were completely frozen over and no amount of scraping with my gloves could clear them. The black leather temple protectors had unfastened in the wind and were dangling along the ear pieces of the glasses. Snow and sleet were smashing into my eyes and face as I snugged the glasses down to peer over them. I pulled my Gore-Tex hood lower and just grinned and beared it.

Sasha led us to what remained of a little abandoned hut at the base of the saddle on the south side of the mountain. At one time, the little hut had been used, but at this point it was in complete ruins, just a few logs stacked like a picket fence. It stopped no wind. Nevertheless, Sasha elected to stop there to work out the next step in getting off the mountain.

To protect us, he ordered us to kneel close behind each other in a line without tangling the rope. We did as he told us. For a moment, I imagined Igor as a German soldier walking behind us and shooting us all in the head, as if we were Jewish prisoners on the way to concentration camps. But Igor was up front with Sasha, trying to light a cigarette while Sasha fiddled with his compass and tried to reach someone on his cell phone. Meanwhile, we were freezing.

After what seemed like hours, Sasha directed us to get up and spread out in a line to make the rope line taut again. Then we headed due east across a very steep slope of deep snow.

I had post-holed in snow before, hitting an occasional soft spot and sinking into the snow up to my knee of thigh. But this was different. Every step taken was into three feet of snow up to our crotches on an angled slope of at least forty-five degrees. It was incredibly tiring and soon my legs were wobbling with fatigue.

When I did step on a firm spot in the snow, my ski pole in my right hand would hit nothing but air to my right. Fortunately, I could not see what it was not hitting because the snow and white-out conditions provided no visibility to my right at all. We were on a ledge walking in the blind. It was just one sheet of white in all directions. I could no longer see Sasha or the Canadian and could barely see Jim in front of me.

Every ten seconds or so, an incredible weight pulled me towards the back of the rope line. The Brit was collapsing and being dragged along through the snow. Or Brent was deliberately sitting down to rest his legs. Each time the rope would come to a complete stop. A few seconds later, Sasha would yell "Go", and we would push forward a few more yards before Brent or the Brit would collapse again.

At this point, I wondered if we would ever make it off the mountain. This was now a matter of survival. I had no feeling anymore. I knew my hands and feet were frozen, but that was of no importance. I could feel my face icing over wherever it was exposed to the elements, but that too was secondary. We were high up on a damned mountain in Southern Russia in a massive snowstorm and the only thing that mattered was getting out of there.

"Come on, damn it," I yelled towards the back of the rope line. "Stay up or die! We've got to get off this mountain."

I waved at Jim to get Sasha to move forward. "Jim, just tell him to go and if necessary we will have to drag the whole ****in' line down the hill!"

I could tell I was losing it, but I really didn't care. There was only one way to safety and that was to keep moving.

My vulgar words of encouragement seemed to do some good. The stops, while they did not disappear, started to become a bit less frequent. After a while, the snow seemed to be getting a little less deep and the wind seemed to be gradually decreasing in intensity.

We passed a series of black rocks to our left and then a large black rock on our right. Suddenly, Sasha had regained his bearings and knew exactly where we were.

"Just a bit more and ve are back on trail to traverse," he said happily, showing his gold-capped tooth for the first time in hours.

Once back on the main path back through the crevasses, the storm let up slightly. After Sasha disengaged us from the rope, we rested for the first time in three hours. I looked around at our team. Sasha was on his cell phone trying to reach friends at the hut to let them know we were on our way out. Igor was already working on his third cigarette of the stop. The Brit looked delirious and appeared unsteady even when sitting down. Brent was tired, but seemed to be recovering. Jim and the Canadian were chatting about something esoteric, and were obviously no worse for the wear, except for Jim's nose, which had swollen up about three times the normal size.

I sucked down a lot of water and managed to get a granola bar to go down. We still had a long way to go, but I knew we had gotten through the worst of it.

For the next three hours, Sasha and Igor supported the Brit on both sides and led him slowly down the mountain. The rest of us plodded behind at the slow pace, getting impatient as the afternoon wore on.

Finally, we saw the Rocks below us. Once there, Sasha quickly escorted the Brit over to a Snow-Cat for transport to the hut.

Jim and I hung together on the hike down from the Rocks as the Canadian and Brent, with renewed energy, zipped ahead of us.

"I'm never doing this again," I said. "We could have been buried up there."

"Yeah, it was pretty intense," Jim replied. "But Sasha earned his stripes up there. Even without GPS."

"We didn't need GPS. All we needed was to come down the way we went up. Going in the virgin snow was a killer."

"All I know is he got us back in one helluva storm. Maybe it will be better weather tomorrow."

"You're kidding me, right," I said. "You want to go back up there at two o'clock tomorrow? That's only nine hours from now."

"Maybe, let's talk to Sasha when we get back to the hut. If not tomorrow, you and I are going to come back next year and kick this mother****ing mountain's ass!"

One year and one month later, Jim and I buckled up our crampons on the bench outside the Diesel Hut under a perfectly clear star-studded and moonlit night. Our friend, Ken, another lawyer from Atlanta, joined us on the porch and shone his headlamp in our direction.

"You won't be needing the torch tonight, Ken. It's clear sailing all the way to the top," I said, as Sasha emerged from the hut.

"Ready for summit?" Sasha asked.

"Sure..." Jim and I said together.

The weather on the day after our ill-fated attempt a year before was even worse than the day we had tried to reach the summit. Even at the Diesel Hut the visibility was almost nil and snow was falling. We took pictures of each other on the hill outside the Diesel Hut and the background was completely white. Then, we had to depart the mountain, as our two day window to summit had passed and we had to be ready for the van ride back to Mineralnevody the next day.

For our second trip to Elbrus, Jim and I had built in a four-day window for our summit attempt, just in case. Luckily we did, as the first two days we could have made the attempt, the weather again did not cooperate. In fact, the weather was rough even when we were acclimatizing. As a result, the Diesel Hut was over-packed with people and many groups were camped in tents outside the hut and all along the ridges up to the Rocks—all waiting for a good day to summit.

In the hut, this time we were upstairs in what turned out to be a toaster oven. The second floor of the Diesel Hut was a large room with platforms on the front and back sides and a couple of picnic tables in between. The room had absolutely no ventilation. If a fire started, we were complete goners.

When we first arrived and set up our sleeping bags, a German group was using the picnic tables. Incredibly, despite the heat, they were boiling water with gas camp stoves on the tables. This was not only an extreme fire hazard, but it also raised the temperature in the attic-like room from a toasty ninety-five degrees, to a roasting one hundred and ten degrees. We quickly learned that to rest, we had to strip to our underwear and lay on the bare mats, completely eschewing the sleeping bags. Even then, it was a sauna, without the luxury of a nice cold pool in which to dip.

The other problem with the crowded conditions in the hut was the insufficiency of the three latrines out back. Inevitably, when people have to go, they have to go. With the lines ten people deep at the latrines at times, climbers started to pee off the front porch or in the rocks above the hut indiscriminately. Privacy was not a concern. Soon the whole place reeked of urine, and Jim and Ken began a slow descent into intestinal hell.

Ken was a serious fitness maniac. He worked out six days a week, primarily using a punishing cardiovascular exercise known as "spinning." He talked about "spinning" with some lady who put him through the toughest workout in Atlanta. Ken could not run anymore due to a prior back injury, but he appeared to be in excellent shape. He had managed to make it to the top of Cheget without breaking a sweat and seemed to handle the altitude on our acclimatization treks up to and beyond the Rocks without any problem. Just another walk in the park.

However, after three days in the bacteria-infested, boiling Diesel Hut, both Ken and Jim were ready to go for the summit and get the hell of there. Their stomachs were upset; diarrhea had set in. They were not the only ones. A whole set of climbers from a Polish group were in various stages of sickness, having been in the hut for five days.

One of the Poles, a rather cute banker from Warsaw, practiced her English on us at dinner the second night we were there. She had been nursing many of the Polish climbers through their nausea, but after a few days she had started to feel ill herself. She worried that she would not even be able to attempt the summit after training for six months. I sympathized with her plight, but blamed most of the bacterial infestation on her comrades who were the worse offenders of urinal hygiene protocols.

I had camped in much worse conditions as a child (don't ask) and seemed to have a certain immunity to the elements. But I also did not crave spending another night in the toaster oven, attempting to sleep shoulder to shoulder with twelve other climbers on a twenty-four foot platform. When Sasha had announced that we would be leaving at 1:00 A.M. the next morning for the summit, we were all relieved.

Unfortunately, since the weather was expected to be good, all the other climbers on the mountain were also heading for the summit. Someone announced that Snow-Cats would be leaving for the Rocks every thirty minutes, starting at midnight until four-thirty. This meant that there would be hundreds of folks ahead of us as we climbed.

But our group would be just the four of us: three lawyer/climbers from Atlanta and Sasha, our guide. No Brit to hold us back. No chain-smoking Russian assistant guide. And this time we prayed for no "whiteout" storm.

None of us needed headlamps as we left the Diesel Hut, just after two o'clock in the morning. The light from the moon and stars filled the skies and the snow on the mountain shone almost as if it were already daylight.

With a clear sky came lower temperatures. From the start, we wore three layers under our Gore-Tex shells, along with gloves and woolen hats. At the Rocks, we would add another layer and switch to double insulated gloves, neck fleeces and balaclavas. Sasha warned us that the weather reports indicated a fifteen hour window of clear skies, but very cold temperatures.

"Stay warm. Keep moving," Sasha said anytime we took a short break for water on our way up to the Rocks.

We moved at a quick pace, but still dozens of Snow-Cats carrying hundreds of climbers churned passed us, their lights leading up the mountain to the Rocks. I couldn't help but feel that we were being cheated, having to follow a bunch of chumps who took advantage of an unfair head start.

Nevertheless, I turned my attention inward and concentrated on the task at hand. Soon I became oblivious to all going on around me. I was directly behind Sasha, matching his footprints step for step and feeling very strong. I still felt fresh as we started up the steep last section to the Rocks.

"Wow," I heard Ken yell from behind me. He was bringing up the rear. I stop, dug in my crampons and turned my head around to see what was going on.

Jim, who had been immediately in front of Ken, was no longer there. When I focused beyond Ken and down the slope, I saw Jim sliding head first on his back at an alarming speed. His arms were just bouncing alongside his body with no movement or effort to slow his fall. He appeared to be unconscious.

About sixty to eighty feet below us, Jim's body somehow shifted sideways and miraculously came to a stop. Sasha and Ken immediately rushed down to where Jim lay. I hesitated, then quickly gathered Jim's ski pole and a water bottle which had come loose in his fall, and worked my way down to them.

When I reached them, Sasha had Jim in a sitting position and was taking to him. Jim was breathing and then started to verbally respond. He had completely blacked out without warning, falling straight backwards. He had no memory of sliding down the mountain at all.

Amazingly, after about five minutes, Jim felt no after-effects. He had no injuries or even a bruise. Sasha advised him to stay seated for a little longer and see how he felt, but Jim turned onto his knees, stood up and started up the hill towards the Rocks. I scrambled after him to give him his ski pole. The three of us followed closely behind him until we were all seated just above the Rocks.

Sasha continued to talk to Jim as we grabbed some hot tea. In my worry about Jim, I forgot to eat anything in the short rest stop.

Once again, as soon as we reached the Rocks and sat down, the wind increased and the temperatures dropped. This time, it was simply too cold to dilly dally around at all, even with Jim's mysterious collapse.

After a few minutes of switching to heavier gloves and adding neck fleeces and balaclavas for further insulation from the freezing conditions, we started up the mountain again. Jim moved into the position immediately behind Sasha, who constantly turned and checked to make sure Jim was okay. I moved back to the third position and Ken remained in the shotgun position in the rear.

Ahead of us on the mountain, we could see hundreds of lights moving slowly up and across the traverse. Climbers were using their headlamps despite the very visible light. It looked like a line of Christmas carolers strolling up the hill.

With three strong climbers and Sasha in our group, we steadily caught up with and passed a number of large groups, including the thirty-plus group of Poles. I noticed the female banker was among them, working her way slowly up the slope. She must have been feeling better.

Jim apparently was also feeling better as well, as he and Sasha slowly pulled away from Ken and me as we crossed the traverse and started to approach the crest to the saddle. By then, the sun was rising to our right and the West Peak of the mountain was glowing in the light. I stopped to take a photo and immediately lost another fifty feet of distance behind Sasha and Jim. Luckily, Ken stayed with me, as Jim and Sasha never looked back. Moments later they crested the hill onto the saddle and disappeared from view. Ken and I kept up a slow but steady pace, assuming that Sasha and Jim would not go beyond the saddle without us.

For some reason, perhaps the fact that I had skipped eating anything at the Rocks and had inadvertently climbed for five hours without any nutrition, I hit the wall. Just as we reached the crest onto the saddle, all energy deserted me and I could hardly move my legs. I took twenty-five steps and then stopped. I hunched over, trying to catch my breath in complete and utter exhaustion.

After a short rest, Ken advised me to take small steps and just keep going, but I disregarded him and took off for twenty-five more determined steps. Then I stopped again, unable to move. I was so weak that I placed my hands on my knees just to stay up. This was getting embarrassing as climbers log-jammed behind me and some worked their way off the beaten path to go around me. Just then, Sasha reappeared in front of me.

"Dah-bid, you must keep going. Ve take rest and eat food in sun," he said, pointing to the other side of the saddle where the early rising sunlight had flooded the mountainside.

Sasha unclipped my day pack from my back.

"I carry, you walk," he said, immediately taking off in front of me.

I did not protest. The weight off my back was minimal, but seemed to make a difference.

If I can only make it over to the sun, then it will be okay.

Slowly, I worked across the saddle, still moving at a snail's pace. At least this time we could see the saddle, a large bowl-like expanse between the two peaks. Down to my left, I could see the logs of the ruined hut where we had tried to take shelter from the storm the year before.

"Keep going, don't stop," Ken said, as I paused to try to figure out the path we had taken the year before to get off the mountain.

"Okay, okay, just stay with me okay?" I responded desperately.

About twenty minutes later, we finally reached the sunlit portion of the saddle just at the base of the West Peak. Jim was seated, drinking hot tea and munching on a high energy bar. I collapsed in the snow next to him and Sasha immediately handed me the thermos of hot tea. As I drank it, I started to shiver. My whole body shook.

What is going on? I was now in the sun and my body should have been warming up, but it felt like it was getting colder and colder. The tea worked its way down and I managed to chew down a Snickers bar while still wondering if the shivering would ever stop. Even though we were in the sun, the temperatures were extreme. The wind swept loose snow across the surface, whipping against my legs and sides as I sat there, trying to regain my energy.

"Dah-bid, ve must get going. Too cold to stop long," Sasha said after about ten minutes rest. "Can you climb?"

"I can try," I replied, not knowing whether I could even stand up.

However, as suddenly as my fatigue had overwhelmed me, it disappeared when I got back on my feet. The shivering stopped and the candy bar kicked in.

"Let's go," I said. "What are you guys waiting for?"

I started to grab my day pack, but Sasha stepped in.

"We leave that here. Take vater. I vill carry. You climb vith no veight."

"Okay, but I have to get my camera for the top," I said, grabbing it and slipping it into one of my pockets.

While we had rested in the sun, dozens of climbers had passed us and were all simultaneously trying to move up the one foot wide diagonal path of stamped in snow up the forty degree slope of the face of the West Peak. Some groups were moving quickly, some slow. Some were roped up, most were not. As the sun melted the hard packed surface, the footing became increasingly slushy and treacherous.

I didn't mind the crowded conditions so much because it gave me ample opportunity to rest. My energy was back, but at over 18,750 feet, climbing a forty degree slope at any speed is tiring.

Ahead of me, however, some climbers began to get impatient. A roped group was stuck and not moving because one climber in the middle was exhausted. Other climbers started to work their way around the rope team, occasionally stepping off the narrow path and onto the slope below. One guy caught his foot and crampons in the rope and tumbled to his right, quickly sliding almost fifty feet down the slope towards the saddle. It looked kind of funny at the time, but we knew that the end of the saddle was riddled with crevasses, so that particular gentleman was lucky to stop and be able to climb back up to the path.

Somehow in the confusion, Sasha, Jim and Ken managed to work their way around the rope team. I could see them moving up the steep path beyond.

Wait up, you jerks!

I was unwilling to pass the stalled rope team on the low side, and the upper side of the path looked too steep to negotiate.

Just then, three guys behind me hopped up on the snow above the path and, with long strides, planted a new path in the deep snow around the impasse.

I did the same, trying to match their footprints. Unfortunately, they were considerably younger and stronger. Halfway around the rope team, I could not keep my momentum going. I lost my balance, then slid down the slope, digging in my crampons on the narrow path and coming to an abrupt stop. Now I was a tangled mess in the middle of the rope team.

Fortunately, I was able to untangle myself and the rest of the rope team elected to step just far enough to the side to let me go ahead.

By now, my team was well ahead and I was exhausted from the added exertion. I struggled mightily to make it up to where the steep section ended in a section of black rocks above. Sasha, Jim and Ken were all waiting for me when I crawled up into the rocky patch, expecting to be able to look to my left and see the summit.

Alas, to my left was yet another path up the back face of the West Peak, steeper than the first.

You have got to be kidding me!

At least this time, the path was relatively clear and our team was back together. After I grabbed a short drink of water and munched a handful of almonds, I plodded along behind Sasha and Jim. The slope was very steep but still firm as we had turned a corner and were no longer in the early morning sun. With solid footing, we seemed to make good progress. Most of the climbers had moved ahead of us or were still blocked below the slow rope team.

However, about half way up the section, the path was not packed in well. I don't know if someone had fallen or whether a patch had melted or what, but when I reached the soft spot, my foot kept sliding back down. I found myself taking steps up and sliding back with no advancement up the slope. Sasha and Jim did not realize my dilemma and just kept moving up, creating a gap between us.

"Just dig the toe of your crampons in," Ken said behind me.

"What do you think I'm doing?" I responded with frustration. "I can't get a foothold."

It was definitely too steep here to try any deviation off the beaten path. I looked down to my right. There was nothing but a sixty degree snow slope going down as far as I could see, then dropping off over a cliff. No way was I going to try the high side to the left again. I was stuck.

"Keep on trying. I'll try to boost you," Ken said after a few moments.

"Alright," I said. "I don't know how Sasha and Jim managed to go right through this."

I gathered all the energy I had left and thrust myself forward. Literally jumping up the path, I made it far enough that this time I slid only halfway back. I jumped again, gaining firm footing. Ken walked up through the same spot without any trouble, making me wonder if I was totally out of it, or just so weak that I was becoming pathetic.

Once past the soft spot, I used all the energy I had left to join Sasha and Jim at the top of the last steep section where they had been waiting for probably ten minutes as I struggled to ascend the path.

I looked again to my left, certain that I would be able to see the summit.

No such luck.

"Thee summit. It's just a little bit further," Sasha assured me. "Just up this hill and across the plateau."

"No ★★★★ing way," I said with no energy left. "I can't walk another yard."

"Come on, Schaeffer, don't be a pansy," Jim said after I had been resting for two minutes. "We didn't come this far to stop a hundred feet from the top."

"A hundred feet? I can't see it. When we get to the top of this hill, there will be another hill, and then another hill. There is no summit up here. It's all a mirage."

"No, Dah-bid, really, thee summit, it is just over that hill. It is easy from here," Sasha said. "Now get up and walk!"

They lifted me up under my shoulders and got me moving in the direction of the next hill. The next hill was actually a very slight rise of only about thirty vertical feet, but it felt like I was climbing straight up at a ninety degree angle. Just like on the saddle, I felt like I could not move my legs. Sasha was close, gently holding my left arm above my elbow, just enough to keep me moving. I closed my eyes and envisioned myself training on the hill on my street in Atlanta.

Just keep a steady pace. Slow and steady. Don't stop.

When I opened my eyes, I saw the summit only two hundred yards away across a flat section. We were crossing the crater rim of the volcano. The summit was a raised ridge at the far side, up a slope of another fifty to sixty vertical feet. Climbers were posing at the very top for pictures. A large group was sitting in the rocks just below and to the left of the summit.

Now that I could actually see the top, I knew I would make it. I pressed forward one step at a time, but still moved very slowly. This time Jim and Ken stayed with me. We would all summit together.

The last incline went quickly and soon we were just a few steps from the top.

"Stop. Ve all step together," Sasha ordered, signaling us to join arms.

The group taking photos cleared the summit and with one big step, all four of us bounded up to the rock that marks the summit of Mt. Elbrus.

"★★★★in' aye! We made it," I screamed at the top of my lungs.

I struggled to hold back the tears as we gave each other bear hugs and slapped each other on the backs. It was 10:15 A.M., just over eight hours since we had left the Diesel Hut.

All around in every direction there was nothing but air. Behind us was a drop off of nearly ten thousand feet down to the slopes below. The sky was clear blue and we could almost see forever. The Top of Europe was everything we had hope it would be. A beautiful, astounding sight. An incredible accomplishment which had taken two years to fulfill.

And a very cold place with winds that threatened to blow us off the precipice.

We quickly took photos as a group, Sasha taking most of the shots as the three of us gloried in our victory. I realized later when I saw the photos that I never took off my goggles at the top and my face is totally unrecognizable in the photos. It was just too cold and I was simply too tired. If not for my blue Gore-Tex jacket and my ice axe held straight up in the air above me, it could be anyone else up there on the summit.

But let me tell it straight. Every month of training, every step up Cheget, every step to the Rocks four times and beyond to acclimatize, every step to the saddle in the "whiteout" and back off the mountain the year before, and every painful step from the Diesel Hut to the summit on our second attempt was a step towards standing on top of the highest mountain in Europe. And we had done it. No tricks, no Snow-Cats, no Diamox, no oxygen, and no questions. God, it felt good.

Just as I had experienced at the top of Orizaba, I felt a huge sense of calm, good will, and personal satisfaction. Only this time, I had friends with whom to share it. Jim and Ken were just as excited as I was but we did not need words to express it.

There simply is no feeling like it.

My law partner, Woodie, is also a mountain climber—much more serious than me. He once turned around only 1500 vertical feet from the top of Everest, having made it that far without oxygen at age 60. On the day before we departed for Russia on our second trip to Elbrus, Woodie returned from a separate trip to Elbrus with his friend and mountain guide, Wally Berg.

Woodie had made it to the top from the Barrel Huts in one day and was no worse for the wear. When he returned to Atlanta, he wouldn't tell me about his trip, wanting me to experience it for myself. Instead, he handed me a piece of paper with a digital photo of a red rock in the middle of a patch of rocks and a drawing on the back—like a pirate's map. The summit of Elbrus was marked with a dotted line down to an "X" in the middle of a group of rocks drawn on the paper.

"When you get to the top, follow this map to the red rock and look under it," he said. "I left something under it for you."

In my joy to make it to the top of Elbrus, I almost forgot about Woodie's map. But I had mentioned it to Sasha, and Sasha reminded me about it as we stepped down from the summit. I quickly dug into my pants to find my wallet and the map.

The rocks below the summit were where most of the climbers who had reached the top were sitting when we crossed the plateau. We scrambled down to find that there were only about a thousand rocks in the area. But very few were red.

We turned over a few red rocks and nothing was under them.

"This is a waste of time," I said, figuring that we were searching for a needle in a haystack. "Let's forget it."

"Ve have a few more minutes, Dah-bid," Sasha shouted up from below me. "Ve find it—yes?"

"Okay, two more minutes," I said. I held up the digital photo once again to try to see where the particular red rock was situated.

"Is this it?" Sasha yelled, holding an object up in his hand.

"What is it?" I yelled.

"Business card. Here you read," Sasha said as he handed it to me.

In my hands, I held my partner's business card, laminated for protection. I turned it over to read the words on the back..

"Good going, Dave. Come home safe."

A simple message that said it all. It was a heck of a job getting to the top of the mountain, but coming home safe to my wife, family, friends and partners was even more important.

"Let's go down," I said. "And let's be careful. More people are hurt going down than going up."

The descent was uneventful—at least at first. As we crossed the plateau, many very fatigued groups were slowly working their way to the top. About twenty-five of the Polish group survived the climb up the face of the West Peak, including the cute banker. I gave her a few words of encouragement as she plodded by us in the direction of the summit. She looked wiped out and bewildered, just as I had thirty minutes earlier. But she too would make it.

The narrow trail down the West Peak was still fairly crowded, but going down was so much easier. When we ran into people climbing up, we were able to easily take the high side and bypass them.

My day pack was still in the same place we had left it at the base of the West Peak about three hours earlier, but was halfway buried in snow. We took a short break for food and water there. But Sasha would not let us dawdle.

"Clouds coming," he said, pointing to the sky. "Ve vaste no time. Get back to Rocks now."

The sky still looked perfectly clear to me, but I did not question Sasha's directions. I was feeling much better and had regained the strength in my legs.

We soon reached the crest where the saddle turned into the traverse and headed down the slope. The Rocks and the Diesel Hut shone in the late morning sun, way down below us. Now we were the dots moving down and across the traverse for those climbers just reaching the mountain and acclimatizing on the lower slopes.

One minute later, a cloud came through, instantly reducing our visibility to ten or fifteen feet. The whole picture changed. Sasha, who had been setting a fast pace ahead of us, disappeared ahead of us. I was closest to him, with Jim and Ken trailing, so I yelled for him to slow down. But I got no response.

I kept walking in the same direction, following the single wands. The cloud cleared and Sasha was only about thirty feet in front of me and waiting.

"Quickly now," he said. "Are you tired?"

"No—well yes, but I'm okay. It's just that we couldn't see you," I said.

"Stay close. But ve hurry down—yes?"

"Sure..." I said mimicking his voice.

Sasha turned and headed down the slope. His pace was even quicker than before.

"Come on guys," I shouted back to Jim and Ken. "Let's get the hell out of here."

There was simply no way to stay up with Sasha. Every time I looked up, he was another fifty feet ahead of us. I was going down the slope at what I considered a pretty good clip, and Jim and Ken had picked up their pace.

Another cloud system closed in on us. Again, we were instantly blinded in all directions. This time it was so thick that I could not see the next wand or even back to Jim and Ken.

"Sasha, wait!" I yelled down the hill. Again, there was no response.

We were down among the crevasses at this point. For some reason, I simply froze in place, unwilling to go up or down. I could not see anything. No wands. No Sasha to follow. No sense of direction. It is easy to understand how someone can become entirely lost on the side of the mountain only minutes after a completely clear day.

I waited, yelling a few more times in Sasha's direction. I could not make myself move.

After several minutes, Jim and Ken caught up with me and waited with me. They said that we had to keep moving. But I refused to move.

"I fell in one crevasse last year with ropes. I'm not risking that again without ropes," I said.

"Come on, we'll all go together. All the crevasses are marked with wands. We will see them," Ken responded.

"Well, you can go first," I said, finally getting up.

For the next five minutes, we moved gingerly down the slope constantly checking our footing and staring into the misty clouds in front of us for any sign of a wand. Every few minutes a single wand would come into view. We never saw any of the crossed wands indicating any crevasses. We also did not see Sasha.

Finally, as quickly as the clouds had descended on us, they lifted and our vision was restored. There was Sasha, maybe fifty feet in front of us, waiting for our arrival. He did not seemed concerned.

"Let's keep together," I pleaded.

"Must hurry," Sasha responded again. "Stay close."

Fortunately, the clouds were behind and above us the rest of the way down. Jim, Ken and I stayed together as Sasha pressed down the slope before us. When we finally reached the Rocks, Sasha took off, with Ken not far behind him. Jim and I stayed together. Jim had not had any more problems, but sensed that he was fading. I knew I should stay with him all the way down.

Something about nearing the bottom of the mountain after a successful but tiring summit day makes one candid and truthful about one's feelings. We were now about twelve hours into our climb up and down Elbrus and there was little energy left. It had been a wonderful, but tough day. Jim had blacked out less than two hours after leaving the

Diesel Hut. I had endured two periods of completely drained energy, almost to the point of turning back. We were both wiped out.

My legs were moving now, not because of any effort on my part, but simply as a result of gravity pulling us down the slope. Jim was sliding and moving at a pace much slower than any of our prior descents from the Rocks.

"I'm never doing this again," Jim said matter-of-factly.

"Me neither," I said. "This was great, but I don't think I can do another mountain like this."

"I just want to go home," Jim continued.

"Yeah," I said.

But then I added, "Let's see how we feel tomorrow."

Back at the Diesel Hut, Sasha had hurried back and organized the gear and provisions for us to leave the mountain that afternoon. Jim and I arrived back at the hut at 2:30 P.M., twelve and a half hours after we left the hut that morning. The last chair lift down was at 4:00 P.M., giving us only an hour and a half to get something to eat, pack and hike the slope down to the Barrel Huts, where the chair lift ended.

Ken was already packing his gear in the roasting attic of the hut. I was ready to be off the mountain, but I did not see how I could possibly do any more hiking that day, even downhill.

"Let's just stay one more night and go down tomorrow morning, nice and easy," I pleaded.

"I'm not staying another minute in this cesspool," Ken responded curtly.

"We're out of here," Jim added.

"Shit," I said, knowing that I was outvoted.

"Exactly," Jim said. "This place is a shit hole and I'm not sleeping here one more night. I've got to get a shower and have a real bed to sleep in tonight."

Thirty minutes later, we were once again sliding and letting gravity pull us down the slope below the Diesel Hut. Sasha arranged for porters to carry our backpacks and gear, so we were only packing our day backs and some water for the trip down. We left at least twenty minutes before Sasha and the porters and the time was getting short as we reached the last slope above the Barrel Huts. The view of the orange Barrel huts below us and the top of the chair lift brought a tidal wave of relief. I navigated the final slope through misty eyes.

When we reached the chairlift with only five minutes to spare, Sasha and the porters were still not in sight. We scanned the last hill above us, hoping to see them. With about two minutes left, Sasha and about five porters came hurdling over the last hill like a small herd of buffalo. They were galloping down the slope almost like skiers, the heavy backpacks shifting back and forth on their backs and boxes bouncing up and down in their arms.

With seconds left, the packs and provisions were loaded on chairs and we were scooped off the mountain for the trip home.

Jim and Ken did not make breakfast the next day. This time we had eschewed the granite chalet of Hotel Cheget and were staying in one of the newer hotels at the end of the gravel area of the Cheget village. Breakfast was at 8:00 A.M., and I had woken up early, with no soreness or signs of fatigue from the prior day's long trek. Amazingly, I felt fine and actually felt raring to go. Because we had reached the summit on our third day of a four day window and not stayed on the mountain that night, we had two extra days at Cheget to enjoy the mountains leisurely.

Sasha joined me a few minutes after I sat down. He asked me how I was feeling and quickly said that a storm had come in overnight. It was good we were off the mountain.

We figured Jim and Ken would join us shortly. But after a delicious breakfast of eggs, sausage, and fruit, they were still nowhere to be seen.

"If it stops raining, do you vant to do short hike today—to glacier or observatory?" Sasha asked as we stood up after breakfast.

"Yes, maybe to the glacier—not to the observatory," I said, knowing that the observatory was a strenuous climb up to a level almost even with the Barrel Huts. I had heard the view from the observatory was spectacular, but I was not about to kill myself. "Let's wait and see how the weather is by ten o'clock and see what Jim and Ken want to do."

"Sure…I'll check back here at ten," Sasha said.

But Jim and Ken did not get out of bed that day. Both had a mystery illness which combined fatigue, nausea, diarrhea and just plain inertia.

They called it the Diesel Hut Syndrome and were unable to get out of bed except to crawl to the toilet and let loose from both ends.

Sasha and I ended up hiking up to a little village nearby, having a small lunch with local friends of his in a tiny house. As the guest of honor, I was allowed to sit in the nicest arm chair. My protests were ignored and I realized that if I did not accept the honor, I would be dishonoring my hosts.

To this day, I cannot tell you what we had to eat for lunch. My mind has effectively blocked out the horror of the taste—something between cat food and sardines spread on bread that could not be swallowed, even after five minutes of agonizing chews. I do remember my sinuses being completely cleared for several days.

After lunch, Sasha and I hiked on, across the main road towards the Elbrus cable cars, and up a dirt road behind a long row of rickety wooden animal shelters. Just as we approached the structures, the rain swept in again, turning the dirt into mud. Soon we were marching through swampy cow dung liberally scattered everywhere. At first, I tried to avoid the piles, but as we got further up the road, there was no unsoiled path to follow. I gave up and plowed right through the bovine excrement until we finally reached a bridge and crossed over into a grassy field leading up a valley towards a large glacier hanging over the edge of the mountain in front of us.

The rain let up and we hiked in a cold drizzle for several hours, steadily ascending towards the glacier. To our right was a field with wild flowers, cattle and some horses scattered across the landscape. To our left was a swiftly flowing stream with grey water cascading down from the glacier. Beyond the stream was a cliff towering above us, made of brown stone with sharp, craggy outcroppings at the top. Despite the rain, it was simply beautiful.

Near the top of the valley on the left side was a gorgeous waterfall, maybe eighty feet high and gushing with water from the glacier and the recent storms. I resisted Sasha's suggestion that we climb the scree slope to get up to the waterfall, as we had already been hiking for about three hours and I was starting to get cold.

On the way back to Cheget Village, Sasha got on his phone several times and arranged for a successful summit celebration party back at a café on the gravel square. He asked me to make sure Jim and Ken joined us, because he wanted all of us to enjoy the Russian tradition.

Alas, my friends were still unable to move out of their beds. I would have to hold up our end of the tradition on my own, along with about five of Sasha's friends.

As it turned out, in that part of the world, the tradition is to celebrate with water melon, chocolate and vodka. Sasha expertly carved up a large watermelon with one of the sharpest butcher knives I've ever seen, before liberally sprinkling vodka over the cut pieces. Then he broke out several large chocolate bars and demonstrated the proper technique for eating the chocolate and washing it down with the spiked watermelon. After we were slightly buzzed from the watermelon, Sasha went to the bar and came back with "shot" glasses, which were really more like small orange juice glasses. The remaining vodka was poured into the glasses and everyone but me chugged theirs in less than a second.

"I don't do vodka shots or appletinis," I said, having learned the hard way in college that a large amount of vodka and my system never did go together. "But I'll take a bottle of Baltika #7," I added quickly, referring to my favorite local beer of the region.

Three Baltika #7's for me and a lot of chocolate and vodka for Sasha and the rest later, the celebration was in full swing. I knew that this was "old hat" for Sasha and his friends. But it was special for this American, making Russian friends and sharing their traditions to celebrate an awesome accomplishment the day before. I only wish Jim and Ken had been there to share it with us.

The storm that day took its toll on climbers high up on Elbrus. A Japanese group of seven climbers, who had shared our platform in the Diesel Hut attic the night we left for the summit, had made their summit push on the same day that Sasha and I had hiked in the rain. They were supported by three Russian guides. At first we heard that the Japanese father had been lost up in the saddle and was feared dead. Then Sasha informed us that it was not a climber, but one of the guides who had been lost. The group had been caught in a "whiteout" and had kept going up, ascending the steep narrow path up the side of the West Peak above the saddle. The missing guide had been in the rear and apparently took a mis-step and slid down the hill towards the saddle, falling into a crevasse somewhere below.

I wondered if it was the same crevasse into which I had almost disappeared the year before.

A search party was dispatched first thing in the morning as the skies cleared. Miraculously, the guide was found and rescued, but one of his arms was so frostbitten that it had to be amputated.

The incident brought me back from the celebration the night before to the stark reality that with every gloriously successful summit, there is a corresponding danger, especially when unnecessary risks are taken. The year before, our group had made the wise decision to turn back in the storm and survived unscathed to climb on a better day. The Japanese group chose another, more risky route, and calamity ensued.

The year before, several weeks before our "whiteout" experience, four Czech climbers had gotten lost in a storm attempting to climb the second leg of the face of the West Peak. Their bodies were found several weeks later by a group led by Wally Berg. Several days later, two Canadian climbers had successfully reached the summit of the West Peak, and, against the instructions and protest of their guides, they decided to try to summit the East Peak the same day. They disappeared, presumably falling into unmarked crevasses on that side of the saddle, their bodies never being recovered.

In May 2006, seven climbers attempting to reach the summit of Elbrus from the remote northern side of the mountain perished in a five day snow storm. It was too early in the season to safely attempt a summit from that side of the mountain, and to add to the danger, there are no huts to which retreat is possible on that side of the mountain. However, they apparently knew the risk and embraced it, a fatal mistake of judgment.

The morale of the story is that every high altitude mountain, no matter where, has risks. The lesson to be learned is that risks can be minimized by proper planning. Choosing the best time of the year to climb is crucial, taking the safest route is wise, making sure you have the right equipment and an experienced guide is critical, and knowing when to turn back and try again another time is probably the most important factor. Otherwise, tragedies which could be avoided will inevitably happen.

For me, the final day in Cheget was wonderful. The skies were clear and blue. All of the mountain tops were shining in the morning sun. The aches and pains from the effort of the week were gone.

This time, both Jim and Ken made it up for breakfast, but both had pale green faces. They picked at their food while Sasha and I discussed our final hike, a climb up to a tongue like glacier hanging down from a mountain to the left of Donguzeran. It would be a spectacular hike and Sasha promised we could climb right up to the ice.

Thirty minutes later, Sasha led Jim, Ken and me along a path next to the main river draining the Cheget basin. After about a half mile, we crossed the river on some logs strategically placed across a narrow section. Soon we were hiking in a forested section of woods on the other side.

Jim and Ken were still complaining about weakness and nausea, but they seemed to be dealing with it. I felt great.

Following a tributary stream, we turned left and started climbing. The trail got very steep as we worked our way up towards a small waterfall.

That was as far as Jim got. He was clearly still too sick to make this climb and his face was an ashen shade of grey-green. Sasha escorted him back down the trail and helped him across the river. Jim spent another day in bed, moaning constantly about the damned Diesel Hut.

After Sasha returned, the three of us worked our way across a gentle slope above the small waterfall. The fields around us were filled with red, yellow, purple and blue flowers of all sorts and sizes, so beautiful that Monet would have loved to paint them.

Straight above us was the tongue-like glacier descending from the mountain top, beckoning us upwards. It was simply a magnificent sight.

Between us and the glacier was a wide expanse of gently rising snow and a steeper rocky section above it. Sasha led us onto the snow which was hard and well packed, almost icy. Without crampons, we slowly traversed the slick surface. Fortunately it had pockets of flat sections to break up the slope.

Looking around, we could see the Cheget village below us and a crystal clear Elbrus beyond it, both peaks entirely unblemished by any clouds. It was another "perfect" summit day.

For me, it was also a perfect day for a picnic on the warm rocks at the base of the glacier. After I devoured some lunch and Ken managed to get something down, we laid back on some rocks and enjoyed a half hour in the sun. I am sure I enjoyed it more than Ken, who was still suffering from the mystery malady. I could not imagine a nicer final day for our Elbrus trip.

The only nicer part of the end of the trip was the hugs and kisses I received from my wife and kids when I arrived safely back in Atlanta two days later.

Only then did I begin to plan my next climb—Kilimanjaro, the tallest mountain in Africa.

KILIMANJARO

"THE MIRACLE WALK"

From the dirt road filled with hundreds of Tanzanian school girls in uniforms heading back from church towards somewhere down the road from our hotel, I gazed upwards, craning my neck towards the sky. There, way above where any solid ground should appear, was the glacier-covered giant of a mountain called Kilimanjaro, majestically shining in the bright morning sun.

I could not take my eyes off the sight. Kilimanjaro, the largest free-standing mountain in the world, loomed over the little town of Moshi, at least 14,000 feet below the summit. The broad, snow-capped peak simply dominated the entire Northern horizon. Several icy glaciers formed tongue-like patterns along the massive volcano's Southern crater rim, creating a mystical and magnetic feel from the ground. I felt the mountain drawing me to it. *Climb me!*

It was February 2005, and Kilimanjaro would be my second of the so-called Seven Summits, after having successfully reached the top of Elbrus six months earlier. Still well-conditioned after my return from Russia, I devoted only three months of training for this climb. My research led me to believe that Kilimanjaro, while over 19,000 feet high, was a relatively easy ascent spread over five to six days. Purportedly, anyone in decent shape could reach the top.

Unlike my prior trips, I had no involvement in arranging the Kilimanjaro trek. My brother Brent, who had accompanied me on my climbs of Orizaba and my first attempt to climb Elbrus, planned the whole thing through a travel agent in South Africa. Brent had successfully climbed "Kili," as the mountain is sometimes affectionately called, about thirty years ago when he was stationed in Kenya with the Peace Corps.

Now his wife, Mpopo, a native of the flat, mostly desert country of Botswana, wanted to climb Kilimanjaro to fulfill a lifelong dream.

I, along with my youngest brother, Eric, who like Brent was working for USAID in Pretoria, South Africa, decided to tag along on the trip. The only thing I had to do was to buy a plane ticket for the fifteen hour non-stop flight to Johannesburg from Atlanta and get a few vaccine shots and malaria pills.

On arrival in Jo'Burg, as they call it there, I wondered whether Mpopo and Eric would be in good shape. I had no concern about Brent, who always seemed to stay trim and physically active. I knew Mpopo had trained for and run in a marathon a few years earlier, so I assumed she would similarly train for this adventure. Eric had scaled the highest peak in the Atlas Mountains in Morocco when he was stationed there and was always the most stubbornly feisty of the Schaeffer boys. But when I had last seen him, he had put on considerable weight.

The Johannesburg airport is a confusing place with an exceedingly long and narrow terminal and very few reliable signs. Once I gathered my bags, I knew I had to meet Brent, Eric, and Mpopo at the ticket counter for Tanzania Airlines for the flight to Dar Es Salaam. However, there were no useful directions anywhere. Everyone I asked seemed just as confused as I was. Fortunately, I had about a four hour layover between the flights, so I didn't panic.

After about twenty minutes of walking around in circles, I finally found the international departure terminal at the opposite end of the airport from my arrival gate. The only problem was that there were no Tanzania Airlines counters among the sixty to seventy consecutively numbered counters in that terminal. I walked up and down, thinking I must have missed it, but Tanzania Airlines simply was not there.

Frustrated, I returned to the central area in the main terminal of the airport and started asking people again. A man with an airport uniform of some sort pointed me back in the direction of the international departure terminal from which I had just come.

"I just left there and there is no Tanzania Airlines counter," I responded. He shrugged his shoulders as if to suggest that I was crazy, then turned to help someone else.

As I was about to throw up my hands and give up, a sweaty young South African lad in an grungy orange vest offered to help. On his vest was a well-worn badge that looked somewhat official.

"Follow me," he said, grabbing my heaviest suitcase and quickly walking away. I scrambled after him, hoping the guy was not stealing my bag.

I immediately realized that following this guy downwind was going to be a challenge. The body odor emanating from the fellow almost made me pass out. I kept him in sight while maintaining a safe distance until he motioned me towards a small elevator door.

"This way—upstairs. Your flight is not open yet," he said as I caught up to him. "You must wait up here until one hour before your flight."

A few seconds later, the elevator door opened and we maneuvered my bags and ourselves into the tiny space. I held my breath as long as I could to avoid the odorous fumes, but the elevator ascended so slowly that I finally had to exhale and breath in some of the putrid air. My eyes were watering when the elevator door opened. I stepped out, grabbing a lungful of moderately fresh oxygen.

My guide stepped quickly ahead of me once again. I dutifully followed him to a waiting area that overlooked the international departure terminal.

"Do you want something to drink while you wait?" he asked in a strangely polite tone.

"No, that's okay, I'm good. Thank you," I said.

He stood there, waiting for about ten seconds, then said, "You have American dollars? I can change them for you over there behind the bar."

"No, no, that's okay," I said quickly, suddenly feeling like I was being played.

Then I finally realized there was no way this young man would leave without some sort of tip. Unfortunately, all I had was a wad of twenty dollar bills.

"Okay, let's go over to the bar. I'll get a drink and change some cash," I said, heading in that direction.

Out of the corner of my eye I saw my guide smile.

"Let me have a Coca Cola, please," I said to the man behind the bar. "I assume you take American dollars."

"Yes," he said, immediately pouring me an 8-ounce Coke and taking a twenty. He glanced knowingly at my ever present bag toter.

For the next five minutes, I watched as the bartender calculated and re-calculated the exchange rate and finally handed me eighty Rands in change. I was never that good at math, but I figured with six Rands to the dollar, I should have gotten at least a hundred twenty Rands, minus maybe twelve Rands for the Coke. But I had just spent about forty Rands, the equivalent of seven bucks, for a miniature Coca Cola, and my local luggage assistant was still waiting with his hand now held out.

Shit. How much is this gonna cost me?

I finally held out twenty Rands, just over three bucks. He smiled and dropped his hand, refusing to take it. I was not getting off that cheap.

A few minutes later, he finally left with sixty Rands and a skip in his step. Oh well, I had just generously contributed ten bucks to the Jo'Burg economy. At least I could breathe again.

About a half hour later, my momentary power nap in the waiting area was interrupted by a familiar voice.

"Doo-fus!" I heard from the direction of the elevator. Eric loved to torture me with my detested childhood nickname.

"Emile!" I responded instantly, using Eric's adopted name from his junior high French class.

A large bear hug ensued, during which I quickly discerned that Eric had not lost much weight for the trip. At five foot seven, he looked to be carrying about 180 pounds, probably twenty to twenty-five pounds overweight.

Brent and Mpopo followed closely behind, dragging more luggage and some large duffel bags. Brent looked svelte as usual, but it was clear Mpopo had not run any marathons recently. During a small lunch, I talked about the importance of endurance and finally asked what training schedule they had followed. To my chagrin, I learned that Eric and Mpopo had devoted only a few weeks to try to get in shape. Their regimen had consisted of a couple of long runs/walks. At least their minimal training had taken place in the mile high city of Pretoria, just an hour north of Jo'Burg, so maybe they had a head start on acclimatizing.

I shrugged my shoulders. "This may not be the hardest mountain to climb, but it's over 19,000 feet. You guys are gonna be dying."

"David, don't worry," Mpopo replied in her crisply clipped African-British accent. "I will make it to the top on sheer will power."

About an hour before our flight, one of the international terminal ticket booths suddenly turned into a Tanzania Air counter. Apparently, there are simply too many internal African air carriers to have permanent counters for each of them. So they share space and have reversible signs which can be adjusted as the flight nears. I had just been there too early.

"I swear there was no Tanzania Air counter here before," I told Brent.

"Sure..." he said giving me a strange look. "You obviously don't travel much outside the States."

Getting through the approval process to get to the departure gate took forever. Mpopo's bags were overweight and an excise tax had to be paid in cash. Rather than pay the cash, we rearranged some of her clothes into our bags, and finally managed to slide through with no penalty.

I noticed that Eric was flirting with the pretty South African ticket lady, but passed it off as a harmless diversion.

The three or four hour flight to Dar Es Salaam was quite uneventful. Eric and I caught up on family matters and I filled him in on the wonders and challenges of having climbed Elbrus. He in turn confided in me the troubles he was having with his marriage. His wife, from whom he was now separated, had actually tried to join us for the expedition, apparently in an attempt to reconcile. Fortunately, Eric had talked her out of it. A mountain climb of this magnitude did not need any distractions. I just hoped that Eric wouldn't dwell on his marital conflicts for the entire trip.

The sun was setting as we landed at Dar Es Salaam Airport, the low lying buildings to the right of the airport hardly making any impression on my memory. The Tanzanian capital looked more like a garden community than a city—at least through the small plane windows at dusk.

As we walked into the terminal and over to the departure gate for our next flight to Kilimanjaro, I realized that most of the group waiting at the gate was part of our expedition. Brent introduced us to Janet, the travel agent from Green Rhino Travel, who had arranged the trip. Though fifty-six years old, she seemed quite fit and had the look of an adventurer. She seemed nice, an outgoing sort. I immediately liked her.

Over the next few minutes, she introduced us to the group.

It turned out that our team of ten climbers consisted of six women and four guys. The ages ranged from twenty-seven to fifty six, the youngest being a banker named Patrick from Mozambique, the only other male besides me and my brothers, and the oldest being Janet, our tour guide. Brent was a week short of fifty-six and Eric was fifty-two years young. Mpopo and I were in our late forties. Then there were Karin and Cherie, two fairly athletic looking women who appeared to be in their early forties, and two younger women with short cropped hair. Probably in their early thirties, their names were Brenda and Joline.

Looking at this rather motley crew, I wondered whether anyone in the group was ready to climb a 19,400 foot mountain. As a reasonably experienced climber, I felt a bit out of place.

However, I soon learned that appearances were deceiving. Brenda and Joline were ultra-marathoners who annually run a 90K race in Durban, South Africa. Joline was a musician and singer who had recorded albums and a theme song for that race. It did not take me long to also realize they were more than just running partners.

Cherie was a regular marathoner who had climbed some more modest mountains in central South Africa. Karin turned out to be another travel agent and had done a lot of adventure traveling.

Suddenly, I began to worry that the rest of the group may actually be more prepared than our family to scale the highest mountain in Africa. I had never even run a half-marathon, let alone a 90K race. Actually, I had never even heard of a race that long.

On the other hand, I had successfully climbed three times to over 18,000 feet without any serious problem. I also knew that some of the most fit marathon runners simply can't handle that type of altitude. Mountain sickness affects people differently and unpredictably, regardless of the level of fitness. So it was dangerous to pre-judge anyone's capabilities. It would be up to the mountain gods.

By the time we landed at Kilimanjaro Airport, I was fading fast. I had been flying or waiting in airports for approximately thirty straight hours and had gotten very little sleep.

But we still had an hour bus drive to our hotel in Moshi.

Alas, sleeping was impossible on the bus. The seats were uncomfortable, the road was rough, and everyone kept thinking they could see Kili to the left or the right of the bus, when in fact no one could see anything but the pitch black night. I didn't even know in which direction I should look to see the mountain. At that point, I really didn't care. I just wanted to have a nice bed on which to crash.

Making matters worse, all of our bags were crammed into the rear seats of the bus where we were sitting, alongside several of the "porters" who had loaded them onto the bus. Once again, I wondered if my nose would survive the ride, as the air became thicker by the minute. Fortunately, the bus had windows which could open. After struggling with a latch, I was able to open one, lean over and suck in some warm, fresh air as we meandered and lurched down the road.

Arriving in Moshi, the bus took a right turn at a large roundabout. The paved road ended a few hundred yards further. Then, for two minutes, I experienced one of the bumpiest bus rides I could ever remember. Potholes which must have been at least eighteen inches deep filled the road from side to side. The bus jerked left and right and up and down, sending us into the aisles and crashing us forward into the seats in front of us. With no seat belts, we had no control over where we were thrown.

Mercifully, the beating lasted only for about a quarter of a mile. The bus slowed, then turned sharply into a gated driveway on our right, pulling up in front of a dingy white building surrounded by shade trees. At last, our hotel.

That is, our un-airconditioned hotel.

After what seemed like an endless check-in process, Eric and I dragged our bags and gear into a room on the second floor on the back right corner of the hotel. The room was toasting hot. We looked for a thermostat or fan, but there was nothing. We opened windows on both outer sides of the room, hoping to get a cross draft of air. However, the outside air was almost as hot as the inside of the room. Nothing seemed to work.

"I saw a bar downstairs. Let's get a brewsky," I said to Eric. "Maybe it will cool down in here if we leave the windows open for a while."

"I don't think so," Eric replied, but followed me out into the hall. My T-shirt was already becoming a moist mess.

Downstairs was almost deserted. All of our team had disappeared into their rooms.

We walked through a dining area, which surprisingly was quite graceful with dark wood paneling and white table clothes. A sprig of freshly cut flowers in small glass vases on the tables added a nice touch to the decor. Beyond the dining area was a smaller room with a billiard table—but no balls or cue sticks. On the right was a glass front beverage refrigerator with Cokes and other drinks in it. Outside was a large patio. Beyond it down some steps, I could see a pool, the greenish water glistening under some floodlights from the building.

Maybe this isn't such a bad place after all.

At the end of the large room behind the pool table was a huge, L-shaped mahogany bar with a few bar stools.

Nice bar, but no bartender.

Once perched atop the stools, we casually glanced around to see if we could get some service. After a few minutes, a woman in a black and white uniform resembling a Southern maid's uniform from years past approached us and informed us that the bar was closed.

But Eric was not taking no for an answer. He started protesting about how far we had come… and how hot it was… and how his brother had traveled all the way from America just to have a beer in this hotel…, and on and on, until the woman relented. Eric is definitely a talented and effective bullshitter when needed.

Moments later, a man slid behind the bar and finally poured us some beers—lukewarm ones that did nothing to cool us down or quench our thirst.

We didn't stay for a second glass.

That night, I tossed and turned in the roasting room, sweating into my pillow and sheets, wondering if I would ever fall asleep. The frustrating thing was that I couldn't figure out if my insomnia was due to the heat or to the fact that I was just too damned tired to sleep.

After a nice breakfast of fruit, cereal, cheese and Danish, I stepped outside to see what the surroundings looked like in the daylight. As I stepped through the front doors of the hotel, all I could heard was the cheerful chattering of what seemed to be thousands of school girls walking down the street in front of the hotel.

Out of curiosity, I stepped out onto the dirt road in front of the hotel. The girls in uniforms filled the street, running and skipping in both directions as far as I could see. The only other movement consisted of a few young boys zipping along the dirt shoulders of the road on dusty bicycles, dodging holes and rocks as they went along.

With my focus on the children, I did not raise my eyes towards the sky in either direction. Then I saw Brent coming back down the road from my right, carrying his camera. I finally looked up.

Oh my God!

I stood completely still, staring into the sky, mesmerized by Kilimanjaro.

In an excellent bit of planning, Janet had scheduled a full rest day in Moshi. This is always prudent in case of baggage losses, late arrivals, and, in my case, a lack of sleep due to intercontinental travel.

After a dry and dusty stroll down the dirt road in the direction of Kili for some early photos of our lofty destination, the hotel pool beckoned. By the time I arrived, Karin and Cheri were already lounging near the pool, staying in the shade of nearby trees. In bathing suits, they looked even more fit.

The trees were certainly nice for blocking the sun on the pool deck. But they also dropped thousands of pieces of what I can only describe as "tree gunk" into the pool, most of which had accumulated in the end nearest the hotel, making the water look very uninviting.

To the left of the pool deck, leaning against one of the trees, was a pool skimmer of sorts. The "basket" at the top of the metal pole was seriously shredded, but after a few attempts, I managed to master a scooping technique which cleared the water of the worst sections of "tree gunk." By the time I completed a barely passable job of skimming the water, I was sweating profusely in the morning sun.

Eric and Brent joined me just as I finished. Together we jumped in like school boys at summer camp.

Regrettably, the water was hot and not the least bit refreshing. However, after a few laps of the pool, I noticed the far end was cooler. Working my way along the far wall of the pool, I found the only cold water feed a few inches below the surface. I pressed my head against the side and let the cool stream cascade against my back. *Nice.*

Within five minutes, a hot breeze had hit the surrounding trees and the pool again was covered in "tree gunk." This time it was Brent's turn to skim, while I found a lounge chair in which to snooze. I nodded off for maybe a half hour before waking up in a sweat and jumping back into the pool.

Lunch was on our own, so Brent, Eric and I decided to venture into town for some local food. Mpopo was nowhere to be seen, apparently still sleeping in her room.

The hotel advertised its ability to get taxis to the town center, but after waiting for ten minutes and seeing no taxi, we elected to walk the approximately one-half mile to town.

It was Sunday morning, and just beyond the large roundabout, church was letting out. Another long stream of humanity poured out of a building on our right, with half of the people heading towards town and half turning in our direction. Suddenly, the street was filled on both sides. The few cars and buses trying to weave their way through the crowds simply had to wait for the throng to disperse.

Brent led the way down the left side of the road, dodging mostly children and women. I noticed that the church was a Lutheran one. For a slight moment I felt guilty for missing the service. My father was a Lutheran pastor, and even on vacations in Europe, we had always managed to find a church to attend on Sundays. I well remember attending a church in Yugoslavia one Sunday in 1964 when I was eight years old. I could not understanding a word said or sung during the service. But back then we were devoted churchgoers no matter what the circumstances.

My guilt was fleeting, however, as moments later, a young man sprinted from a market on the right of the road, followed closely behind by a mob of angry men yelling at the top of their lungs. We stepped back against a wall as the young man went flying passed us, fleeing for his life. The mob behind him slowly gained ground, like the peloton in the Tour de France reeling in a breakaway rider at the end of a stage.

About a quarter mile down the road, the mob caught up to its quarry, then beat the living daylights out of him. Apparently, the young man had snitched an item from the market without paying for it, and the vigilantes had exacted their revenge. Fortunately for the thief, after a few minutes of pounding, the mob dragged him off to the nearby police station where he could be charged and receive well-needed medical attention.

And we thought it was going to be a boring trip to the town center for some lunch!

That afternoon, our group met for an orientation session led by our head mountain guide, Michael. Michael was a native Tanzanian who had worked his way up the various levels of porters, obtained basic first aid and mountain guide training, and had guided dozens of groups successfully to the top of Kilimanjaro.

In this part of Tanzania, the head mountain guides are demi-gods upon which all of the porters, cooks, assistant guides and bus drivers depend for their livelihoods. The head guide had the exclusive contact with the climbers and expedition leaders, so he would receive all of the payment for every porter and assistant. It was against standard protocol for climbers to tip or pay individual porters, as it was up to the head guide to dole out the money at the end of the trip, depending on how well each of the porters performed. Michael emphasized these points at our first meeting, making sure to solidify his place at the top of the heap.

The rest of the session included directions on what to bring on the climb and how to pack it for the porters, repeated admonishments to climb slowly at all times, a brief outline of the six days anticipated on the mountain, and a rundown of equipment that could be rented from Michael at a "reasonable" price.

We were to carry only our own day packs, with water bottles, a few layers of extra clothing and a snack or two. Everything else was to be packed in a single large duffel bag or case that could be carried on the head of a single porter who would be assigned to each climber. No traditional back packs were allowed to be used. Apparently, porters did not like to carry climber's things on their backs. We later learned that most of them had very small day packs to carry their own change of clothes on their backs while carrying our stuff on their heads.

I had brought a huge blue Slazenger duffel bag which could hold my sleeping bag, an inflatable pad, all of my clothes and cold weather climbing gear, and a substantial amount of extra food in case the grub provided by the cook was not satisfactory.

At this first meeting, we were also introduced to the phrase that would be our mantra for the next six days—"Po-le, Po-le"—meaning slowly, slowly. Michael explained that on Kilimanjaro, there is no hurry. Every day on the climb is carefully spaced out and important for acclimatization. Those who go too fast pay for it with nausea and headaches. They do not make it to the top.

"Everyone in my group will make it to the crater rim—a successful climb—if they remember po-le, po-le," Michael said at the end of his talk.

The crater rim? What about the summit?

I knew from my research that, on the Machame route we were taking, we would reach the rim of the Kibo central volcanic crater on the fifth day of the climb at a spot called Stella Point. But the highest point on the crater rim was Uhuru Peak, another 700 feet above and to the west of Stella Point. Just making it to the crater rim would not be a successful climb for me. I wanted to make sure we planned on continuing on to the true summit.

"For those who are willing and able, yes, we will go to Uhuru Peak," Michael assured us. Yet, to me, his tone and demeanor said that, just looking at us, he had serious doubts about the fitness of our group. He was already downplaying expectations.

Nervous excitement was in the air as we loaded the bus the next morning for our bus ride to the Machame Gate trail head, approximately one and one-half hours from our hotel.

As the bus zoomed along the highway running parallel to the southern side of Kilimanjaro, heading towards the western end of the mountain, I couldn't help but notice that the agriculture in the region was still almost medieval. Farmers were toiling in the large flat fields at the base of the mountain, digging up clods of dirt with hoes made from long sticks and sharp rocks attached only by small ropes or strings. Acres and acres of farmland appeared to have been plowed by hand with these rudimentary, makeshift tools. There were a few farms with tractors and mechanized plows, but by far the more pervasive method was the old fashioned way. In Tanzania, even farming was "Po-le, po-le."

After turning right and heading straight towards the mountain, the bus quickly started to climb. Soon we were beyond the flat farm and heading up a gravel road through forested hills. Both sides of the road were sporadically lined with huts and small houses, interrupted by a few concrete-walled stores or restaurants.

Interestingly, almost all of the dwellings or structures within fifty feet of the road had large red X's painted on their walls. Upon inquiry, Michael informed us that the Tanzanian government intended, sometime in the future, to widen and pave the road to improve tourism. Each of the houses or stores marked with the red X were to be demolished to make room for the new road. From our vantage, that appeared to be about ninety percent of all the structures along the road. We wondered how the local inhabitants would be able to afford to rebuild if the road project ever occurred. Michael told us that it would probably be another ten years before the project got underway. Meanwhile, no one was building any new homes or maintaining any of the existing structures within the right of way. This explained why the buildings all looked dirty and neglected.

As the road got steeper, the tires of the bus dug in for traction. Soon the dust was coming up through the floor boards and vents of the bus. Closing the windows did no good whatsoever. The only defense was to cover our faces with bandannas and breathe through the cloth. By the time we finally pulled up in front of some buildings marking the end of the road and the entry to the Machame Gate, we were covered in a thick layer of orange dust which seemed to cling tightly to everything it touched. But at least we had finally arrived. I, for one, was ready to escape the planes and buses and start climbing.

The trail head compound was a bustling place, with climbers, guides and souvenir hawkers milling around everywhere. Aggressive shirt and hat sellers pressed against us as we disembarked from the bus. Michael shooed them off and led us quickly through a large A-frame gate, beyond which the merchandise pushers were not allowed. They continued to wave hats, T-shirts, and packs of Kili photos through the gate, begging us to buy something.

Once inside the gate, to the right was a small cottage with a covered entrance leading to a window with bars, through which all permits had to be processed. That is, once it became our group's turn. When we arrived, at least a hundred people were lined up and none of them appeared to moving anywhere fast.

"Po-le, po-le," Michael said, smiling. "Find some shade and get a snack. If you need to go to the bathroom, go now. I'll let you know when it is time to get in line for the permits. Stay close and be ready."

An hour later, we had snacked, peed, stretched, re-stretched and were still waiting in the shade. Our group was getting restless.

Two hours later, we were getting downright impatient. We watched as countless other groups completed the process and headed up towards the beginning of the trail. Porters were loading provisions and baggage onto their heads and moving up the trail. Groups of fresh climbers, looking like they were out for a Sunday afternoon stroll, disappeared into the woods. Yet, our group was going nowhere, still cooling our heels under some shade trees. *Come on already!*

At about 1:30 P.M., Michael finally motioned us into line at the permit hut. One by one we moved to the window, filled out a single line with name, address, and passport numbers, showed our passports and were issued permits, all of which were immediately handed over to Michael. We couldn't figure out why it had taken so long to complete this simple registration process. The only explanation is that in Tanzania, nothing happens fast.

Moments later, we followed Michael up to the beginning of the trail. There he informed us that he would organize the porters for the climb and his first assistant would lead us up to the first camp, a climb of approximately five hours through the "rain forest."

I had seen a documentary on Kilimanjaro and watched video of climbers struggling to climb up muddy slopes in torrential downpours on the first day of their trip up this same trail. But on this day in February, 2005, the path was dry and the weather warm, without a cloud in the sky.

In fact, the first mile or so was on a wide, gravel service road, like a stroll in the park. Then, passing through a gate, we started up a gradually rising trail which was so manicured that we could have been walking on a botanical garden path at Callaway Gardens. On each side of the five or six foot wide trail were wooden supports lined along the path, creating a drainage ditch to the left and the right. Between the wooden supports, dirt and wood chips had been tramped in, creating easy and smooth footing. Orange, yellow and purple flowers seemed to have been sprinkled along both sides of the path.

"Geez," I said to Eric. "This is tough, huh?"

"Yeah," he replied, "but at least we are finally moving. I thought we'd never get going."

The only dangerous activity during the first day of the climb was trying to avoid being run over by porters or breathing in the noxious fumes as they passed by on their furious assault up the mountain. "Po-le, po-le" did not apply to the porters, all of whom climb Kilimanjaro year round, usually taking only a day or two off between climbs. They are permanently acclimatized and zip up the mountain as if running downhill, despite carrying tremendous loads on their heads and backs.

"Porters, coming," we heard from behind us after about an hour of climbing, leading us to quickly move to one side of the trail. Within seconds, ten or twelve porters hurried by, most of them wearing some sort of Western clothing, typically NFL jerseys. All of them wore wrong-sized, soft shoes of some sort. How they managed to avoid ankle sprains is beyond me.

Without exception, all of the porters left a wake of fumes nearly strong enough to knock us over.

During an extended snack break almost half way to the first camp, we watched our individual duffel bags go by on the heads of the porters assigned to our group. My blue Slazenger bag was nicely perched on the head of a very strong looking six foot two porter who was several inches taller than most of the others. On top of the bag was a large table the porter held with one hand above his head. On his back was another pack, presumably containing his own gear. My stuff looked to be in good hands.

Other less senior porters were assigned the job of carrying large water and food baskets, which were the heaviest of the lot. Some of the guys were barely five feet four and probably 125 pounds. Yet, everyone of them was strong and determined, constantly competing with each other to move up the trail faster and faster. This was their job and they appeared very good at it.

We expected Michael to follow close behind the porters, but there was no sign of him. His assistant, who did not speak much English, motioned us forward and we followed him at a slow and steady pace.

About four hours into the climb, the trail started to get a bit steeper. Soon the constant, cheerful chatter which had marked the first part of the trail began to disappear. Occasional groans could be heard from several of the women. But they kept moving. Mpopo and Brent were bringing up the rear. From time to time I could hear Mpopo mumbling something in a Setswana dialect which did not need to be translated to understand that she was tiring.

At the top of a particularly steep section, Cherie stopped and pulled off her boots. Her heels were already blistering. She had made the mistake of wearing a single pair of fairly thin socks, thinking that the first day's hike would be easy. This was a serious mistake.

I immediately suggested that she cover her heels in athletic tape to protect them. I offered a roll of white tape I had stuck in my day pack for emergencies. However, she declined, instead using some cream offered by one of the other women to put on her heels. In my experience, this was not a good idea, but my opinion did not carry the day.

Unfortunately, she had put her thick socks in her duffel bag which had already passed us on the head of her porter. No one else had any spare socks to lend her. So the back of her boots continued to rub the blistering wounds on her heels as we pushed up to Camp I.

About one-half hour before we reached the first camp site, Michael appeared from the rear. He looked as if he had not broken a sweat.

"Nice of you to drop in," I said somewhat sarcastically. "We have been po-le, po-le-ing it all the way up. I think everyone is doing pretty well, except one of the ladies has some pretty bad blisters over there."

I nodded towards Cherie, who was now noticeably limping.

"Thanks," he replied. "I'll take a look at it once we get to the camp."

The sun was just about to set when we reached Machame Camp, our first stop. Michael led us through some large pamphus-like grass clumps into a clear area just to the right of the path. As we emerged, we saw that our camp had already been set up by the porters. Michael pointed out several nearby outhouses and then announced that dinner would be served in the large green tent in thirty minutes. At the mention of food, I realized that I was starving.

Mpopo immediately collapsed to the ground in front of one of the tents and took off her boots, again mildly cursing in her native language.

"Sheer will power," I said, teasing her.

"David, you have seen nothing yet," she said confidently, her crisp accent emphasizing the "t" on the end of "yet."

"Okay," I replied.

"I haven't even tapped into my will power," she continued. "I'll let you know when that is needed."

I smiled and hoped that her will power was indeed as strong as her confidence. I had a feeling that the first day had been a cakewalk compared what lay ahead of us. I had barely breathed hard the entire day, but I could tell that it had not been that easy a hike for some of the others, including my sister-in-law.

After picking out one of the two man tents for Eric and me, I walked around to scout out the area. I had been told that the Machame Route was less crowded than the most direct and popular Marangu Route. That route, which is sometimes referred to as the "Coca Cola"

Route, goes straight up the mountain from the east and is lined with permanent huts. I had expected that on our more remote trail, there would be at most four or five groups like our own. In fact, we had not seen very many climbers on the way up, probably because we were one of the last to get started. However, to my surprise, the whole hillside was covered in encampments.

By estimate, there were probably seven hundred people staying at Camp 1 that night, well over two-thirds of them porters and guides. This trek would be a massive migration, like a community of nomads, moving from one camp to the next, working their way up the mountain. After counting heads, I realized that our group of just ten climbers had twenty-seven porters and guides carrying all of our gear, tents, tables, folding stools, provisions, water, fuel, and food for thirty-seven people for six days. This was an enormous undertaking. And probably twenty other groups just like ours were doing exactly the same thing at the same time. One day later, another seven hundred people would take our place at Camp 1, and follow us to the top, separated only by the passage of twenty-four hours.

This would not be an isolated journey in the wilderness at all. Rather, the climb would be a collective social experience with groups from all over the globe marching on the same trail, going in the same direction, and all with the same goal in mind – to set foot on the highest point in Africa.

After dinner, the cool night air began to descend. As the sky darkened to a deep shade of purple, Kili's central mass, called "Kibo", with its tongue-like glaciers, loomed over the horizon, now only about 9000 feet above us.

I actually slept very well the first night out. Though the temperature dropped to below freezing in the early morning hours, it was snug inside the tent. The only impediment to sleep was Eric's continued tale of marital woes, followed finally by his loud breathing and periodic passing of gas. Eric assured me that I was as much of a culprit as him. This was not the first time I had been accused of snoring up a storm or farting in my sleep. And it would not be the last.

The banging of pots outside woke us up. I stuck my head outside and noticed that the porters had filled bowls with warm water so that we could wash our faces and hands before breakfast. This unexpected luxury was well appreciated, especially by Mpopo.

Our meals were served in the green tent at a long table surrounded by little, foldable camp stools. Breakfast, consisting of eggs, fruit, bread and oatmeal, washed down with coffee, tea or hot chocolate, was quite good. After each breakfast and dinner, Michael made the rounds to each climber, attaching a clothespin-like device to our index fingers to measure heart rates. He methodically recorded the rates in a log book, along with any comments about any headaches or other signs of altitude sickness. At various stages along the trail he had to present his log book to mountain officials, who presumably were checking to make sure everyone moving up the mountain was medically ready to do so.

As soon as the breakfast plates were cleared, Michael informed us that we would hit the trail in twenty minutes. All we had to do was pack our duffel bags and leave them out in the open for the porters, then ready our day packs for the hike. The cook gave us each a bag of goodies for lunch. Nothing fancy. Just a boiled egg, a sandwich, a plantain, and some cookies. Water bottles were re-filled, and then we were off.

The trail leading up from Camp I was considerably more rocky than the day before. And it was noticeably steeper from the get-go. Our legs were fresh from the night's rest, but our calves quickly began to tighten as we moved up the first section. Mpopo and the others began breathing harder than at any time the prior day.

"Po-le, po-le," Michael reminded us, as we paused to let some porters from another group pass by. "We've got a long way to go to the Shira Plateau today, so take it slowly."

He demonstrated the art of breathing out the carbon dioxide with a strong, swooshing sound, but most of our team did not seem to get the hang of it.

So slowly we went. Most of the day, climbers from other groups passed us and headed up the trail. Only a Canadian group and a group of women from England seemed to be traveling at our plodding speed. One woman from Leeds, who did not seem to be having any problem with the altitude, constantly chattered away about anything and everything under the sun.

"Geez, is that woman ever going to shut up," Eric whispered to me several hours into the climb. "If I was married to her, I would go crazy in less than a day."

"Yeah, she's a bit obnoxious, but she seems to be having a great time," I replied.

Since we were going so slowly, we had ample time to enjoy the changing flora surrounding us. The rain forest had given way to what seemed more like a Scottish highlands environment, with scattered small-petaled cool-weather plants, such as small yellow daisies and faintly purple blossomed thistles. By far the most exotic were the Lobilias, which I find very hard to describe. The bottom portion of the plants, about the size of a cabbage, are formed by hundreds of reed-like narrow curved leaves. From the center of the plant rises a large, phallic plume, sometimes four or five feet high, posing like small cacti in the mist. They reminded me of the Silverswords I had seen inside the Haleakala crater on the Hawaiian island of Maui, on another memorable trip.

As we worked the steeper hills leading up the increasingly rocky mountainside, the occasional, light moisture from swirling clouds added dampness to our misery. The sun periodically filtered through the mist, adding to the surreal feel.

The Shira Plateau is a relatively flat shoulder of land on the western end of the mountain at almost 13,000 feet. To get to it, we had to climb through a particularly steep section of wet rocks. Soon we were scrambling to find good hand and foot holds to hoist ourselves up along the trail. The porters, of course, seemed to fly up the rocks with total abandon, their feet barely touching the ground. However, each member of our team made sure every grip was solid and every footstep secure. Needless to say, our progress was painstakingly slow.

The easy ascent from the first day was a memory. Now the climb was real work. Still, no one complained, no one whined, and no one lost focus. Cherie was still limping a bit from her blistered heels but did not voice any discomfort. Janet, Karin, Brenda and Joline seemed to be doing well and kept up a steady pace. I was duly impressed by the positive attitude and persistence of the members of our group—all day long.

Finally at about five o'clock in the afternoon, we crawled over the last steep wall which, at the top, crested onto the Shira Plateau. The final thirty minutes of that day's hike was actually downhill to the Shira camp, a nice transition from the tough uphill climb. From our vantage point, we could see at least twenty occupied encampments already set up below us. We were the last to arrive.

As Michael marched us all the way through each of the other encampments, I swore under my breath. I knew we had to climb back up the way we came the next day. The lower we went, the more we would have to climb on day three.

Just as we were about to drop, Michael entered into a small cratered area, where I recognized our tents huddled in the middle. Beyond them, gleaming in on the horizon was a huge mountain forming a perfect volcanic cone, split by a narrow wisp of cloud crossing just below its peak. The sun was setting behind it, creating a postcard-worthy photo opportunity. Brent quickly informed us that it was Mt. Meru, another volcano he remembered from his Peace Corps days.

On the rocks forming the crater around us sat what can only be described as Kilimanjaro "vultures," large black scavenger birds with white rings around their necks. There were hundreds of them, watching and waiting for the opportunity to devour any food, candy wrapper, or popcorn kernel left on the ground. With over seven hundred sloppy humans camped out for the night, the pickings would be plenty.

On the eastern end of our camp, barely visible above the rocky wall forming the side of the small crater, we could see Kibo and the glaciers above us. But the view lasted only for a moment, as the clouds came in, obscuring the peak. After a warm dinner of mystery-meat stew, rice and bread, our group was quite ready to call it a night.

Unfortunately, my sleep was interrupted around 2:00 A.M. by wretching sounds from the tent next to ours. Mpopo was already vomiting, not an unusual occurrence for climbers unaccustomed to sleeping at 13,000 feet, but still a foreshadowing of problems to come.

We woke up early the next morning knowing that we faced an even longer hike on the third day. Breakfast at daybreak, followed by a quick getaway, was Michael's plan.

The temperature was much cooler as I stuck me head out of the tent. I immediately advised Eric that at least three layers would be in order, along with some gloves and woolen hats. I bundled up in a nice fleece jacket and grabbed some toilet paper for a very chilly trip to the closest one-holer.

When I returned, Mpopo was moving around the camp slowly. Bundled up in a large coat and scarf and not looking too well, she claimed that her overnight sickness was due to the food and not the altitude. I had my doubts, but I held my tongue. It could have been the mystery meat, as that night Eric came down with a mild case of diarrhea. However, I had read in the literature that quite a few climbers get sick at the Shira Camp, simply because they ascend from 5000 feet altitude at the hotel to almost 13,000 feet on the Shira Plateau in just two days. For even those used to high altitude climbing, a certain level of nausea was inevitable. Thankfully, I felt fine.

On day three, the plan was to climb up to Lava Tower, a volcanic monolith just below the glaciers at about 16,000 feet, then to descend to another camp at 13,000 feet near the Barranco wall. The Lava Tower route is optional and some climbers choose to forego it to take a more level route across the landscape to the Barranco Camp. However, climbing high and then camping low is the key to good acclimatization, so I definitely wanted to climb to the Lava Tower. But I worried whether ascending 3000 feet then climbing back down to almost our starting elevation that day would be too difficult for Mpopo and some of the other women on our team.

News that Mpopo had been sick overnight spread quickly among the group. It also earned her the position directly behind Michael on the climb. He wanted to keep a close eye on her. I settled into line immediately behind Mpopo, constantly giving her verbal encouragement and support as we worked our way up the Shira Plateau and began the more vigorous climb towards the Lava Tower. There was nothing that could be done to affect Mpopo's physical condition, but her mental attitude was the key to her continued success on the trek.

Fortunately, Mpopo's overnight sickness did not return on the trail. She remained slightly weak, but amazingly, she kept on going, "po-le, po-le." I wondered if the "sheer will power" was starting to kick in.

After about four hours of climbing, in the middle of a flatter section of scattered volcanic rocks and scree, we reached a junction in the trail. The left fork went directly up to the Lava Tower and the right fork traversed across the mountainside, then down towards the Barranco Camp, a shorter route staying at lower altitudes. We could not see very far in either direction as a cloudy, cool mist obscured any vision beyond about fifty yards.

Michael signaled for the lunch break. Everyone automatically dropped their day packs and found a lava rock on which to sit. Mpopo simply collapsed in place, folding her legs under her. I reached for my pre-packed boiled egg and sandwich and began munching away as Michael walked around to each climber, asking them how they were doing. Overall, it was a tired looking lot. Three days of hiking, the last two mostly in slightly moist conditions, was taking its toll. We had started at about 6000 feet and at this point were already at 14,500 feet.

I still felt good. The pace had been slow and my legs were strong. I was experiencing no problem breathing and did not even have the slightest headache. Brent and Eric also showed no signs of weariness. But Janet looked pretty spent, admitting that her head was throbbing. Surprisingly, Joline, the younger of the two ultra-marathoners, who up to that point seemed to be one of the strongest of the climbers, was feeling "a bit woozie."

After analyzing the situation, Michael announced that his head assistant guide would lead the wearier group down the trail to the right and Michael would continue up the left fork to the Lava Tower with the stronger climbers. The group was split exactly in two, with Eric, me, Patrick, Karin and Brenda taking the left fork up and Mpopo, Brent, Janet, Joline and Cherie, still suffering with the blistered heels, turning right and going down towards the next camp. Brent, despite feeling no ill-effects himself, was staying with Mpopo no matter what. He later told me that he was actually quite happy to skip the Lava Tower that day.

I hated for the group not to stay together, but there was no reason for those beginning to feel the altitude to push their luck by going higher.

Hopefully, by descending for the night, they could recover sufficiently to push up to the final pre-summit camp the following night.

Michael picked the pace up slightly once our group split off after lunch. Without the other climbers holding us back, we could move a bit quicker, though still in the "po-le, po-le" tradition.

Throughout the almost two hour climb to the Lava Tower, the temperature dropped steadily as the winds began to pick up. I stopped to add a windstopping fleece to the three relatively thin layers which had served me well up to that point.

The landscape was eerie. No plants to speak of. Certainly no trees. Just large and small lava rocks dotted among the scree. I knew that directly above us to the left was the steep wall of Kibo and the tongue-like glaciers, but due to the heavy clouds hugging the mountainside, we could see none of it. Down to our right was just light grey mist.

"There," Michael said suddenly, pointing straight ahead.

I could see nothing in front of us.

"There," he said again, as the wind shifted just slightly.

My eyes squinted tightly, trying to see whatever it was. Then, just for a moment, the top edge of the Lava Tower came into view. Just as quickly, it disappeared.

For the next five minutes as we slowly approached, the Lava Tower played peekaboo with us. The haze partially cleared, giving us a momentary glimpse of the volcanic formation.

Eric pulled out his camera, but Michael advised him to wait.

"It will clear. It always does."

Sure enough, a few minutes later a fresh gust of wind moved the clouds to the left, exposing the entire Lava Tower to our view. At least eighty to a hundred feet high and probably half a football field wide, it dwarfed any lava rocks we had seen on the mountainside. Apparently, the "tower" was really what remained of a large lava flow from the side of the Kibo crater eons ago. Over the centuries, water and wind had eaten away at the ridge of lava, creating the freestanding block of lava forming the monolithic "tower".

As we approached the tower, I noticed several tents scattered among the rocks to our left. To our right, climbers were scaling the side of the Lava Tower with ropes attached. I had no desire to join them.

Beyond the tents, and up through the mist, we could see the bottom of the tongues of glaciers. We were only 3000 feet below the summit, which was almost straight above us. Michael showed us a very steep route between the glacier tongues that some more daring climbers take as a short cut to the top, but it looked way too dangerous to attempt without technical equipment and ropes.

As I stared up at some of the rock climbers, all at once I felt a headache coming on. Within minutes, my head felt like it had a dagger thrust into it, pounding and throbbing uncontrollably.

Woah, what's going on?

I took a few deep breaths and rubbed my temples, trying to settle the pain. Thinking that I may have gotten a bit dehydrated moving up the last 1500 feet from the trail junction, I drank almost a liter of water, trying to stem the migraine misery. When that didn't work, I pulled out my first aid kit and downed two extra strength Tylenol tablets. Suddenly I needed to urinate as well.

Great, I've lost control of my body. And it's only day three.

The latrine was hidden behind some rocks to our left. As I maneuvered myself over the rocks, my head felt like it was about to blow up. Once inside the one-holer, I noticed that my yellow pee was much darker than normal, a clear sign of dehydration. Yet, I hadn't felt tired or weak at all until five minutes ago and had been drinking fluids regularly all day during the climb.

Back with the others, I drank another half liter of water. Finally, the Tylenol started to kick in. I told Michael that I had a splitting headache, but that it seemed to be under control.

"Let's get going then," he replied. "It's all down hill to the camp. You'll be fine as soon as we go down a bit."

Sure enough, the headache disappeared as quickly as it had arrived as soon as we descended about a hundred feet on the far side of the Lava Tower.

The descent to the Barranco Camp was extraordinarily beautiful. Glacial streams dissected the mountainside, feeding exotic plants and creating a natural botanical garden unlike anything I had ever seen. The stark, lava rock-filled scree which had been our environment all day, gave way to lush, craggy valleys filled with babbling brooks and wild flora.

My favorite was the Senecia plants. These huge trees, growing as high as thirty feet, somehow reminded me of broccoli spears. In the mist, they resembled jolly green giants with palm-like hats or maybe the walking trees in the movie version of the Lord of the Rings. Hiking down between them was a mystical experience to say the least.

The mist and glacial streams created other problems for the downward hike. Frequently, the trail disappeared into loose rocks and water and the occasional small waterfall. Footing was slick, and at times we found ourselves almost sliding down sections of wet rock or jumping down five or six feet to more firm soil below. On one slippery section which Michael had navigated nimbly ahead of me, I lost my balance as my right foot slid out from under me. My hiking stick also skidded outwards, leaving me no option but to brace my fall with my hand. Seconds later I landed on the ground on my feet, but my butt and right leg of my pants were soaked through with water and several pieces of flesh across the knuckles on my right hand were missing. Within moments, my hand was covered in bright red blood. Apparently, the altitude does not diminish the vividness of its color. Gratefully, the wounds were fairly superficial and band-aids were sufficient to stem the flow. Keeping the band-aids on was a greater challenge, given the wetness of the conditions, but after ten or fifteen minutes I was able to concentrate on enjoying the hike again.

My thighs were aching from the downhill trek by the time we crested a hill and looked down on the Barranco Camp. We had been climbing upwards to the Lava Tower for almost six hours and then downwards for another three. For me, the downhill section, with its steep drops and slick footing, had been much tougher than the steady plod uphill. And the next day, we would have to gain every foot of elevation back!

Once again, by the time we stepped into the camp, most, if not all of the other groups had already arrived and were well into dinner preparations. Our campsite was set up with the familiar yellow tents surrounding the two green tents in the middle of an area unprotected from the wind. As soon as I arrived and was no longer moving, I had to add multiple layers to avoid the chill invading my bones.

Surprisingly, the rest of our group had not yet arrived. One would have thought that taking the short cut would have cut their trek by one or two hours. But there was no sign of Brent, Mpopo or the others. I hoped that they were okay.

While I waited, I decided to explore the camp. The Barranco Camp has been billed as one of the most beautiful back-country campsites in the world. If it were not so crowded, I might have agreed with that description.

The camp sits at the end of a narrow valley, through which we had come. Even at the bottom of the valley, the vegetation was still amazing, an endless variety of sizes, colors and shapes. In the dusk, some of the plants resembled sentries, guarding the campsites and the ubiquitous one-hole outhouses scattered throughout the area.

Looking out away from the mountain, I could see all the way down to the plains below. The houses of Moshi were glistening in the late afternoon sun. Later, as the sky turned dark and the stars twinkled above, the lights of Moshi were clearly visible, some 10,000 feet below us.

To the left or eastern side of the valley, I stared at the Barranco Wall, a huge rocky buttress extending outward from the Kibo peak. Between the Wall and our camp was a rather impressive stream, carrying thousands of gallons of melting glacial water off the mountain every minute. I realized that we would have to cross it in the morning.

Immediately behind me, just to the left and above where the Barranco Wall split out from the mountain, soared the Kibo peak. This was, to date, the most impressive view of what lay ahead. From this vantage point, the central volcanic core of Kilimanjaro appeared cold and isolated, an almost impenetrable fortress above us. The steep sides of the mountain looked much rockier and less glacier-covered than before. For just a moment, I wondered if it was even possible to make it to the top.

Just take it one day at a time. It's only six thousand more feet. For now just enjoy the scenery!

The other half of our team finally staggered into the camp as darkness was descending on us. The bedraggled group was completely silent—no words of greeting or explanation. Each of them went directly to their tents and disappeared. Only Brent ventured out to tell me that the entire afternoon had been a constant struggle to keep them going.

Mpopo was dragging and had gotten nauseous again, Joline was getting sick, and Cherie's blistered heels were hurting so much that she could barely keep going. Brent described long stops and such painstakingly slow progress that he wondered how it was possible for the group to make it over the Barranco Wall in the morning.

"Let's wait and see how everyone feels after a warm dinner," I said. "I was pretty beat when we made it into camp tonight as well."

That night, there was plenty of room in the mess tent. Cherie never made it for dinner, Joline stuck her head in to let us know that she was too nauseous to eat anything, but that she hoped to get some soup down back in her tent, and Brent and Mpopo showed up late. To my surprise, Mpopo seemed fine after her nap in the tent. She was bundled up because of the cold, but her appetite had returned.

Eric was at the top of his game that evening, keeping everyone in good spirits with his sordid banter and "fart" jokes. My brother was a Borat before Borat became popular!

After a long, tiring day, a few bellyaching laughs at gross humor gave us something to take our minds off our sore legs and bodies. That and some amazingly delicious banana fritters the cook fried up for dessert.

Bright and early the next morning, Michael led us single file down the slope towards the Barranco Wall. First we had to cross the raging stream over a series of rocks strategically placed about a yard apart. Due to several groups traversing the stream ahead of us, the rocks were already wet and looked quite slippery.

Michael bounded across like a kitten crossing the top of a couch—no problem at all. Mpopo was next, but I opted to go ahead of her so Brent and I could both support her from the front and the back. I stepped across to the second boulder in the water and looked back just in time to see Mpopo slip on the side of the stream and drop straight down on her buttocks in about four inches of water.She had not even made it to the first rock.

"Get up quickly! The water is going to soak through your pants," I scolded her gently. But for a moment, she just sat there apparently frozen with embarrassment.

Finally, she rose, swiping the moisture on her legs with her gloved hand. Had she been wearing Gore-Tex pants, the water probably would not have permeated, but it became obvious that the sweatpants she had selected for that day were not waterproof and the glacial water from the stream had soaked in completely.

"You're gonna have to keep moving, Mma," Brent said affectionately, but with a simultaneous tone of authority.

"All at my own time,' Mpopo responded. Then with Brent's and my help, and renewed focus, she worked her way across the stream without further incident.

The Barranco Wall loomed ahead of us. We could see other climbers working their way diagonally up the rocks to our right. It looked extremely steep, but once on the ledges, it was quite manageable. Michael led us up several switchbacks between the rocks and soon we were climbing the jagged rocks, using well-worn hand and foot holds, just like thousands of climbers before us. I pointed out the best spots for Mpopo to brace herself whenever she hesitated. Surprisingly, she moved up the wall steadily and without complaint.

Every ten minutes or so, a bottleneck developed at a particularly steep section. Our group chose to wait as other groups and hoards of porters moved through, the porters smartly balancing huge loads on their heads while climbing up through narrow cracks in the cliffs above.

I couldn't help but become frustrated. I felt like a slow foursome at a golf course, letting groups go through on the par threes. Embarrassing to say the least. I also knew that we would be heading for the summit that night and I wanted to get to the high camp early enough to get some rest before the grueling summit push. But there we were, going nowhere, while literally hundreds of others cut in front of us.

After about three hours of slow torture, we reached the top of the wall. The sun was filtering through the mist and we sat down for a mid-morning brunch of gorp and candy bars. As we sat there, porters crossed in front of us, their silhouettes forming artistically graceful shadows against the grey mist beyond the edge of the wall. Unfortunately, my photographs of this surreal scene did not do it justice.

The rest of the day was a long slog. At first, we slowly descended across the Karanga Valley. This was the easiest section of the mountain since the first day. By lunchtime, it was hot and we had stripped down to one or two layers on top and shorts below. We all talked and joked, relieved to be on a wide and gentle trail for the first time in three days. Off in the distance about 2000 feet above us, we could see the Barafu High Camp. A snakelike trail dissected the long rise ahead of us, then turned sharply to the left up a steep ridge to the camp. Barafu looked fairly close, but appearances can be deceiving. I knew it would be another four hours before we got there.

Okay, five and half hours. The last ridge up to the camp was another slow burn and torture for our group. After nine hours of hiking, no one wanted to finish on a steep rise of rocky switchbacks that seemed to never end. But we had no choice. We had to get to the camp, which sat up at the top of the ridge at just over 16,000 feet.

Shortly before six o'clock, after the sun had set behind the mountain peak, our group trudged into the Barafu Camp, ready to collapse. I felt fatigued myself, so I know the rest of the team was suffering.

We finally found our tent encampment up on the right. Apparently, our porters had not gotten a favorable pick of sites, because our tents were set up on thousands of large sheets of slate, off to the side of the flatter portion of the camp. I had heard of several disasters at this camp, occurring as a result of small tremors creating avalanches of slate. Unsuspecting campers had been crushed while sleeping in their tents. However, on this day, my only concern was getting a few hours of sleep. As I began to crawl inside my mummy sleeping bag, I groaned. Even with a foam mattress and thin air mat beneath me, the floor of the tent was rough and uncomfortable. I opted to lie down on top of my sleeping bag to get a bit more cushioning, hoping to get a few minutes of rest. Time would be short before we were climbing again—to the summit.

My back was sore when the porters woke us at 11:00 P.M. Not really falling asleep, I had just wrestled to try to get comfortable for three hours. The damned slate beneath us not only poked up into the mats below me, it also cracked and crinkled whenever I or Eric rolled over or anyone passed by outside. Someone may as well have been crushing aluminum foil into balls next to my ears all evening. But there was no use crying over lost sleep. We had a summit to reach.

This was the first time during the trip that we had gotten up in darkness. Without my contacts in, I was a bit disoriented, being almost completely blind without glasses or contacts—20/800 in both eyes. I struggled to find my larger headlamp to light the inside of the tent so I could dress and put in my contacts. I had already donned most of my summit gear, except for the Gore-Tex outer shell and boots, so dressing was not too difficult. However, trying to clean and rinse my contacts inside the tent and getting them on my eyeballs with poor lighting and no mirror always posed a challenge. Finally, I managed to get them in and my vision was restored. Once outside, I stretched and rubbed my back, trying to get my body moving. If I was stiff from the one day hike from Barranco and after resting for three hours, I wondered how everyone else was faring.

It was definitely a lot colder outside at 11:15 P.M. I blew smoke rings with my breath as I exhaled into the night air. After jumping up and down a bit to get my circulation going, I decided it might be warmer inside the dining tent.

Once inside, I saw that the porters had hot chocolate, coffee and sugar cookies ready for us, a nice last snack and energy boost for the summit push. I had enjoyed hot vegetable soup and bread shortly after arriving at the Barafu Camp four hours earlier, but I was still hungry.

Michael entered the dining tent looking to see who was ready. Only Janet, Patrick, and I were there at the designated time. Michael huffed out and went to roust the others. This night he was all business. He had told me earlier that he wanted our team to start up the steep rocky switchbacks above us by midnight, ahead of all the other groups, because we would be moving slowly. We would need the head start. Before that could happen, all members of our team had to be up, dressed, fed and tested for pulse rates and blood pressures.

One by one our climbers straggled into the dining tent. Heads were down and no one had anything pleasant to say.

"Today's the day!" I said cheerfully.

"I feel awful," Karin responded. The rest just shrugged and ignored me.

"Alright…" I replied. "Don't forget to bring some snacks for the climb. It's gonna be a long day."

I had already lined my jacket with six Snickers bars—one for every two hours on the anticipated twelve hour round trip to the top and back. I was not about to make the same mistake I had made on Elbrus.

I strolled outside and looked. I could not see the summit from the high camp, and the dark mountain and rocks above us were certainly ominous. The temperature was also a concern. I felt the wind picking up. Even with three layers of fleece and long johns beneath my Gore-Tex jacket, I wondered if I should put on a fourth layer. Instead, I kept moving, built up some internal heat, and the chill seemed to subside.

Just in case, I pulled another light fleece from the tent and packed it on the top of my day pack. I adjusted my headlamp and was ready to go by 11:45 P.M. If only the rest of our team was there.

Come on. We've got to get going.

Finally after much cajoling from Michael, our ten person team lined up single file for the ascent. Everyone but Brent and Mpopo had headlamps. Mpopo would be second in line, directly behind Michael. I was behind her. She would rely on my headlamp for footing. That seemed like a workable plan, but once we started, I soon realized that I was craning my neck sideways to make sure she had light in front of her. Within ten minutes, my upper back and shoulders were getting sore in the process.

I knew Brent and Mpopo should have rented headlamps from Michael back at the hotel, but they declined to shell out the extra money. Oh well, we could get by, even if it meant a sore neck for me.

We were actually the second team to begin the march up from the high camp. The first group quickly zoomed ahead, the flickering headlamps soon disappearing beyond the rocks above us. It was impossible to see the mountain with any clarity, so I found myself never looking up. I just concentrated on the ground and each step. We hiked on a fairly steep but doable sandy/gravel trail, working up very short switchbacks between the large rocks. Left and right we went, steadily gaining elevation. Occasionally, the trail would seem to disappear and we would have to crawl or climb over large boulders to regain the path. After a while, I realized that there was not really any major trail up through the rocks. Various guides just followed their instincts on the best course, creating a maze of semi-obscured trails that only the guides could decipher.

After about fifteen minutes of adjusting to the cold air and upward movement, several other teams caught up and passed us through alternate routes among the rocks. Within minutes, the entire mountain above us was filled with twinkling lights moving rapidly away from us.

The stream of climbers passing us never really let up for the next two or three hours. We were making continuous, but slow progress—"Po-le, po-le." We could only go as fast as Mpopo could manage. But nothing Mpopo was doing or thinking could be considered "fast." She was starting to show signs of exhaustion and could barely put one foot in front of the other. Occasionally she would stumble and I reached out to steady her. I wondered how long she would last. If she was using "sheer will power," it surely was at a torturously slow pace.

After four hours of plodding up steep switchbacks through the rocky face above Barafu Camp, Michael signaled for an extended rest stop at a wide section of the "trail" near a ledge. We had stopped momentarily for water breaks five or six times before that and had rested several times as other faster groups squeezed past us. But this time he told us to take off our packs, sit and get a snack. I had already snuck a Snickers into my system on a water break a few hours before, so this time I pulled out a couple of meat sticks I had stashed in my day pack. I had to remove my gloves to rip open the package, and for the first time on the entire trip, I suddenly felt very cold. I rapidly removed one of the long meat sticks and stuffed the package back in my day pack. Then I quickly re-gloved and wriggled my fingers and right hand for a few seconds to gain warmth inside. Fortunately, I could easily eat the meat stick with gloves on. I finished my picnic with another Snickers, savoring the chocolate and caramel.

Looking around, I saw that some of the team members were struggling with their day packs and food, digging in to find items deep inside their bags, while the wind whipped around us. After a few minutes of chewing, I finished up the candy bar and washed it down with some very cold water from one of my four Nalgene bottles. I could feel the sub-freezing temperatures seeping into my torso as we sat there on the windy ledge in the dark.

"Michael, let's get going. I'm getting cold," I shouted over in his direction.

Several of our group nodded agreement. A few others mumbled, "Just a few more minutes."

Michael did not respond. Huddled at the other end of the rest stop, he appeared to be having intense discussions with his two assistants. Finally, they stopped whispering and Michael addressed the whole team.

"Okay," he said, "we will need to break into two groups. The first group will go with me and my first assistant. One slower group will follow with my second assistant. Mpopo, you need to go with the slower group. You can go further if you feel good or you can turn around if you are too tired. I think you will not make it to crater rim today."

He then asked who would go in the second group. Only Brent indicated that he would stay with Mpopo. Everyone else claimed to be fine. All of them wanted to stay with the first group. I didn't blame them. But I wondered if the pace would pick up much with eight climbers still in tow. I gave Mpopo a hug and whispered to Brent to watch her carefully. She had done alright up to that point, but she clearly was tiring. Over the last hour, her energy level had noticeably diminished. Michael and I had constantly had to encourage her forward.

"If she can't keep going, turn around and get back down," I finally said to my brother.

"David, I don't think she'll listen to me one way or the other, but I'll keep a close eye on her," Brent replied. I knew that Mpopo was an independent, strong-willed woman. But I hoped that she would listen to her husband if things got rough. I figured she had maybe one more hour in her and then they would turn around and head back to Barafu.

The pace picked up slightly after we left Mpopo and Brent behind. I felt a sense of earnestness in the group, knowing that everyone had committed to going in the faster group. There was no talking any more, just the panting and breathing and an occasional scrape or sliding of rocks underfoot. We still had a long way to go and it did not look to me like we would make the crater rim by dawn—the normal goal for most groups.

However, we soon learned the value of going slow. Several times in the next half hour we saw headlamps flickering down the mountain towards us.

Surely no one could have reached the summit and was already started heading down—could they?

No, they couldn't. In fact, these poor souls had ascended too quickly and were suffering from acute mountain sickness, complete with dizziness, nausea and vomiting. Now they were having to descend quickly to avoid getting sicker, completely ruining their chances of reaching the top of Africa.

There is a reason for "Po-le, po-le."

Several hours later, we were still in the steep rocky section when the sky started to turn pink on the horizon just beyond a secondary peak called Mawenzi to our east. Dawn on Kilimanjaro was truly a majestic sight, but Michael did not slow up or stop for a photo op.

Just as we reached the top of the rocks at about 18,000 feet and faced the next hurdle, a steep section of pure scree, the sun rose above the peak of Mawenzi, bathing us all in rosy orange light.

Here Eric stopped to take a few pictures with his digital camera and fell behind the group by fifty feet or so, as Michael again did not stop. Eric had been laboring a bit after ascending over 17,500 feet. He had never been above 14,500 feet before, so he had already eclipsed his personal best.

An assistant guide/porter stayed back with Eric as he got the photos of the rising sun and I assumed he would reel Eric back up to the group in a matter of minutes. However, on the scree slope, footing was much softer, almost like hiking up a sand dune. Eric's laboring became a slow, agonizing deterioration into pure exhaustion. Each time I looked back, he seemed to have lost another ten yards. Soon it became apparent that he would not be able to catch up.

The sunlight had its advantages and its drawbacks. It felt good to warm up after the very chilly ascent for the last five or six hours. However, after about one-half hour, the heat was causing us to sweat. I zippered down the side vents on my Gore-Tex jacket, then pulled my hood down to keep from overheating. Eventually, I even stripped off my outer mitts and switched to a set of single layer Black Diamond gloves.

By now we were working our way up long winding switchbacks in the scree and watching as other climbers began sliding down the scree after having reached the summit at dawn. We could see the edge of the crater rim several hundred vertical feet above us and I was sure that we would reach the rim within another thirty minutes. Au contraire. It took another hour and a half. But we finally trudged onto the crest of the crater rim at Stella Point at 8:30 A.M. We were now at 18,750 feet.

The view in front of us was amazing. The vast crater of Kilimanjaro's central Kibo core must be three or four miles wide. The crater itself was not terribly deep, but it was huge. Snowfields were randomly scattered across it. Nothing in the volcanic crater looked remotely active. Down to our right was Gilman's Point, where climbers reached the crater rim on the Marangu/Coca Cola route, maybe 300 vertical feet below us. To our left, the crater rim slowly rose in a crescent towards Uhuru Peak, the actual summit, still 700 vertical feet above us.

Behind us, I looked back down the scree slope. Step by step, Eric was moving in our direction, still several hundred yards behind. It would take him another twenty minutes to arrive at the crater rim, totally exhausted.

Meanwhile, the seven members of our team hugged and celebrated the achievement of reaching the rim. For many, the rim is treated as a successful summit. In fact, everyone who reached the rim got a certificate indicating they had reached the top. Group and individual photos were taken behind a sorry looking wooden sign with the altitude in meters written on it. The crater and the summit ridge made a nice backdrop for the pictures. After Eric arrived and rested for a few minutes collapsed on his back, another set of photos had to be taken. I only wished that Brent and Mpopo had been there to join in the glory. But I assumed they had long since turned back.

After less than thirty minutes at Stella Point, Michael announced that anyone wanting to climb the rest of the way to Uhuru Peak, the true summit, must leave with him in two minutes, as it was getting late. He explained that we had to descend to a camp several hours below Barafu before sundown.

Janet, Karin and Cherie instantly begged off. They were finished. The euphoria of reaching the crater rim and the dread of pushing back into the unknown, coupled with mental and physical exhaustion simply overcame their desire to go any further. That, in addition to some very wobbly legs still suffering from the trudge up the scree slope. I could only imagine how much pain Cherie must have been with the wounds on her heels.

We were down to four climbers from that point on. Patrick, Brenda, Joline, and I stepped back in line behind Michael and started out up the slope to our left. We carried only water and cameras, leaving our day packs safely with one of the assistants. Eric was still laying on his back with his head on his pack when we left Stella Point. When he realized we were leaving for the summit, he managed to get up, adjusted his jacket and tried to follow us. After about fifty feet, he recognized that he had reached his limit and could go no further. He turned back, dejected, but still proud of how high he had gone.

I was feeling pretty good, especially after the long rest at Stella Point, and began to pick up the pace. However, Michael quickly put a "governor" on the speed of our ascent.

"Still 'po-le, po-le' here, David. Don't overdo it. We have another hour to the summit."

The next forty-five minutes was alternatively wonderful and frustrating.

The wonderful part was seeing the top of the glaciers just below us to our left. The edge of the glacier on the upper side must have been eighty to a hundred feet high. The top of the glacier was very flat, extending out for what looked like a quarter mile before falling off the side of the mountain in the long tongues we had seen from below. As we scanned the glacier towards the left from whence we had come, the top of the glacier cascaded off in a series of steppe-like ice rinks conjoined by gentle frozen waterfalls. It was impossible to photo the entire scene without a panoramic lens, so I took a series of shots from left to right to splice together later.

The frustrating part was that we kept thinking that the summit was the next high ridge to the right of our path. We headed up towards each ridge, just knowing it was the one, only to find out that the next ridge beyond it was higher. They say fool me once, but you can't fool me twice. Well, this damned mountain rim fooled us at least three times before we finally saw the wooden summit sign we had seen in all the pictures.

Just before we got there, maybe two hundred yards away, a rosy cheeked young lady was being led down towards us by a porter or assistant guide from another group. I remembered her from the English group on the lower slopes. At first I thought she was smiling, but as she got closer, I realized that she was in trouble. She was barely cognizant of where she was and the porter had a firm grip on her arm. She was basically a walking zombie. The woman had made it to the top, but had used up everything to do it. Now she was almost unable to move. Luckily she had help to get down.

Once she passed us, we almost skipped the rest of the way to the summit. We were the last to arrive. Everyone else had come and gone or never reached the ultimate destination of the climb. The highest point on the continent of Africa was completely deserted except for the five of us.

We hugged, slapped backs, and gave each other high fives, then lined up under the summit sign for photos. In bright yellow letters, the sign read: "CONGRATULATIONS! YOU ARE NOW AT UHURU PEAK, TANZANIA, 5895 M. AMSL, AFRICA'S HIGHEST POINT, WORLD'S LARGEST FREE-STANDING MOUNTAIN, ONE OF THE WORLD'S LARGEST VOLCANOS—WELCOME."

Somehow it was not quite the same feeling as reaching the top or Orizaba or Elbrus. Kili had been more of an experience than a challenge, a pleasant climb rather than a difficult, physically and mentally exhausting ascent. Still, it was glorious to stand at the top of Africa, with not a cloud in the sky and stunning glaciers on all sides. Once again I felt an overwhelming sense of accomplishment. Amazingly warm, I ditched my gloves and wool hat for the photos and actually never put them back on the rest of the day.

I had seen pictures of the top of Kilimanjaro with lots of snow and high winds, but on that day we had never stepped near any snow and there was no wind. Just a warm sun in which to bask at the glorious summit.

After less than fifteen minutes at the top, Michael motioned for us to start our descent. We had a good five hours back to Barafu Camp, followed by a short rest and then another two hour march down the trail to a lower camp on the Mweka Trail. We had to get going.

I remember very little about the hike back down to Stella Point, but do recall vividly rejoining Eric there. The look on his face was one of worry and panic.

"You won't believe it, David, but Mpopo made it to the rim—crawling the last one hundred yards," he said. "But now she's in real trouble. She can't move her legs and she's totally out of it."

"Where is she?" I asked.

"The porters started dragging her down about ten minutes ago. Brent is with them."

Upon hearing this, Michael swooped into action.

"We have to get her down, quickly," he said, as he waved for us to follow him.

Within seconds he was sliding down the scree on his feet, throwing dust up behind him. Instantly my eyes became full of sediment from his wake, almost blinding me.

I rubbed my tearing eyes until I could keep them open, then swapped out my glacier sunglasses for a pair of wraparound goggles. Once able to visualize again, I could see that Michael had already caught up to Mpopo, Brent and the porters about five hundred feet below us. He appeared to be examining her while the rest looked on.

I hurried down the scree, leaving a series of skidding marks and a plume of dust behind me. Thank God for my gaiters. Otherwise, my boots would have been full of rocks and sediment.

Once I arrived at the group, I could see that Mpopo's face had swollen noticeably. In her light blue down jacket, she looked a bit like the Michelin Tire guy. Michael lifted her legs, but they flopped back down, completely flaccid. She was mumbling words, but nothing very understandable.

"She's bad off—probably pulmonary edema," Michael finally said. "We must get her off the mountain. Now! I will get a rescue team. Stay with her and get her down one—two thousand feet, whatever you can, until help arrives."

With that, Michael turned and shussed down the scree slope like a Tanzanian Jean-Claude Killy. Within minutes, he was out of sight.

The two porters then raised Mpopo up, lifting her from under her shoulders. With amazing strength and balance, they carried her another hundred feet down the steep slope, her legs dragging and bouncing awkwardly behind her. When the porters reached exhaustion, they were careful to cushion Mpopo as the three of them crashed to the ground in an explosion of dust. After about three minutes, they repeated the sequence, dragging her down another thirty to forty yards.

Brent, Eric, Patrick and I followed slowly behind, trying to figure out how to help. Brent kept talking to Mpopo, sometimes in English, sometimes in Setswana, in an attempt to keep her spirits up. Every third carry or so, we would spell the porters, who clearly were getting fatigued trying to mange my sister-in-law's deadweight. While sheer will power had carried her to the crater rim, now she was fading fast. Her breathing was becoming shallower and more strained by the minute. Her legs were totally useless. We had to get her down.

By now the sun was almost straight overhead and we were beginning to bake. At that altitude there is little atmosphere to shield solar rays. As uncomfortable and dusty as I was becoming, I knew that Mpopo was truly suffering. She was no longer talking, just moaning as the porters dragged her down the scree, yard by yard.

After about two hours, we had moved Mpopo approximately 1500 feet below the crater rim, but were still probably above 17,000 feet. Another woman to the right side of the scree slope was also being assisted down by porters and a few fellow climbers. They seemed to be having as much difficulty as we were, but yelled over and said that a rescue team was on its way.

A short time later, a group of eight porters carrying a large blanket and moving rapidly up the slope approached us from below. Our hopes were heightened as they neared, but dashed when they headed in the other woman's direction. Within minutes, the woman had been hoisted up on the blanket and the porters were effortlessly running her straight down the slope and out of sight. We later learned that the woman on the blanket was the same rosy cheeked young lady from the English group whom we had seen just below the summit.

Mpopo's spirits deteriorated further as the other women was rescued. She broke into uncontrollable tears and refused to move. After what seemed like an endless series of sobs, she mumbled to Brent that she needed to go to the bathroom. We looked around and there was nowhere she could go privately. No rocks, no plants, nothing to hide behind. To our left was a slight ditch, maybe thirty feet away, so Brent and one of the porters slid her over until she was sitting in the depression. Then Brent worked to get Mpopo's pants down. The porters turned their backs, looking sheepishly down the slope. Eric, Patrick, and I decided to walk down the slope a bit to give her as much privacy as possible under the circumstances.

Where the hell is the rescue team? It's been over two hours!

I really wasn't thinking too straight because even if Michael had been able to get down to the Barafu Camp and organize a rescue team in a few hours or by radio, the team would have to climb up from the high camp. We were probably still at a level amounting to a five hour climb for our group from Barafu Camp. Even if porters could cut that time in half, it would take considerably longer for them to arrive.

In any case, we could see at least a thousand feet down the scree slope and there was no rescue team in sight. Time seemed to be marching on and we were making very little progress. Mpopo was stopped in her tracks with no mental motivation to move. I began to wonder if we would ever get Mpopo off the mountain.

Once done with her potty break, Mpopo's sobs returned. I could hear her moaning even from my vantage point about 100 feet down the slope. Brent again tried to console her, his body language giving away his frustration and his mounting concern for her safety. Mpopo had not moved herself in over an hour. Her legs were complete mush. The situation looked hopeless.

Suddenly, Mpopo stopped crying and pushed Brent away.

"Help me up. It's time to go," she said. She mumbled something to Brent in Setswana.

The porters and Brent hoisted her up into a standing position, supporting her under her shoulders. Once again she pushed them away.

Incredibly, she started walking down the slope with no support from anyone except God above, her arms stretched out for balance.

"Catch her—she'll crash," I yelled from below. I rushed up the slope in her direction, expecting her to collapse any second. But I could make no headway in the soft sand. Mpopo kept coming, striding and stumbling down the mountain, somehow staying on her feet. I had never seen a miracle before, but now I believe in them.

At least one hundred yards from where she started, Mpopo came to a stop. She stood there, barely maintaining her balance for a few seconds, then collapsed onto her back in the soft sand. We all rushed to see if she was alright. Remarkably, she was no worse for the wear.

"My sister spoke to me and told me that I had to walk," Mpopo said triumphantly.

That was the only explanation we were given for her amazing feat, but it was good enough for me. Brent later confirmed that Mpopo had mentioned her sister in Setswana just before her miracle walk on the slopes of Kilimanjaro.

From that point on, Mpopo was able to assist the porters as they carried her down the slope. The progress was noticeable. Still, there was no rescue party and the sun was starting to descend towards the rocks above us.

Eric, Patrick, and I were providing very little help with Mpopo at this point. After consulting with Brent, we made the decision to go for help. Cutting over to the edge of the rocks to our right, we followed the direction taken by the other rescue team. Soon we were in the steep rocky section we had climbed up in the wee hours of that morning. Unfortunately, we were still at least two hours above Barafu Camp and it seemed like a hopeless task to get there in time to check on the rescue team.

We rushed down, scraping our legs, almost wiping out on the rocks. Time was of the essence and I had an unrelenting and sinking feeling of doom as we descended.

Where is the rescue party? Wouldn't they be coming up this way?

Finally, we spotted the yellow and blue tents below us and knew we were close. The rocks gave way to slate, signaling the outskirts of the encampment. We rushed over to the familiar yellow tents of our camp and searched in vain for Michael. The rest of our team had made it back to the camp and were napping in their tents, so they were of no help.

After a few minutes, which seemed like an eternity, Michael appeared from the direction of the medical tent.

"Where's the damned rescue party?" I asked him a bit harshly. "It's been hours and Mpopo is still up there. We've seen nobody."

Michael's face crunched up a bit, revealing concern.

"I sent them up to find you three hours ago. Where did you last see Mpopo?" he said in a calm voice, regaining his composure.

"We've dragged her down, probably 2500 feet below Stella Point, straight down the scree. They are probably even further down by now, because it took us almost two hours to get here from there."

"Okay, the rescue team was going up the scree directly. They will find them."

Michael turned and walked away. Moments later, I saw him on a radio, speaking heatedly. Once he concluded his call, Michael came back to our tent.

"They are close. Don't worry," he said. "They'll have her back to the camp in no time. Then she will have to be evaluated by the rangers. They will decide if she has to go off the mountain tonight or if she can wait until the morning."

He advised us to get some rest. Regardless of what would happen with Mpopo, our whole group had to march to another camp two hours further down the mountain before dark.

In my tent, I couldn't sleep. I felt I had let everyone down. I began to second-guess my decision to leave Mpopo with Brent and the porters to go for help. After tossing and turning for a an hour or more, I finally decided that I would be better off pacing outside on the slate.

To my surprise, as I stuck my head out of the tent, I saw Brent rummaging into his tent a few feet away.

"You're back. Where's Mpopo?" I asked quickly.

"They're looking at her over at the main tent. They're saying she'll have to be taken off the mountain tonight."

"How are they going do that—helicopter?"

"No, nothing that sophisticated. The porters will carry her down on a wheeled stretcher."

"You're kidding. That's a long way down."

"Yeah, but that's how they do it. They were taking another girl down just when we arrived."

Brent gathered up some water bottles and Mpopo's overnight kit and hurried back to the tent where Mpopo was resting. Moments later we watched as four porters hoisted Mpopo's stretcher up on their shoulders. They began running down the trail, Mpopo's torso bouncing up and down as they disappeared around a corner. Four more porters ran after them, ready to take their turn carrying her once the first group got exhausted.

Smart girl, that Mpopo. She managed to avoid having to climb off the mountain. The taxi service was a bit rudimentary and the ride bumpy, but by 11:00 P.M. that night she was in the local hospital in Moshi.

At five o'clock, our team (less one) started down the trail to a lower camp. The glory of reaching the summit earlier that day seemed so far away. Getting Mpopo down safely had taken over all our thoughts. Now we wondered if she would be okay. There were no cell phones or radios to check on her condition.

I could only imagine what Brent must have been going through. He had initially suggested that he go down with the Mpopo and the porters, but Michael and the camp doctor had convinced him that he would only slow them down and that it could put Mpopo's life in danger. Plus, Brent was physically and mentally exhausted having pitched in to help the porters hoist Mpopo up so they could drag her down the scree. So Brent, like the rest of us, worked his way slowly down the mountain. He would have to wait until the next day to check on his wife's condition.

Once down the steep switchbacks below Barafu Camp, we took the left fork onto the Mweka Trail which leads straight out of the park. The Machame Trail back over to Barranco was now to our right. In the very organized system at Kili, the Machame Trail is really a one-way trail for those going up only. It seems that everyone exits via the Mweka Trail.

As the sun set behind the mountain, we straggled into the lower camp, which did not even have an official name. The porters had rushed by us about thirty minutes earlier and had already pitched the tents. The cook was boiling water and preparing our last dinner. The porters remained incredibly efficient to the end, despite all the turmoil around them.

We sat on some stools, pulled off our boots, and closed our eyes. We had been hiking up or down or dragging Mpopo down the scree since midnight, a full nineteen hours ago. Everyone in our group had made it to the crater rim or the summit—both successful climbs in the books at Kili. All but one had made it down under his or her own power. Not bad for a group of co-ed novices ranging in ages from 27 to 56. The job was done. Now only one more night in the tents and a five or six hour descent in the morning was all that was left of our Kilimanjaro experience.

Dawn came early the next morning. Stiff legs and backs were the main complaints among the group. After breakfast, Cherie finally showed off the deep and very inflamed wounds to her heels, gaining significant sympathy from the group. To this day, it is hard for me to imagine the pain she must have endured day after day, all the way up to the crater rim.

With the peak of Kilimanjaro directly behind us, we lined up in front of the green dining tent for our final group photo op. Michael began to lose patience as cameras appeared from everywhere and dozens of photos had to be taken to satisfy everyone's needs. My camera had actually malfunctioned on the second day of the climb, so I had to rely on Brent's and Eric's cameras the rest of the way. Fortunately, I had taken Eric's digital to the summit and have excellent photos of the top of Africa. Brent's camera was used for the final group shots.

Five and a half hours later, a tired, but profoundly happy group of nine climbers reached the trail head and souvenir village at the bottom of the Mweka Trail. Our only stop had been at the Mweka Camp after about two hours, a memorable rest area primarily due to the availability of ice cold Coca Colas in old timey, long glass bottles. To this day, my favorite photo of the trip is of me drinking that wonderful tasting soda with my head tilted back and the peak of Kilimanjaro in the background!

For the last mile before the trail head, small children in tattered clothes, some with shoes and some without, ran along with us, constantly begging for money or trying to sell us t-shirts or carved figures of one sort or another. The asking prices seemed high at first, but as we got closer to the trail head, the prices started dropping in their desperate attempt to make a sale before we reached the souvenir village.

Eric and I gave several of the younger children some dollar bills. Eric even bought some trinkets from one particularly persistent lad. In seconds, the word was out. Children appeared from right and left, almost mobbing us.

This section of Tanzania, so close to one of the most amazing wonders of the world, is, sadly, very impoverished. Parents work the fields all day, trying to eke out enough food to subsist, while their children, starting at age three or four, work just as hard, trying to convince climbers to hand over any spare cash available. It was impossible to say no and we were generous with our spare cash, but we could not help them all.

Once down in the souvenir village, the pressure to buy is even more intense, so much that the bus parking area has a special roped off safe haven to which climbers can retreat. There they can buy a soda or beer from an official vendor.

But the highlight of our last steps on the mountain occurred just before we reached the souvenir village. Eric and I had picked up the pace with Brenda and Joline as we approached the end of the trail. As we came around a bend, on the right we saw a small house with a flower garden and a sign asking the climbers to check-off the mountain—a de-registry of sorts.

As we stepped into the garden, to our surprise, there was Mpopo, wearing a bright colored, flowered shirt, shorts, and sandals, looking as good as new. We hugged and laughed with joy. She told us that she had been released from the hospital after a short observation period and had been waiting for us to arrive all morning.

Mpopo and I immediately wandered back onto the trail, looking for Brent.

After a few minutes, he came into view, his discernable gait and silly looking floppy hat unmistakable in the distance. At first he did not see Mpopo, continuing down the path at a casual pace.

"Brent, look who's here!" I yelled up in his direction.

His ears perked up. His hand rose to shield his eyes from the sun. Only then did he realize who was waiting for him beside me.

Instantly, Brent's slow walk turned into a galloping run. He was moving so fast that his hat flew off. He threw his hands up in the air, skidding to a stop and retracing his steps to retrieve it. Then he ran full tilt down the hill, one hand holding his hat on his head and the other wrapped backwards around his pack to minimize the jostling.

He didn't stop until his arms were around Mpopo, hugging her with all his might. Neither would let go.

The scene was straight out of the movies. Everyone around was clapping and smiling with delight. I imagined a movie camera circling them 360 degrees over and over again taking in every ounce of the emotions being shared, as the credits rolled.

I looked over at Eric and realized that both of us were crying. We always liked Mpopo, but until that moment we never knew the depth of our brother's love for her.

Kilimanjaro is a magical place, a life-time experience for many, a challenging climb for most, a hallowed ground for some. For me, it was a chance to re-kindle my relationship with my overseas brothers and sister-in-law, to enjoy the wonderment of so many different climates, and to see the grit and determination of my climbing partners, who never gave up, never complained when the going got rough, and who all made it down safely. They climbed Kilimanjaro as much with their hearts as their legs.

I went to Kili to bag my second of the Seven Summits, and certainly I accomplished that goal. On the way, I discovered the merits of "po-le, po-le," the virtue of patience, and once again, the danger of climbers not being prepared. But most of all, I witnessed a miracle walk that has not been able to be explained by any logical reasoning and the incredible love and affection between my oldest brother and his bride—the one with all the "sheer will power."

I will never forget our week on Kilimanjaro.

ACONCAGUA

"FLYING HIGH"

R eaching the top of a mountain is only half the job. Getting down is not only sometimes more dangerous than ascending, but, as master climber Ed Viesters says, "It's mandatory."

The day after I stood atop Aconcagua in the Andes mountain range in Argentina, at 22,845 feet, the highest point in the Southern and Western Hemispheres, I learned that lesson well.

Aconcagua is well-known for its fierce weather conditions. Indeed, on our ascent we had experienced strong winds and stormy conditions which had stalled our progress at the lower camps and had dumped twenty-four inches of snow on the upper half of the mountain. On summit day, we experienced seventy to eighty mile per hour winds for about forty-five minutes on one ridge below the final, steep Caneleta, but had managed to sidestep most of the worst winds as we climbed to the top.

No avoidance was possible the next day. The winds were relentless and brutal.

I awoke to seventy mile per hour winds blasting our tent, now half buried in the snow at Camp Four. Spindrift snow inside the vestibule piled two feet high, completely covering my double plastic boots and other stowed gear. Even exiting the tent was a Houdini act.

At 20,600 feet, the thin air makes it tough enough to dismantle tents, even in calm weather conditions. However, on the morning after our summit success, packing up the tents was a Herculean task. Once outside in the frigid air, I discovered all tent lines by which the fly was tethered were buried beneath large boulders iced in by the storm. Windblown snow added thickness to the ice coverings by the minute. One of the other climbers named Stephane and I hacked away with our ice axes, trying to pry the rocks loose in order to free up the strings. As I chiseled and wrestled with the boulders, my face was constantly battered by small particles of snow swept across the mountainside by the harsh winds. Impossible to dodge, the winds seemed to appear from all sides indiscriminately.

But we had no choice. We had to help get the tents down before anyone could start the descent. Everyone had to do their part.

After an exhausting process, we finally loosened the fly on the first tent. I quickly began stuffing it into the tent bag. Before that job was completed, a particularly strong gust of wind almost sent the main body of the tent airborne. Stephane and I jumped onto the tent body to keep it from flying away. At the same time, I struggled to pry some of the remaining poles loose from the ground straps so the tent could be flattened on the ground. Our guide, Eric, seemingly unfazed by the wind, expertly slid the six black poles out from the tent as I hung on for dear life. The windblown snow blasted me across my face and body.

This task was repeated two more times until the third tent was safely stowed in its bag. What should have taken less than fifteen minutes took us almost an hour in the windy, icy conditions. My face was stinging cold and coated with snow particles. Rubbing with my gloves did no good, as they too were icy. I just had to "grin and bear it."

As soon as the third tent was stuffed into its bag, Eric divvied up the tents, pots and pans, fuel canisters and burners, and all surplus food among us, as all the gear and supplies had to be stuffed in our back packs and carried off the mountain. Even though another team from our guide group would be heading up the mountain over the next few days, nothing could be left behind at the higher camps. Everything had to go. This meant that on our seven thousand foot descent to base camp we would be carrying the heaviest packs yet.

I watched as one of our team members took all three sets of tent poles. I quickly took a tent body and fly, a large plastic bag of extra food, and some cooking utensils, struggling to stuff them in or strap them onto my backpack. I had already crammed all the rest of my clothing, foam mattress, Thermarest, sleeping bag, eating bowls/cups, water bottles and personal items in the pack before getting out of the tent. My pack, which had been almost empty for the ascent to the summit only hours before, was now bulging at the seams. I estimated it weighed at least sixty-five pounds, but the others may have been even heavier.

Luckily, we are going downhill, so it will be easier, right?

Not in a "viento blanco," or "white wind," as they call it down in Argentina, in which the entire top of the mountain is surrounded by lenticular clouds, with gusts up to 100 mph.

Between Camp Four and Camp Three, only 1400 feet below, we had to descend a steep traverse filled with almost completely fresh snow drifts in fierce winds. The surface was not quite packed sufficiently to hold my weight. Every other step for me created a post hole into which my double plastics and gaiters disappeared under a foot or more of snow. Sometimes I sunk in above my knees. To make matters worse, the gusts were swirling, alternately pushing me off balance from behind and then, without warning, blasting me straight in the face. I pulled up my neck fleece so it covered everything but my nose, then cinched down my Gore-Tex hood for added protection.

Slowly, we pushed ourselves down the steeply sloping snow fields. I blocked the wind the best I could with my back, shoulders, Gore-Tex hood, and goggles. At times the wind simply stopped me in my tracks; at times, it threw me sideways off balance. Sometimes I simply had to crouch and take cover. Still, we pressed on and made progress as our legs were still relatively fresh.

The frozen ponds of Camp Three kept getting closer and closer. However, it seemed to take forever to reach them. What should have been a simple descent took almost two hours. We were already way behind schedule. But time was becoming increasingly irrelevant. I just wanted to get out of the wind.

Finally, we turned left off the snowy traverse, descending on some harder scree and rocks to the camp, perched on a wide ledge at 19,200 feet. I felt a bit disoriented and clumsy on the rocky surface, but focused on just getting to the team's one tent left at Camp Three.

There I collapsed, hoping for a well-deserved rest. Alas, there was no place to escape the brutal winds. Another guide and the one member of our team, who still planned to make a second summit attempt via the Polish Glacier were already inside the tent, along with a lot of provisions.

We had to wait outside while our guide, Eric, worked out the next logistics.

Constant blasts of eighty mile per hour winds beat against my back as I sat on my backpack, trying to regain my energy and hydration with snacks and water. Even though I was sitting just in front of the tent and a windbreak of rocks, the wind was undeterred. The few times I looked back to see what our guides were doing, my face was blasted by icy winds from behind us. So I faced forward in a slumped crouch, just trying to stay warm.

I had four layers of fleece or fleece underwear covered by a Gore-Tex shell jacket and a full down parka on my upper body. My face was protected by a neck fleece up to my nose, high altitude goggles, a Mountain Wear Windstopper hat and the hood of my Gore-Tex jacket. Somewhere along the way I had misplaced my balaclava purchased just for this trip, resulting in my nose remaining partially exposed. I had three layers of fleece and Gore-Tex on my legs, plus three layers of socks inside my double plastic Koflach boots and gaiters on top of that.

Incredibly, despite the violent winds, I stayed relatively warm as long as I did not take off my double insulated gloves. The few times I did, in a matter of moments, my fingers were numb and almost brittle from the wind-chilled conditions.

While I managed to avoid becoming a human popsicle, I still could not get any rest. Every bit of energy saved by sitting was used up in trying to create a shield against the scathing winds.

"Let's just go," I kept yelling. "It's senseless to sit here in this wind. The sooner we get going, the sooner we will get off this damned mountain." But no one seemed to listen as we sat there for at least forty-five minutes, slowly getting the hell beaten out of us. The glorious summit of the day before was now a distant memory.

Finally, after adding some more weight to our bags from items cached at Camp Three, including our "Wag Bags"—plastic baggies with our now frozen waste to be carried back to base camp—we set off for Camp Two, another 1500 feet below.

Soon after gingerly squeezing by a particularly narrow ledge of exposed and icy scree around a rock outcropping, I was met by blasts of wind that constantly slammed me down to the ground. I had no idea the speed of the wind, but its power was devastating. The support of a ski pole and ice axe were simply no match for the onslaught. I repeatedly found myself collapsing into a kneeling position, my toe crampons locked into the snow or scree just to anchor myself.

I crept forward and down, inch by inch, foot by foot, and yard by yard, just trying to stay vertical. The other climbers were not faring much better, though Eric and Stephane, who was one of the strongest but thinnest guys in our group, seemed to be cutting through the wind a bit easier than the rest of us.

I thought that surely the winds would subside below Camp Three and soon we would be casually descending the rest of the way. But as we approached the knob above Camp Two, which sits on an open col between Aconcagua and the neighboring 19,000 foot peak of Ameghino, the blasts intensified even further.

By this time, Eric and Stephane had moved down about fifty vertical feet below us and were scrambling down the almost snow-free, wind-swept scree. One of the lightest guys in our group, Tom, and I were struggling to keep up with the rest. We had fallen about thirty yards behind the lead group. A momentary break in the wind gave me the opportunity to catch up some ground. I hustled down the scree hoping that the wind would stay still for just a bit longer.

"WOAH!" I yelled, as an incredibly powerful blast of wind came out of nowhere, lifting me completely off my feet and slamming my face and right knee into the scree about fifteen feet to the right of where I had just been walking. I saw Tom hit the ground simultaneously.

"Holy shit!" I screamed with no guilt or hesitation. Before crash-landing, I had not even had time to get my arm up in front of my face, which was now filled with dust and small rocky particles.

Fortunately, my scree landing area was soft and I had avoided any boulders. My goggles had sufficiently protected my face from harm. My right knee, now buried deep into the scree, felt uninjured. After a few seconds to regain my composure, I fought back up into a four point stance against the wind, with my two legs, a ski pole and an ice axe supporting my hunched body three feet above the surface. Dazed, but unhurt, I took a deep breath, turned and returned to the path with a stiff shoulder into the wind. I was determined to get down to the col at Camp Two without hitting the ground again.

Not a chance.

Four or five more times, the wind forced me to the ground. At least it did not pick me up and throw me across the scree again.

Struggling just to stay on my feet as we trudged into Camp Two, I slid my backpack off and slumped to the ground next to the large windbreak of rocks. This time I covered my legs with my backpack as the wind continued to pummel me. The windbreak was useless on this day.

I sat there, frozen in place, not wanting to go any further. Confused and disoriented, my brain was checking out, a casualty of the constant pounding of the wind or maybe it was just plain exhaustion. I'm not sure which. The air was still very thin at just under 18,000 feet and I'm sure my condition was also weakened by sleep deprivation over the previous two weeks.

But most of all, I had just been thrown airborne across the scree and really did not want to be there anymore. I had to get off the mountain.

Can someone fly in with a helicopter and take me out of this mess?

Our guide, Eric, reminded me to eat and drink. Like a robot, I followed his directions without thinking, struggling to munch on a few almonds and a cookie from my snack bag. Though my water bottles were starting to freeze, I managed to drain a few ounces of water into my system. However, I felt no boost of energy and still did not feel like moving another inch.

No more walking and no more wind – please!

After a rest of only about fifteen minutes, we were forced to get up and add more "Wag Bags" to our load from the Camp Two cache. Now I regretted ever having gone #2 on this mountain.

That crap weighs a ton.

Moments later, Eric commanded us to head down the slope for Camp One. At this point we responded only to sharp commands, not to mere suggestions. To our surprise, Eric went off in the opposite direction to cache a white gas container for the next group in a designated spot to our left. Now we were on our own—at least for a while. It didn't matter to me. I simply followed the others like a pack mule following the lead caballero.

The week before, after our first "carry" up to Camp Two, we had descended the dry scree to Camp One in twenty minutes, like alpine skiers moving down a slalom course. That was before the first snowstorm had dropped eighteen inches of snow on this section of the mountain. Still, I figured we should be able to get down this section of the descent in thirty or forty minutes.

Wrong again.

Murphy's Law kicked in. Just as we left Camp Two, the Thermarest that I had strapped onto the side of my pack flew off and skeetered down the snow in front of us. Luckily Tom was able to spear it with his ski pole. Unwilling to unload and repack my backpack, I opted to stuff the Thermarest inside my down parka until the next camp. With the extra padding, I must have looked pretty fat, but I didn't care.

At first I thought the wind was starting to subside, because we walked a few hundred yards without being slammed to the ground. The air was still for a few seconds. Then the strongest gust of wind of the day hit me flush from the left.

With no warning or defense, the one hundred miles per hour blast walloped my body, instantly lifting me completely off the ground. With my pack acting almost like a parasail, I was thrown sideways twenty-five feet through the air, my feet desperately reaching down to try to regain contact with the ground. As I hurtled to my right, I saw Tom rolling out of control across the same ridge just below me.

The expletives that escaped my mouth during this second involuntary flight are not repeatable in print.

I crash-landed in a snow bank, my head and right shoulder leading the way. Fortunately, my pack partially cushioned the impact.

Instantly covered with ice and snow, I was amazed to find that I was unhurt. Thank God for the deep drift into which I had tumbled.

Looking down, I noticed the impact had knocked the crampons off of my right climbing boot. Luckily, the dangling metal spikes did not pierce my leg. But my gaiters, which had been developing rips all morning, were now in shreds.

For what seemed like minutes, I lay there, contemplating my fate as I tried to disgorge the snow from inside my hood. For some reason it seemed like I was just knocking more snow inside my jacket. I wondered if I should try to get up. But the snow was soft, and, while I was down, the wind seemed to have disappeared.

Maybe I should just lay here for awhile longer. It's so comfortable.

Once more, my mind was not fully registering. I was probably on the ground for only a few seconds, yet it seemed like forever.

The next thing I remember, was hobbling down the slope trying to stay vertical with one crampons on my left boot, a ski pole in my right hand, and an ice axe and the other set crampons in my left hand. This was not a good combination, but it never dawned on me to sit down and put on the other crampons. For some reason, I didn't feel I could do it. My mind simply was not connecting with the rest of my body.

So I limped down the hill, falling down every time my right boot hit a slippery, icy spot. Any time the wind picked up, I just hit the ground to avoid being thrown around. Depending on one's point of view, I had either learned my lesson or was totally intimidated. Either way, it was slow going.

Soon Eric and my fellow climbers were considerably below me, quickly descending. I don't remember Eric rejoining us at all, but I was glad to see him. I yelled in his direction to wait and give me some help, but he was too far ahead to hear me. Finally, Tom, who seemingly had recovered from his involuntary roll, caught up to Eric and pointed his ski pole in my direction. At last, our guide waited for me to catch up. I remember feeling silly that I had not been able to fix my own crampons. But I was glad to have professional help and to rest my body and mind while he re-strapped the spikes onto my boot. Soon I was back on my feet with both crampons working. I felt like a new man.

A good two hours after leaving Camp Two and at least twenty minutes after the other guys had arrived, I staggered into Camp One, this time for a real rest. We still had the final trek down to base camp, another two hours in milder winds, but I knew then that I would make it off Aconcagua and live to climb again.

After climbing Kilimanjaro in February 2005, I had successfully reached the highest points in the 48 states, Mexico, Europe and Africa. The next logical step was to conquer either Denali/Mt. McKinley, the highest point in North America up in Alaska, or Aconcagua, the tallest mountain in South America, which, at 22,840 feet, also happens to be the highest point in the Southern and Western Hemispheres. Simply put, one has to go to the Himalayas in Asia to find any higher mountain.

I had friends who had attempted Denali, some successfully and some not. All of them described severe snowstorms causing dangerous conditions and multiple days "hunkered down" in tents or snow caves at high altitudes. I had also heard of many fatalities and instances of frost bite among Denali climbers over the years. One law school classmate had warned me never to try Denali. His experience there led him to drop high altitude climbing as a sport completely.

Aconcagua, as related to me by several experienced climbers, was a long and steady slog through dusty, dirty scree—an overwhelmingly boring and unpleasant climb. Because Aconcagua is rarely snowbound, many climbers regard it as an ugly mountain. The "Stone Sentinel," as Aconcagua is sometimes named, was said to simply be "a big rock that anyone stupid enough to put up with fifteen days of dust and dirt can climb."

I guess that makes me stupid.

As was my usual practice, I searched the internet for information, photos, and guide information for both Denali and Aconcagua. Since both are part of the Seven Summits series, there were plenty of web pages from which to pick.

Denali was all snow, partially technical, and expensive. The climb starts with a flight on a small plane fitted with skis up onto a glacier and goes up from there, with climbers pulling sleds and carrying backpacks up to a series of high camps under very cold and snowy conditions. Not for me.

Aconcagua looked rocky with snow patches here and there, and was described as a pure "walk-up" requiring nothing more than crampons and ice axe, unless one wanted to climb the Polish Glacier to the top, a much more technical climb. Again, as a regular guy, I was not interested in making things more difficult and had no desire to tackle the Polish Glacier. Best of all, Aconcagua cost only $4,000 to go with the best guide group available, which I determined to be Alpine Ascents International. AAI, as it is called, was planning five expeditions and had a permanent base camp presence for the whole December to February season. It utilized a fourth camp above base camp to assure proper acclimatization and to maximize the chance of successfully reaching the summit.

It looked to be the most organized and well-supported guide group on the mountain, so I quickly moved it to the top of the stack.

Other commitments precluded me from making a trip in the winter of 2005-2006, so I set my sights on January 2007 to head for Argentina and climb the "ugly" Aconcagua.

With all of 2006 to prepare, I carefully laid out a ten month training schedule, including a trip to Colorado to climb a 14,000er as a mid-term test in August.

I started in March, with my usual regimen of hill-running on my street, starting with ten hills, followed by sit-ups and crunches on my den floor. With over a year since I had climbed Kilimanjaro, my diet had gone to hell in a handbasket, and I knew I had to lose weight. But with ten months to train, I only slowly decreased my intake of Cokes, chips, chocolate and desserts and merely moved from regular beer to lite beer for the first few months. No need to kill myself immediately. But the weaning needed to begin.

By May, I was taking my calorie intake a bit more seriously and had increased my hill work to fifteen then twenty hills. I added four and five mile runs on the weekends, and soon my extra weight from months of laziness began to melt away. However, the workouts were becoming much more difficult as the hot Atlanta summer descended on us. I found myself in a holding pattern at twenty hills for several months.

David, maybe you're getting too old for this...No, just work harder, you lazy moron.

As August approached, I felt a renewed purpose, especially since I had decided to take my seventeen year old son and fifteen year old daughter with me to Colorado to climb Long's Peak. At 14,246 feet, Long's Peak is the highest point in Rocky Mountain National Park. I definitely did not want to falter on that climb, given my children's unreasonably high regard for my climbing ability. The fear of embarrassment is a high motivator, especially in front of one's teenage kids.

So I pushed the hill work to twenty five hills in the blazing summer heat, several times wondering if I would be able to make it back up my driveway and into my house without collapsing. To make sure I was ready, I also added several nine mile runs to my itinerary—but made sure I ran them early in the morning before the temperatures were prohibitive.

Meanwhile, my kids relied on their soccer practices and general youthful vigor for their training.

It really is not fair.

My daughter, Lora, was truly excited about finally being able to make a climb with her dad. Daniel, a few years older than his sister, had already made two climbs with me, one an overnight hike in the Tetons culminating in a trek across a snowy pass at just over 11,000 feet when he was fourteen, and the other, a climb up to the Boulderfield at 13,000 feet on the same Long's Peak the prior June. On that trip, it was too early in the season to make a try for the top as the snow and ice on the exposed ledges below the summit made it too dangerous.

Lora felt a bit left out on the prior occasions, though she enjoyed riding horses with my wife in the lower hills both at the Tetons and Long's Peak. She had been hinting at the opportunity to make a hike with me for a few years. After a trip to REI to outfit her with some suitable clothes for the trip, she was all set.

To give us the best chance of success, I carefully laid out plans to acclimatize for two days before making the assault on Long's Peak.

The first day in Colorado, we drove straight to Rocky Mountain National Park and headed up the Trail Ridge Road to two short trails at over 12,000 feet. At first the kids did not notice the thin air and altitude, but after panting a bit, they paid a bit more attention to my advice to take it easy and walk at a slow pace even on the easy trails.

The second day we got up early for an acclimatization hike, hitting the trail up to Sky Pond at 6:30 A.M. The first part of that glorious day took us by the swiftly flowing Alberta Falls, a mirror-like Loch Lake, and a lovely 40 foot cascading waterfall called Timberline Falls. Next to the falls was a very steep, somewhat slippery climb on granite rocks, a barrier to most everyday climbers that afternoon. However, Daniel, Lora and I scampered up the slick rocks and were rewarded several minutes later with the breathtaking view of the Lake of Glass. Still further up the mountain, we finally reached Sky Pond, the final lake in the valley surrounded by a semicircular amphitheater of 13,000 foot snow-covered peaks and ridges. We sat by the water, enjoyed a leisurely lunch of meat sticks, gorp, carrots, Snickers, and apples, and let the warm sun and the fresh mountain air refresh our souls. By one o'clock in the afternoon, we were back at our car and heading for the motel room to rest up for the big climb the next day.

The alarm clock at 1:00 A.M. came way too early. But we had to be on the trail by two o'clock to be sure of having sufficient time to reach the summit and get off of Long's Peak before the usual afternoon thunderstorms. Daniel and Lora were a bit grumpy about the early hour, but I could tell they were excited to finally start the real climb.

I expected more cars at the trail head parking lot, but was happy to be able to pick a spot directly across from the little ranger hut next to the trail sign. At 1:50 A.M., we clipped on the straps to our backpacks, adjusted our head lamps and started out at a steady pace. Like Michael on Kili, I reminded my kids about the virtues of "Po-le, po-le."

We hiked through the woods for about three hours, taking short water breaks and one good snack break on the way up to a flat area known as the Boulderfield. Almost no one passed us on the trail, and most of the time we walked quietly, the silence interrupted only by our breathing and exhaling of the still chilly air. Then as we turned right at the Chasm Lake trail junction to traverse the long rise to the Boulderfield, other groups began overtaking us. I worried if they were going too high too fast. Sure enough, before we even got to the Boulderfield, several climbers were bent over, already nauseated.

Fortunately, we had kept a very steady pace, and with the acclimatization hike the day before, were in pretty good shape when we reached the Boulderfield, a huge plateau between ridges on both sides and the diamond shaped cliff of the top of Long's Peak straight ahead.

After a long rest stop, the going got very tough as we ascended the boulders and large granite rocks up to the "Keyhole," an eye-like notch at the top of the ridge above the right end of the Boulderfield. I had not remembered this section being so steep and difficult when Daniel and I had been there the year before. I lagged behind Lora and Daniel as we approached the hole in the ridge.

The "Keyhole" itself is a narrow ledge with very little space to rest. Several climbers were taking refuge there, but they did not look comfortable in the wind. The other side of the "Keyhole" is a whole other world. The Boulderfield side is a safe, sheltered plateau. Beyond the "Keyhole" is a sheer, exposed drop off of 1500 feet, with astonishing views of snow-capped peaks across the valley. I admired the beautiful vista, but quickly focused my attention to my left. The next stage of our climb was to navigate across the "Ledges."

The "Ledges" is a section of narrow sills which cross almost vertical walls of granite like a roller coaster. Red and yellow bulls-eyes were painted along the best route. I watched other groups slowly edge their way, climbing up and down and across the side of the granite walls.

If they are able to do it, it must be safe, right?

Daniel and Lora looked a bit apprehensive as I suggested that we get going. To make it easier, we followed another group that included a few young teenage boys. Unfortunately, we almost immediately ran into a log-jam at one particularly narrow spot which was blocked by a large boulder. One had to squeeze through a narrow space on the inside of the boulder or hang on the outside of the boulder over a 1500 foot drop to get past. We opted to wait for the squeeze through, but lost about fifteen minutes while others ahead of us contemplated turning back.

At the end of the "Ledges" is a steep couloir called the "Trough," an almost vertical gulch filled with boulders of all sizes, going straight up towards the peak. Looking up, we could see several dozen climbers crawling on all fours from rock to rock. Lora, who has always loved climbing on rocks and boulders and who had virtually no weight in her pack, assumed the lead on this section. Like a spider climbing a gutter spout, she seemed to glide up the steepest sections with ease, her long legs and arms spread out and constantly moving to the next handhold. Daniel stayed close behind her. I watched helplessly as they zoomed up and then sat on rocks waiting for me to catch up.

"Po-le, po-le," I sputtered, pretending to be deliberately taking it at a slow pace. The truth was that I was struggling just to stay within shouting distance. A fifty year old trying to keep up with a couple of teenagers is a losing battle!

Just when we thought we were reaching the top of the "Trough," we realized that it bent at a slight angle to the right and kept going. We were only half way up it. The second part looked even steeper.

I had no idea that the top of this mountain was as difficult as it turned out to be. I was completely wasted by the time we finally climbed the last particularly steep rocks of the "Trough."

The good news was that the next section was flat. The bad news was the trail meandered along even narrower ledges, appropriately dubbed the "Narrows." At one extremely narrow "overlook," metal bars are drilled into the side of the mountain for footholds above a thousand foot drop off. Once across that drop off, I thought the worst was behind us.

Wrong again.

At the end of the "Narrows," we encountered the "Homestretch," a section of granite which in the website pictures looked like a gradual slope to the summit. In real life, however, the "Homestretch" is a couple of cracks in a 400 foot cliff going straight up. At first, I simply muttered that there was no possible way I was going up that thing. Daniel and Lora's eyes were also as big as saucers, their minds boggled at the prospect of scaling that wall of granite.

If we had been there by ourselves, I am sure we would have turned back. But after watching several dozen other climbers of various ages, shapes and sizes going up the crack on the right side of the cliff with no ropes, we fell in behind them and started up.

Now it was absolutely essential not to look down. It was too frightening for that.

Just concentrate on going up. Worrying about getting down later.

Amazingly, after the initial shock from the steepness of the climb, I realized that there were very conveniently spaced foot holds. Soon it was not much different than going straight up an extension ladder. Only there were several sections that required embarrassingly spastic, spread legged, squirming techniques to reach the next step on the "ladder," scraping the "family jewels" along the way. Fortunately, my wife and I had already decided not to have more children.

While we were slowly moving up the right crack, climbers descending from the top were coming down a smaller crack next to a knee high wall of granite to our left. Some moved slowly and deliberately, making sure to grasp safe handholds and footholds every step of the way. Others moved faster, sliding down sections precariously.

Crazy bastards!

At 11:15 A.M. almost nine and a half hours after stepping onto the trail that morning, we reached the summit of Long's Peak.

Lora screamed in delight, threw her hands up in the air, and hugged Daniel and me with great glee. Daniel and I slapped each other's backs. A job well-done.

My feeling of personal accomplishment was strong once again, but somehow I was not as euphoric this time—at least not for myself. This climb was for my kids and I stood and watched them celebrate with great satisfaction. I was so proud of them making it to the top. They had just kept on keeping on, refusing to turn back despite some rather intimidating terrain, even for me.

The fact that they did it with me, and to some degree, *for* me, was priceless.

We worked our way over the flat, football field size top of Long's Peak to the official registry to make sure our names were signed in at the summit, took a few photos on the highest boulder, then collapsed on some flat rocks. Lora almost immediately fell into a light sleep and Dan and I scrounged into our backpacks for some food for a quick lunch.

We did not rest long. The clouds were already starting to close in on us and a few people mentioned a rainstorm approaching. I knew that we needed to get some sustenance, but instinctively, I began to sense an urgency to get off the mountain.

I roused Lora after a few minutes and urged her to eat some food. She managed to get a few bites down, but mostly just wanted to sip on some water.

"We are only halfway done, guys. Going down should be easier, but we have to stay focused," I warned them.

I had no idea at that moment just how difficult the next three hours would be.

The winds picked up and I felt the temperature drop. Moments later, water droplets began splattering on my cheeks. Instantly, the remaining seventy-five or so climbers at the summit began doffing rain gear and grabbing their packs. We quickly joined them and headed back over to the top of the "Homestretch."

The rain was coming harder as we stepped off the edge of the summit plateau and gingerly down the right hand crack of the "Homestretch." Daniel went first, quickly descending about thirty feet. Then he waited for Lora and me to drop down to his level.

The granite beneath us, which had been bone dry on our way up, was now seriously slippery. Lora grabbed onto my arm as we worked our way down along the crack, holding onto the short wall to our right with both hands. Clearly, my daughter was no longer as comfortable as a spider on a water spout. Neither was I.

Section by section we lowered ourselves, sometimes sliding, sometimes grabbing on to each other or the side wall, always jamming the toes of our boots into the crack at the bottom of the wall. Behind and above us were fifty or sixty other similarly struggling climbers. I offered for others to go past us, but they indicated that they were more than happy to stay at Lora's pace. Five or six times we simply had to resort to controlled slides on our butts, digging in our heels or toes as well as possible and just praying we would stop at cracks or protruding edges of rocks.

Finally, with the mist and rain still moistening our faces, we reached the bottom of the "Homestretch." Turning to our right, we almost raced across the "Narrows," only to run into a huge traffic jam at the top of the "Trough." There, the twenty foot high section of steeply angled rocks, which when dry had been passable, was now a sheet of sheer slickness. Dozens of climbers were refusing to going down. One guy was lowering a woman on a rope and offered to do the same for others. But there was not enough rope for all the climbers—not unless everyone was willing to wait for an hour or more to get down.

An alternate route was soon discovered, but it involved about a twelve foot drop off a slick ledge to a flat area below. It was too high to just hang and jump down. However, one brave guy did just that. Then, one by one, each climber helped the next one down. Daniel zipped over the edge and a climber grabbed his legs and lowered him down. Lora was next, but she hesitated at the top of the ledge. Eventually, with others pressing behind her, she slid her legs over until Daniel could reach up and

Pico de Orizaba, Mexico

David on Lower Section of Jamapa Glacier, Pico de Orizaba

Self-photo of David at Pico de Orizaba Summit

Mt. Elbrus, Russia, Highest Point in Europe

Summit of Mt. Elbrus, Ken, David and Jim

Kilimanjaro from Moshi, Tanzania

David at Uhuru Peak, Kilimanjaro Summit
Highest Point in Africa

Aconcagua, Highest Point in South America
Polish Glacier View

David at Aconcagua Summit
South Face in Background

Aconcagua Summit, Al, Stephane, Paul and David

Aconcagua, South Face

Mt. Vinson (Peak in Background) from Vinson Base Camp

David at Vinson Summit

Vinson Summit, David, Johan (front), Jim and Vern

Mt. Koscuiszko, Highest Point in Australia

David at Mt. Koscuiszko Summit

support her ankles above his head. I held her wrists for support as she dangled there, still clinging onto the ledge with her hands. But then she wouldn't let go.

"Trust us," I said. "We're not going to let you fall. Just let go."

"No!" she said and just grabbed on harder.

"Okay, then Dan and I are going on without you," I responded quickly in my most serious sounding voice.

Her hands immediately loosened and she slid down the rock into Dan's arms.

"Now that wasn't so hard, was it?" I quipped with a smile.

Lora did not smile back. I slid down the ledge and dropped the five feet to the ground below and gave her a hug.

From that point on, the climb down the "Trough" was a constant torture on the legs, but was relatively uneventful. Once again, Daniel kept moving down ahead of us, while I hung back with Lora, taking each rock and boulder very carefully. She was being an unbelievable trooper.

We were nearly the last climbers to reach the bottom of the "Trough." Surprisingly, some climbers were still working their way up towards the summit, obviously against all warnings. Only idiots would try to go up the slick granite once it was wet, especially with more potential bad weather coming.

Treacherous is the only way I can describe the "Ledges" after the rain. The level parts were not so bad, but the roller coaster rises and drops towards the end proved to be the most dangerous section of the entire climb.

It didn't help that Lora and I were pretty wiped out. Daniel seemed no worse for the wear, a young guy with no end to his endurance. At least he wasn't gloating.

At one point, where another steep drop off in the trail caused a bottleneck, the fellow in front of Daniel made a detour around a huge boulder to our left, almost instantly appearing on the other side of the logjam. Daniel followed him around the boulder and moments later he too appeared on the other side. Lora followed me around the boulder onto a very narrow ledge with a thousand foot drop just to our left.

Just before we could re-join the main trail, we encountered a three foot gap with the thousand foot chasm below it. The only way across was to lean our entire bodies against a bulging boulder, inch our way across a pencil thin crack at our feet, then jump across. Daniel was already across, so I knew we could do it. Making sure the edge of my boots were secure on the edge of the crack, I straddled the gap with my left foot and reached back to help Lora across. Once more she balked. I found myself precariously balancing one foot on the firm ground, one foot on the tiny crack and pressing my body against the boulder, reaching back for my daughter. Once I was able to securely grab onto Lora's arm, she leaned in my direction. With what she later described as a vice grip on her arm, I forcefully pulled her across the chasm, the two of us sprawling on the ground on the other side, with Lora on top of me. I was still holding the left arm of her light blue jacket with all my strength.

"Okay, we are not doing that again," I said, with a sigh of relief. Lora looked stunned, but got up, dusted herself off and headed down the next ledge without a word.

Moments later, we climbed through the "Keyhole" and back to the safe side of the mountain. If only we didn't have a good four hours' hike back to the trail head and our car.

After a hearty snack and fresh water (as fresh as iodinized water can be) at the Boulderfield, we headed out. With only safe, wide, downhill trails ahead of us, Daniel and I were ready to pick up the pace and get the heck off the mountain. But Lora's feet ached and there was nothing we could do to make her feel better. She would take it one step at a time, at her own pace. At the Chasm Lake trail junction where we stopped for a rest break, she refused to get up. I began to worry that I had pushed her too hard.

I wished that I could carry her off the mountain, but that was not an option. It had been many years since I had been able to carry her "piggyback."

The last two hours were a constant struggle. I promised Lora a big steak dinner at the best place in Estes Park if she would just keep going. Then I started complaining about blisters I thought I could feel developing on my feet—just to give her some company in misery. To her credit, she finally resolved to finish the trek despite her painful feet. The last mile through the woods above the parking area seemed to last forever, but finally we emerged from the trees and found ourselves moaning with pleasure and pain as we pulled our boots off at the car.

It was 6:30 P.M. We had been hiking for 16 1/2 hours from trail head to summit and back, an incredible feat for a seventeen year old son and a fifteen year old daughter. But I don't think either of them was any more tired or relieved to be back safe than their old man. I had successfully completed my mid-term test of conditioning for Aconcagua, but only by a hair.

It was all we could do to stay awake long enough to eat the promised steaks that night. I just remember that the milkshakes tasted mighty fine. And I'll never forget the closeness I experienced with my two children on our climb of Long's Peak.

Once back from Colorado, my training intensified as the fall weather approached. Soon I was running thirty and thirty-five hills two or three evenings a week and jogging six and eight miles on the weekends. My stomach was flattening, my legs were strengthening. I felt great.

At the same time, my correspondence with Alpine Ascents increased as I fine-tuned the gear I needed for Aconcagua.

I quickly learned that my trusty Salomon 8 leather expedition boots that had served me so well on Orizaba and Elbrus would be insufficient on Aconcagua. Double plastics were required. Three hundred and fifty dollars later, I was well outfitted with a pair of Koflach boots. Now I really looked silly marching up and down my hill in a bright yellow pair of ski boots and running shorts!

A twenty below sleeping bag was next on my list. Fortunately, a friend who had just come back from Elbrus had one and graciously offered it for my use. I did my best to persuade him to join me on the Aconcagua trip, but his wife and boss vetoed it. At least his sleeping bag took a nice trip to above 20,000 feet!

Alpine Ascents also sent an equipment list requiring one of two specific types and sizes of backpacks. I knew that my old grey, external support backpack was too small and outdated for the trip, so I splurged on the most expensive Whitney Expedition pack on the guide list. Of course, it had so many zips, pockets, strings, and covers that it took me weeks to figure out all the compartments and the endless variety of ways to strap things on. Actually, it wasn't until I got to base camp that one of the guides who used to design these types of packs showed me all the tricks for snugging up and balancing the pack for the most comfort.

I ended my buying spree with a blue Mountain Hardware down jacket which could stuff into a pouch the size of a large grapefruit, a pair of extremely warm Black Diamond gloves, new fleece Patagonia longjohns, a large quick drying floppy sun hat from REI, a cheap pair of Teva sandals for the river crossings, and a very warm-looking balaclava.

No one could accuse me of not having warm enough gear for this trip. My wife wondered if I was going to Mars.

The first week of December, I reached my goal of forty hills (I almost died) and then backed off a bit to make sure I didn't burn myself out before the trip. The final tune-up was my usual twenty-two mile round-trip hike to the top of Rabun's Bald in the North Georgia mountains, which I completed twice for good measure, once before Christmas and once on the day before New Year's Eve. As usual, I could get no one to go with me. Somehow a nine hour hike in the mountains in the dead of winter just is not too inviting for most folks.

I was ready for the challenge. I could not wait to go to South America for the first time in my life—just to climb the highest mountain on the continent! My only regret was that I had not been able to convince anyone to go with me. Besides the sleeping bag donor, I had met with several friends of friends, including a couple from Tennessee, who were going to climb Aconcagua. but they had already committed to another team led by famed mountaineer Wally Berg, whose trip included a "two-fer," starting with the tallest mountain in Chile, then concluding with Aconcagua. I was not up for that. So for this trip I was on my own. I just hoped the rest of the team would be friendly and capable.

Getting to South America proved to be a bit of a challenge. On the day I was to depart, a midday thunderstorm and tornados in the area closed down Atlanta's Hartsfield Airport for over two hours, leaving the flight schedules in shambles. The first leg of my trip, a short flight to Miami, was delayed "at least four hours" according to the woman at the ticket counter.

ACONCAGUA

Luckily, a morning flight which had been scheduled to leave before I even got to the airport still was on the ground and had a few extra seats open. After a rather heated argument with a ticket agent who thought I would still have plenty of time to catch my connecting flight in Miami if I waited for my original flight and wanted me to defer to "more urgent" passengers, I snagged a ticket on the earlier flight. As much as I would have liked to help out other delayed travelers, I could not afford to miss the Miami flight to Santiago, Chile, that evening, and the weather still did not look promising. I had to take the first flight available.

I'm glad I insisted, as I arrived in Miami just long enough ahead of my flight to grab a bit of dinner and jump on the plane. I did not begin to relax until the LAN Chile jet was airborne and heading over the Gulf of Mexico.

Unfortunately, the flight to Santiago was packed. Every seat was taken.

The couple next to me were from Toronto. They were heading to Chile for a two month beach vacation. *Sounds nice.* When I told them where I was going, they quickly said that I must be crazy, then proceeded to cuddle and neck most of the rest of the flight. Ignoring their public display of affection, I tried to get some sleep. However, several crying babies made it almost impossible to get any meaningful shut-eye, so I spent most of the nine hour flight watching movies and eating. LAN Chile is not like Delta. The food keeps coming and coming.

The highlight of the flight was about ten minutes before we landed in the wee dawn hours. To our left was the Andes mountain range, stretching as far as we could see. Suddenly, across the horizon loomed a peak four thousand feet above the rest.

Aconcagua.

My stomach tightened at the sight.

Once in the terminal in Santiago, I followed the signs to "IN TRANSIT" to avoid having to go through customs, all the while praying that my bags would arrive safely at my final destination in Mendoza, Argentina, as I had checked them all the way from Atlanta. Just in case, I had a change of clothes and my light hiking boots with me just in case I had to go a few days without my main gear.

The Santiago airport is actually quite nice, with lots of places to eat, a huge duty-free store, and a nice variety of art, jewelry, clothing and souvenir shops. On the way to my departure gate for Mendoza, I spied a very nice lapis necklace which looked like it was made for my wife's neck. But it was too early in the morning; the shop was closed. I made a mental note to find that store again on my return trip.

I finally fell asleep on some rather hard couches in the international departure gate area. I remember watching some very scantily clothed Latino singers on the overhead TV and the next thing I knew, it was two hours later. Fortunately I had a four hour layover.

Refreshed by the nap, I started to notice a few other American-looking travelers straggling into the same area. I was anxious to make connections with members of my team.

"Are you here with Alpine Ascents," I asked a few guys with backpacks. They looked at me quizzically and then walked away speaking rapidly in some Portuguese-sounding dialect.

I did not know what any of the Alpine Ascents climbers looked like. They had sent a roster of the nine people in our group. It looked like seven guys and two women, though I later learned that the second seemingly female name, Stephane, was actually a guy.

About forty minutes before my flight, I noticed a couple walking in wearing small packs and hiking boots. This time, they were part of the group—Mike and Jen from Falls Church, Virginia, the one couple on the team. We quickly introduced ourselves. They had climbed Elbrus and Kilimanjaro with Alpine Ascents and had high praises for the organization. Both were dedicated runners, completing three or four marathons a year. Jen, a nice looking blonde, appeared fit, but was taller and larger than most female long distance runners. From the start, I sensed an inner toughness in both Mike and Jen. Neither looked even the least bit fragile. I liked them immediately.

A few minutes later, another member of our team named Brian arrived at the gate. Though it was quite warm in the terminal and I had already stripped down to shorts and a T-shirt, Brian was decked out in white long johns under some hiking shorts, a black fleece jacket, and woolen hat with warmer flaps over his ears. He had all sorts of electronic gadgetry, including a GPS device, a SAT radio, an iPod, a cell phone and camera. However, looking him over, I realized that not all his bulges were digital equipment. He too had apparently climbed to the top of Elbrus with Alpine Ascents, but I immediately wondered if he had put in any training for this climb. Brian was a self-effacing single guy from New York with a dry sense of humor. One couldn't help but like him. But I had no idea how he could possibly climb an almost 23,000 foot mountain with that much weight. Obviously, he planned on giving it a try. With longjohns in the 85 degree terminal, maybe he would sweat off some pounds on the way to Mendoza!

The short flight to Mendoza was spectacular. As we flew directly over the Andes Mountain range, snowcapped peaks filled the horizon to the right and the left. I had a window seat looking north, just where Aconcagua should be. However, spotting the highest peak from 10,000 feet above it is harder than it looks. There were so many peaks that I was not sure which one was Aconcagua. One thing I knew for sure: This was going to be one helluva climb and the scenery was going to be awesome.

Once past the mountains, the plane almost immediately began its descent into Mendoza Airport. The entire flight took less than thirty minutes.

Though Mendoza is a large city and the center of a huge wine region, famous for its Malbec wines, its airport is tiny. With only one terminal and two gates, it would be impossible to get lost. Once inside, we wound our way through a couple of corridors, cleared customs, and waited at a small baggage claim area.

I began to get nervous when my equipment bag and backpack were missing from the first batch of new luggage on the conveyor belt. Mike and Jen also anxiously waited for their bags to arrive.

Finally, their yellow North Face bags appeared, followed by their packs. Still no sign of my stuff. I sweated it out for another few minutes until at last I spied my green Whitney backpack and the blue duffel bag containing my climbing gear.

Moments later, we emerged from the baggage claim area. Scanning the myriad of cardboard signs being held up by dozens of men standing behind a rope, I realized that none had "Alpine Ascents" on it.

As Mike, Jen and Brian arrived with their bags on a rolling cart, I asked one of the English speaking sign holders if he knew where the Alpine Ascents guide was.

"He was here a minute ago," came the response.

Just then a tall, dark-haired guy in flip-flops appeared, scanning the crowd of arrivals.

"There he is," the sign holder said, pointing in his direction.

I recognized our guide, Eric, from the photos of the Alpine Ascents guides in its brochures. He was at least six foot four, and thin from top to bottom. Most climbing guides I had met were much shorter. But he certainly looked fit and had a confident air about him.

He moved casually towards us as I raised my hand and started pointing to our group.

Quickly, we realized that the flight also included another member of our team, a stocky, balding guy in his fifties. He was also decidedly bow-legged. I was instantly glad there was someone of my vintage in the group. Al was his name. He had experienced all sorts of problems flying in from Denver. I don't remember the details, but it involved several missed or cancelled flights, a detour to Lima, Peru, and about twice the time scheduled. He had planned to arrive the day before. Luckily, his luggage had somehow arrived without incident.

Eric immediately escorted us to a small white bus in front of the terminal. The temperature was at least ninety degrees outside under very blue skies. The air conditioning felt good as I settled into a seat in the back of the bus.

Soon we were in heavy traffic heading for the center of town. The outskirts of town appeared very similar to Mexican cities to which I had traveled—dusty plaster buildings with concrete block walls in front of them. There was really nothing too extraordinary to catch my eye.

On our way, Eric explained that three members of our group, Tom, Paul, and Mitch, had already arrived and another, Stephane, had gotten delayed and was going to join us later that night. We would have a total of nine climbers and three guides on our team. A tenth climber, a man from Seattle, had cancelled due to severe storm damage to his house earlier in the week.

About thirty minutes later, we pulled up in front of the Nutibara, a rather unimpressive looking hotel with three golden stars on its marquee. It was obviously chosen for its location, not its name.

Inside the double glass front doors was a large room with couches, an elevated flat screen TV and a pool table to the left, the registration desk to our right, and a bar and restaurant towards the rear. Beyond that, through glass doors and windows, I could see palm trees and a pool which looked like it had been built in the sixties. Not exactly the Ritz, but it seemed nice enough, especially since we wouldn't be there long.

Our bags and equipment filled most of the open floor in front of the registration desk, but blocking egress and ingress did not seem to be a problem.

Eventually, room assignments were made and keys distributed. I was paired with Al from Denver. Naturally, they put the old guys together.

Eric instructed us to take our non-climbing gear and clothes up to our rooms, but to leave everything we planned on taking up on the mountain downstairs, because the first order of business was an equipment check. He wanted to be sure we had everything we needed, and if not, there were several local stores where we could purchase additional gear or clothing that afternoon.

About ten minutes later, in an open air garage area beyond the pool table, we scattered all of our gear and clothes in separate piles for the inspection. By then Paul and Tom had joined us. Mitch and Stephane were still missing.

I quickly noticed that everyone had really serious duffel bags made of heavy material, most with recognizable brand name labels on them. My duffel bag was the same beat up, large Slazenger tennis bag which had carried all my clothes and extra gear on Kilimanjaro. Eric asked me where my large weather proof duffel bag was, and I sheepishly said that was it. He gave me a strange look as if he had already pegged me as a problem.

Before the real inspection began, Eric gathered us into a circle. He first introduced Brent, a short, athletic guy who looked to be in his mid-twenties, as his assistant guide. Brent quickly confessed that this would be his first high altitude climb after having done a lot of rock and ice climb guiding in the United States. He was "looking forward to experiencing the climb with us."

Eric then assured us that he had personally led eleven prior climbs on Aconcagua and that we were in good hands. A third, "high camp" guide named Dave, would join us once we got to the third camp above base camp. Then it was the climbers' turn to introduce themselves.

Paul and Tom, both computer engineers, were friends and business colleagues from Vermont who had climbed together several times before. They had trekked or climbed 20,000 foot peaks in Nepal and, from the looks of their equipment piles, seemed to be quite experienced. They excitedly explained they planned to climb the Polish Glacier route to the summit as an add-on after a normal summit trip with us. After Jen, Mike, Brian and I introduced ourselves, it was Al's turn.

"I'm a sheet metal worker from Denver," he said in a gruff voice. "Just looking forward to climbing with you young guys."

I immediately wondered how a sheet metal worker could afford to travel across the globe to climb mountains, but decided I could find out the answer to that question later.

Amazingly, my pile of gear passed the inspection. Eric pointed out several items that I would not need, one of them an alpine harness I had worn when roped on Elbrus.

"We won't be roped at any time on this mountain?" I asked him.

"Nope—no ropes," he responded.

Rather than make me nervous, that comment actually increased my confidence.

If we don't need ropes, it can't be that steep.

A few other pieces of my clothing and an extra pair of fleece gloves were deemed to be unnecessary and pulled out by Eric. He explained that it was essential that we eliminate every possible ounce of weight from our packs, as, on the way up, every pound would feel like a ton, and on the way down, we would have to carry everything at one time.

Of course, I had carefully packed everything the way I wanted it before I had left Atlanta. But now, every item had to be re-packed in a different sequence. We would need clothes for the day before starting the hike, then light hiking gear for the three day trek to base camp. Everything we didn't need for those four days had to be packed in our large duffel bags, which would be loaded on mules for the trip to base camp.

Since I didn't have a huge duffel bag like the rest, the main gear had to be split between my Slazenger bag and my backpack. I would have to get by with my small day pack for the other four days. Fortunately, Eric informed us that the mules would be stopping at the two initial camps on the way to base camp, so we could access the bigger bags each night.

After what seemed like an hour, I finally got all of my gear re-arranged and back in the bags and struggled to get them up to the room on the second floor. Once inside the narrow room, there was almost nowhere to walk for all the bags. I was sweating like a pig and felt like taking a nap. But it was already past lunchtime and the group was planning to find some food down in Mendoza.

Al begged off, claiming jet lag. By the time I got to the lobby, only Mike and Jen were ready for lunch. So the three of us headed in the direction of the central square of Mendoza.

In the blazing heat in the middle of the day, I expected to be very uncomfortable outside. However, the sidewalks in Mendoza are all lined with shade trees fed by an ingenuous irrigation system. The central park or square had large fountains in the middle and a semicircular row of trees and arts and craft tables along a curved path on the right side. We followed the path in the cool shade, then turned right down a pedestrian only, tree-lined avenue. Small shops, banks and refreshment stands lined both sides of the street. Men and women walked quickly along the way.

One block further down, we could see outdoor cafés with bright colored umbrellas. As we approached them, a band began to play Latino music from a gazebo-like stage in the center of the café district. All in all, it was a surprisingly picturesque scene.

We chose a table under some green umbrellas outside one café. The restaurants all looked the same, but with different color umbrellas and table clothes. I noticed that all the waiters were men, most of them smoking when not serving the food.

Jen and Mike ordered a pizza and beers, and I ordered something akin to cheese toast and a Coke. The waiter brought Pepsi, which was really unacceptable to this Atlantan, but I managed to endure the sweeter taste.

Without anything to do that afternoon, we lingered at the café, watching the local people scurry busily on their way while we swapped tales about our climbs on Elbrus and Kilimanjaro. I wondered out loud how the three experienced guides, as advertised by Alpine Ascents, had been reduced to one experienced guide, a novice guide, and a "high camp" guide we had not yet met.

"I'm sure they are all very capable," Jen assured me. "Alpine Ascents always has great guides and the best set up everywhere we've gone. They've never let us down."

"I hope so. It worries me a bit when I've climbed five higher mountains than one of our guides. Who knows how Brent will adapt to the high altitude once he gets above 14,000 feet?"

"I'm not worried about him," Mike said. "I just hope we all stay healthy and that we can keep going."

"Yeah, it is going to be a long climb," I replied. "I know I can make it to 18,000 or 19,000 feet. Never gotten sick with the altitude. But I have a feeling that the last 4000 feet is going to be tough even if we are feeling good."

"Let's just take it one day at a time," Jen advised, and we all agreed.

When we got back to the hotel, we met a husband and wife who had been part of Alpine Ascents' first or second team that season. Unfortunately, the guy had suffered unexplained seizure-like symptoms at Camp Three and had to be evacuated off the mountain. His wife abandoned her summit attempt to stay with him and now they were back at the hotel with about a week to go before their team would return to Mendoza. They put up a good facade about the situation, but I could tell they were bitterly disappointed. I could not imagine how I would feel to put in that type of training and then have to turn back well short of the goal.

We commiserated with them for a while, but I did not want to get depressed, so I excused myself and headed upstairs to take a nap, joining Al who was already well into a three hour sleep.

After about an hour or so, we both woke up and started chatting about our jobs and families, getting to know each other. As it turns out Al was not exactly a sheet metal worker. He actually was a business owner, with a number of companies in the heating and air conditioning business. As the conversation went along, I learned that his companies had major subcontracts all over the globe, including very sophisticated air conditioning systems for off shore-oil rigs. From the descriptions he used, it was obvious that Al had a strong engineering background. His folksy appearance belied a savvy businessman.

Once he learned that I was a litigation attorney, he started to pepper me with questions and stories of lawsuits he had been in over the years. In the process, I got a good idea of the scope of some of his businesses and the troubles he had encountered over the years. But I never did get a good handle on how many different companies he owned or how big they were.

After about an hour of legal quizzing, I reminded Al that I was on vacation and really wanted to turn my mind off for a while. He quickly obliged and we caught another half hour nap.

That night, the whole group had an orientation dinner at a local steak house called Don Pablo's. Though we arrived at about 8:00 P.M., the place was completely empty. Like Europeans, Argentinians eat dinner very late, many times not even getting started until 9:30 or 10:00 P.M.

By now Mitch and Stephane had arrived. Mitch was a nickname, a shortened version of his last name, "Mitchell." I confess that I do not remember his first name. He was about 5' 11" with a solid frame and a surprisingly dark tan for January. It turns out that he had arrived in Argentina a week earlier and had gotten his tan in Buenas Aires and on a trip across the country to Mendoza. Also from Denver, he was an insurance adjuster and his climbing experience was mostly rock and ice climbing in Colorado. He had done no prior high altitude climbing.

Stephane clearly was a male rather than a female as I had originally presumed. He owned a high-end fabric company in New York, had climbed in a number of exotic places all over the world, especially in the Alps and curiously, in Outer Mongolia. He exuded the air of a jet-setter, and from the beginning he almost never stopped talking.

Dinner at Don Pablo's was absolutely amazing. Argentina is known for its steaks and we were treated to some of the biggest and best. Brent ordered the "Grande," a hunk of meat at least twenty ounces large. I ordered the regular filet mignon which was only about sixteen ounces. I struggled to get it down. But the piece de resistance was the dessert. Most at the table ordered enormous ice cream concoctions with wafers and chocolate piled eight inches high on a plate with fruit and caramel aplenty. Still swooning from the size of my steak, I ordered a bowl of fruit instead. Even still, the portions of fresh pineapple, strawberries, grapes and a couple of melons I did not recognize filled me until I was almost ready to burst.

Just as we were finishing our desserts, another group of climbers arrived at the restaurant and settled in at the next table over. They looked completely whipped, their shoulders drooping and their cheeks bright red. Some still had full beards from the climb. From their appearances, I could not tell whether they had reached the top of Aconcagua or not. However, after their leader ordered a round of beers for them, it quickly became apparent that they were celebrating a successful summit.

Still, it was a bit disturbing to see how subdued they were. I wondered if they had run into problems or whether they were just so tired that they could only managed a half-hearted celebration.

Shortly thereafter, we waddled out of the restaurant, crammed ourselves back into a couple of taxis and headed back for a well needed night of sleep at the Nutibara. I just hoped my snoring would not keep Al up all night.

The next day our destination was Los Penitentes, a small ski village near the Vacas Valley trail head three days' hike from the Aconcagua base camp. But before we could leave on the three hour drive to the mountains, we had to get our permits. Located in the Bureau of Tourism in downtown Mendoza, the little permit room for Aconcagua was crammed with other groups trying to register. Two Argentine women were handling hundreds of permits very very slowly. No one was going anywhere fast.

Eric handed out forms for us to fill out. Some of the questions called for information we did not have, like the policy numbers for our evacuation insurance policy and the telephone numbers of the hotel where we would be staying for the next three weeks.

Eric told us to just fill in numbers randomly. "It doesn't matter. Just make sure you have the Alpine Ascents headquarters phone number and your home phone number and everything will be okay."

We did as he told us and at some point he took the forms and our passports into the permit room for processing.

We waited. Then we waited some more. At one point, Brent, the assistant guide decided he was bored and started to climb up the side of the bureau building, digging his fingers into cracks and pulling himself up. Impressively, he quickly moved ten or twelve feet up the wall before sliding back down to the sidewalk. The marks where he disturbed decades of soot and dust above the decorative marble along the top of the first section of the wall are probably still there. Of course, Brent's hands and the entire front of his pants and shirt were also covered in soot from the effort. And there was nowhere to clean off.

After almost two hours, Eric finally emerged from the permit room with a folder of permits. We each retrieved our passports, and moments later we were fighting traffic to get out of town and head for the mountains. I felt a surge of excitement when our buses took a turn off an expressway and the Andes were suddenly straight ahead.

The bus ride was more interesting than I had anticipated. For the first half hour, we zoomed along flat roads with vineyards on both sides of the street. Rows of grapevines loaded with luscious-looking grapes filled the fields for as far as we could see. Every few hundred yards was another ornate entrance signifying the wine maker. I recognized a few of the larger brand names, but most were local brands of which I had never heard.

As we approached the mountains, the lush, irrigated vineyards gave way to desert-like wasteland split on our right by a very fast moving and rough river of churning muddy waters coming from the mountains. The river had eroded the landscape, forming a deep canyon which looked impossible to cross. Occasionally, bridges spanned the river and the gorge, the roads seemingly aiming for nowhere on the other side.

After about one and a half hours, we reached a fertile valley on the way up the slopes. The river was now on our left, but it was shielded by a row of tall thin trees which also acted as a windbreak for the little town in the center of the valley. The bus driver pulled into a gravel parking lot next to a shop/restaurant on our right, and Eric announced that it was lunch time.

This time, the menus were strictly in Spanish and ordering in English was not an option. I managed to figure out what I hoped was a ham and cheese omelet and pointed it out to the waitress. Brent and Eric had some linguistic aptitude and helped the rest with their orders. What came out on my plate was in fact an omelet of some sort, but the key ingredient was clearly a lot of grease in which the yellowish mass was floating. It actually had a reasonably good flavor, but I only risked a few bites. I had started on my prophylactic doses of Cipro the day before and the antibiotic would be working overtime the rest of the day.

The rest of the trip to Los Penitentes was through hot, dry, dusty, and very unmemorable scenery. We mostly slept in the air conditioned bus. Some of the guys were zoned out with their iPods plugged into their ears. Only Stephane could be heard chattering away with Eric in the front of the bus.

A few miles before our destination and just across a small river, we passed what looked like a supply or ranger station on our left and a flat loading yard with a small bunker on our right. "There's the trail head where we start tomorrow," Eric said, pointing to the right of the bus.

All I could see was a dirt road heading in the direction of a narrow chasm between two high ridges with a grey river running along it. There were no snow-capped peaks anywhere to be seen. Obviously, the thirty mile hike to base camp had to start somewhere, but this certainly was not an impressive place to begin.

Past the trail head, the bus climbed several hairpin curves and within ten minutes we pulled into the little village of Los Penitentes. The village consisted of approximately eight to ten small hotels. Only two of them on the left side of the road were open for summer business.

Once out of the bus, we could see ski lifts rising up the ridge on the right side of the road, disappearing about a 1000 vertical feet above us. With no snow in sight, it was hard to imagine this being a ski resort, but Eric assured us that in the winter, the whole area was packed with snow.

After only a few minutes in the sun, I was already starting to sweat.

The first task was to get all our gear and food packed for loading onto the mules the next morning. Eric led us down some stairs and a ramp into the basement of a building just up from our hotel. There we found dozens of round blue canisters into which all of the food for our trip would be crammed by the guides. Our job was to weigh and mark each of our duffel bags with the number of kilograms, as there were strict regulations limiting the weight for each mule. The cost of the portage was also to be determined by the size of the load.

The guys hoisted all of the gear while Jen, who we all chauvinistically assumed had the best handwriting, wrote out the labels. My gear in the Slazenger bag and my large backpack were thrown inside a large blue canvas bag and tied snugly at the top with rope and wire. Even combined, they were lighter than most of the other duffel bags.

By the time we had the duffel bags weighed and marked, Eric and Brent had stuffed most of the blue barrels. Each of them had to be weighed and marked as well. The only food left out was what Eric estimated we would eat for lunch on the trail to base camp. The entire process took approximately two hours, but at the end, we had one very large pile for the mules to carry. I was glad that we did not have to carry all that weight for the first three days.

With the rest of the afternoon to kill and the group anxious to stretch their legs, Paul and Tom suggested that we take a short hike up the ridge behind the hotel. Someone had told Paul that Aconcagua was "clearly visible" at the top of the ridge and he was going to check it out.

All nine climbers agreed to get some exercise and soon we had crossed a small bridge across a rushing stream behind the hotel and were heading across a cow pasture towards a steep ridge. Paul and Al led the way at a pretty good clip. Feeling a bit winded almost immediately, I started to warn them with the Kili chant, "Po-le, po-le." But they barely slowed down.

Once across the pasture, the trail led steeply up, diagonally traversing the flank of the bluff. Already panting hard, I managed to get the group to stop for water twice. But soon we were gaining serious altitude and about half the group started falling off the pace. Paul, Al, Tom and I kept going, periodically looking back across the valley towards where Aconcagua was supposed to be.

We were at least 750 feet above the hotel when I decided that there was no way we could see Aconcagua over the nearby ridges. With the sun starting to drop toward the horizon and the shadows creeping across the narrow trench we were climbing, I advised the others to turn back. However, Paul was persistent and Al appeared determined to match him step for step. Tom and I reluctantly worked our way up behind them to a crest, where I stopped and turned around. We could now see some snow-capped peaks, but surely none of them were Aconcagua.

I saw a path on the other side of the dry gulch we had been climbing along and decided to go back an alternate route. I thought Tom was following me, but after I dropped about fifty vertical feet and looked back up, I saw him heading up the mountain in pursuit of Paul and Al. Eventually, the three of them stopped at a big rock perch high up on the ridge. They later said they may have seen Aconcagua, but the pictures they took from that vantage point certainly did not look like it.

The climb was a bit treacherous on the way down. At one point I found myself sliding down some very steep mule paths and then having to cross between paths to find a trail back to the cow pasture. Once off the worn paths, the thorns in the dry plants scraped my calves and the burrs collected all over my socks and the laces to my leather hiking boots. By the time I reached the cow pasture, my right leg had a nice stream of blood working its way down from a scratch and my boots were almost green with burrs.

As I reached the pasture, a guy and a girl came running down the side of the steep bluff, the dust flying up behind them. They were both huffing and puffing as they reached the bottom. The guy was shirtless and quite toned. The shapely girl was blonde and pretty. I couldn't help but notice her tanned shoulders soaking in the late afternoon sun rays.

"Okay," as my wife says, "No harm in looking at the menu."

After hearing them laugh and chatter in English, I asked them where they were from.

"Montreal," the pretty one answered.

"Do they teach you to run down mountains like that in Montreal?" I asked. "You guys must be crazy."

"It's the fastest way down, mate," the guy responded.

He turned and began jogging at a good clip towards the bridge to the hotel. The girl ran after him, but could not keep up.

I was not about to run, but I picked up my pace, enjoying the rear view of the figure in front of me. When I reached the bridge, the Canadian couple was walking arm and arm up the hill on the other side.

Once back at the hotel, I learned that the couple was part of a team of emergency room physicians who planned to climb Aconcagua simultaneously with our group. They were taking the same route to the same base camp (there are actually four base camps to choose from) and hoped to reach the summit at the same time as us. I wondered where the rest of their group was.

An hour later, I finally finished picking the thorns and burrs out of my skin, socks, and bootlaces and went inside for a well-deserved shower. Unfortunately, four burr thorns remained embedded in the soft tissues of my left thumb, causing me much pain over the next three days. I finally cut them out with a Swiss Army Knife at base camp.

Mitch and I enjoyed some local beer under some red umbrellas outside a nearby pizza café before the whole group enjoyed pizzas for dinner that night. The pizzas were surprisingly good, with thick creamy cheese, tomatoes and mystery meat. Again, I was thankful that my doctor friend had prescribed a healthy dose of Cipro to avoid intestinal infections on the trip.

Breakfast at the hotel the next morning was pathetic. I had envisioned a nice final meal of sausage, omelets and fresh fruit. Instead we were given a few hard biscuits which were a chore to force down, followed by a small saucer of really scrambled egg crumbs about a quarter inch high. It was as if they had taken three regular sized helpings and rationed it into eleven servings. I kept waiting for them to bring more, but it never came. Luckily, I had stashed some extra almonds and raisins in my small pack, so I was able to avoid complete starvation before starting out on the trail.

A mix-up on the transportation from the hotel to the trail head caused a delay of almost a half hour. Finally, Eric decided to split the group up and shuttle us and our small packs to the Vacas Valley trail head. Six of us, plus Eric and the driver, crammed into a small red Jeep with a little luggage trailer behind it containing our packs. Tom, Paul, Stephane and Brent waited behind for the next trip.

The drive to the trail head was only about eight miles, but the driver almost flipped the vehicle over on the curves about five times. We all started to lean in the direction of the hairpin curves to help stabilize the damned thing as the driver just kept speeding down the road. I was very relieved when we finally pulled off the road and into the flat, dusty loading area at the trail head.

There we adjusted our trekking poles, added a bit more sun block to our legs and faces, and to my surprise started up the trail without waiting for the second group.

"There's a nice place to wait for the others just up the way," Eric assured us.

Sure enough, after about a quarter of a mile, he led us up a side path to a fortified bunker hidden by the last shade trees we would see for the next eighteen days. A small irrigation ditch filled with grey water ran by the bunker and added to the coolness of the spot.

I was anxious to get going as I knew we had almost ten miles of trail to cover before the first camp, and it was already almost noon. But it took at least a half hour for the rest of our group to join us. Only then did Eric give us instructions for the day. The only part I remember is that he said we would hike for an hour at a time, take several rest stops and enjoy a picnic lunch, but "take it easy" all afternoon. He said it was impossible to get lost because we would just be following the river to our right until we got to the first camp.

The only warning he gave us was to keep an eye out for mules, and if we saw some coming, to get off the trail as they would just keep coming.

At first the trail was easy, alternating hiking up well worn paths up fairly gentle hills to walking along the river beds or through gorgeous fields of yellow flowers as high as our waists. Occasionally, I spied a lizard squirming off the path or behind rocks as we approached, but for the most part, the land was dry and lifeless.

Shortly before lunch, the emergency room physicians' group passed us, the Montreal couple laughing a bit obnoxiously as they went. Their group was led by a thin bearded guy and a petite dark-haired woman, both of whom obviously knew our guide, Eric. There was one other young woman in their group besides the Montreal blonde. The rest looked like very fit guys, mostly in their thirties from their appearance. They were moving at a slightly faster pace than us, but I was content to plod along. We were going to the same place and both groups would be there well before sunset.

For lunch, Eric pulled out fresh tomatoes, cheese, cucumbers, and sliced meat. I helped with the slicing of the tomatoes while others re-filled water jugs at a nearby side stream. With a beautiful view of the river below, we gorged on juicy sandwiches made up of all of the above and garnished with either mayonnaise or a more spicy reddish spread which I carefully avoided. There were also cookies and fruit to complete the small smorgasbord, laid out on a square red tarp. Much nicer than I had expected.

After lunch, the hiking became a bit more serious, with several extended rises that tested my leg strength and my cardiovascular conditioning. Breathing hard, I started to get used to the rhythm, taking water on the move as I needed it.

Eric was not kidding. Once we started hiking we did not stop for an hour no matter who was asking for a rest. Then, almost to the minute on each hour, we stopped for a ten minute water break.

By the time we finally made it to the first camp, called Pampa de Lenas, my feet were sore, my body was covered in dust and grime, and I was almost out of water. But there was nothing to do but wait, as the mules had not passed us on the trail and had not arrived.

Eric showed us around the camp, which was nestled on a broad plateau between a sheer ridge/cliff to our left and the river to our right. The flat area of the camp was about the size of a small football field, and indeed, shortly after we arrived, the ER doctors were tossing a Koosh football around, periodically tripping and falling over boulders or stones strewn throughout the area. I was just waiting for one of them to turn an ankle. The other female climber in the group, another blonde, seemed very athletic, choosing to punt the football thirty or forty yards and laughing infectiously as her friends scrambled through the rocks to try to catch it.

Closer to the river was a rock-walled cabin flanked by two tent-like structures. In front of them was the end of a long hose pulling water from a nearby water source. Eric warned us to start using water tablets or to filter the water as the water source was near where the mules relieved themselves after the long trip in. The best part of the tour was the outhouses, scattered back near the cliff away from the river. At least we would have a small amount of privacy to take a dump after dinner.

With nothing to do, I chatted with Al and munched on some almonds and gorp, while Brent, Paul, and Mitch matched rock climbing skills on a large boulder in the middle of the camp. We watched as Brent masterfully worked his way up the most difficult side of the rock, his fingers locking onto whatever cracks and bumps were available. Just before he reached the top, his grip failed. To everyone's surprise, he did a back flop straight onto the hard ground from about twelve feet up.

Woah, that must have hurt!

Al and I shared a slight grin at Brent's expense. We were content to sit back and let the younger guys expend energy on useless pursuits.

Brent's ego was probably hurt more than his body, but I think the fall knocked the wind out of him—at least momentarily.

Paul and Mitch took turns trying to go up the same side as Brent had fallen from, abandoning their efforts about halfway up.

The female guide from the ER doc group joined them, but wisely chose the opposite side of the boulder. Within seconds, she was standing atop the rock. Soon, all three rock climbers from our group joined her. But Brent slid down after a few moments and resumed his attempt on the more difficult side. This time he made it, instantly regaining his reputation as the best rock climber in the group, and the most impetuous.

Finally the mules arrived, along with our tents and gear. Once unloaded, the mules were tied into groups of four and led off by the caballeros. Some were more cooperative than others. One white mule got away and headed for the river, only to be caught by another gaucho on a faster mule.

Our attention was focused on Eric, as he instructed us, in great detail, how to properly set up the tents. With the winds above, he explained that it was critical to secure the tent lines exactly the way he showed us. No small rocks would do. Each line had to be attached to a large rock and then the large rock had to be covered with other large rocks.

After we set up one tent, Eric went around tugging hard on the lines, instantly sending our rock piles tumbling and leaving the line loose.

"Not good enough. This tent just flew off the mountain with you in it," he said. "Try it again."

After a few more tries, we got the message. Soon Al was dragging fifty pound boulders over to secure the lines to our tent. Eventually all the tents passed inspection and Eric announced that he had arranged a special dinner for us on our first night out.

"Carne," he said, pointing in the direction of the rock hut. There behind the hut, several caballeros were working on a fire and the smoke was wafting in our direction.

About a half hour later, just as it was getting dark, our team sat in a semi-circle around the fire watching the cowboy expertly cut up juicy thick steaks with a very sharp knife and handing us generous chunks to eat with our fingers. *Succulent.*

A tangy salad of tomatoes, cucumbers, onions and herbs balanced the meal, but we kept going back for more of the delicious carne, cooked right on a metal rack on top of the fire.

Midway through the meal, two climbers and a guide from the first Alpine Ascents team arrived from the other side of the camp. The guide, a short Asian fellow, quickly embraced Eric, who introduced him only as "Lakpa."

Lakpa had successfully led the two climbers, one male and one female, to the summit only three days earlier. That day, they had hiked the twenty miles from base camp to Pampa de Lenas. After a few bites of carne and some sips of hot chocolate, they were ready to tell us about their summit experience.

Incredibly, they had reached the top without ever having to put on crampons. The young guy, who confessed he was just twenty-one years old, described the climb as "tough, but very doable." They had occasionally crossed some very short sections of snow, but not enough to need crampons. It was just a long, dusty scree climb. I was reminded of the comments from other climbers who had said Aconcagua was just a miserable, bone-dry trudge.

After giving us the basic details, both climbers begged off answering the rest of our questions. I thought that they would be ecstatic. But they were quite bland and not animated at all. In retrospect, I realize now that they were simply too exhausted to exhibit much enthusiasm. But they were happy for some really good food and anxious to get to a hotel to take a shower.

Lakpa was all smiles and looked no worse for the wear. Apparently, a twenty mile trek three days after reaching the summit of the highest mountain in the Western Hemisphere was not that big of a deal for him. Upon inquiry, I learned that he was actually a sherpa from Nepal, but now lived in Seattle, while continuing to help guide Alpine Ascents climbers in South America and in the Himalayas. I only discovered later that he had already successfully reached the top of Everest nine times!

The next morning, we were up at dawn. Al, Eric and Brent had opted to spend the night under the stars in just sleeping bags. I shared a tent with Brian, but did not have much of a chance to talk to him since we crashed a few minutes after laying down after the carne feast.

Brian, a vegetarian, was the only one who did not partake of the scrumptious steak. He simply did not know what he was missing. However, his idiosyncracy was the key to the name we selected for our Alpine Ascents Team 3. We became Team "Carne Plus One" for the rest of the trip.

After a breakfast of rather greasy but tasty ham and cheese between grilled tortillas, one of Eric's specialties, we quickly packed up the tents and hit the trail.

The first obstacle was getting across the river to the other bank. Fortunately, a small metal bridge which had been washed out a few weeks earlier was back in place about a half mile up from Pampa de Lenas.

In a mild test of courage, each member of our group crossed the rickety narrow bridge above the rushing river below as pictures were taken to document the feat. It really was not particularly dangerous, but the two foot wide metal plank swayed a bit as we crossed, and the only handhold was a loose wire at thigh level on one side of the bridge.

Brian looked especially grim as he worked his way slowly across the span, but smiled like a Cheshire cat once on the far bank.

After the crossing, the going got much tougher as we immediately began to work our way up some steep bluffs, requiring the ascent of several switchbacks. Making it a bit more difficult, Brent was assigned to lead us for the first segment of day two on the trail. His gait was steady, but slightly faster than Eric's pace the first day.

Soon it became apparent that our group would not always stay together as a team all the time. The first group of Al, Stephane, Paul, Tom and I kept in close formation behind Brent. Sometimes Mitch stayed with us; sometimes he dropped back a bit. Mike and Jen kept up a good pace, keeping within contact. Brian started falling considerably behind and struggled to catch up during the breaks. In proper guide etiquette, one of our two guides always brought up the rear, usually staying right behind Brian, encouraging him as he moved along.

It didn't help that in the hot, desert-like conditions, Brian was still wearing long johns, a woolen hat and a long sleeved fleece.

Once up on the bluffs above the river, the conditions were extremely dry. Parched, cracked dirt and rocky sections were interrupted only by a few dry gulches. Yet, mysteriously, every hour or so, a thin green patch would appear, where a small stream worked its way across the wasteland. There we would stop, fill water bottles and get snacks along the way, always remembering to add iodine pills to the bottles.

Lunch that day was at the end of a long gradually rising slope, where, to the left of the trail were three large flat rocks, perfect for setting up the daily picnic. I soon realized that the meal would be the same as the day before—tomatoes, cucumbers and ham and cheese sandwiches with the same tube spread mayonnaise and alternate reddish stuff. Just as we get settled in, the ER doc group arrived at the same picnic site. We moved some of our stuff to give them one of the rock "tables."

Somehow the pleasant setting did not seem as nice once they arrived, especially after the Montreal couple began making a spectacle of themselves, making out by the trail.

For better or worse, they would be moving up the mountain in tandem with our group. They clearly were making faster time than us, as before we finished our lunch, they had packed up were heading up the trail.

Midway through the afternoon, the trail returned to the side of the river. For miles, we hiked directly on the rocky river beds which were sometimes several hundred yards wide. This was tremendously rough on our feet, as there was no flat trail to follow. I was thankful to be wearing a nice pair of Asolo trekking boots with very sturdy soles and ankle support. I could not understand how or why Brent was hiking over the same rocks in a pair of light sneakers with no socks.

A couple of times the trail was squeezed onto a steep pile of scree immediately rising from the water's edge. We found ourselves leaning into the rocks and away from the water while trying to avoid sliding off the narrow section of path into the water. Eric resumed the lead during this section, which was the most precarious yet, but still "doable." The other option was to work our way up steep bluffs, only to return to the river after expending considerable energy to climb them.

Here, our group fragmented, with Mike, Jen and Brian falling significantly behind.

But, once we made it through the narrow section and after a particularly windy crossing of a wide river bed, Eric lead us to a sheltered embankment for a rest stop. The team was reunited.

That rest was an extended one, as the next section of the trail led us up a long traverse up the side of a bluff several hundred feet above the river. We could see the ER docs almost at the top of the ridge, moving slowly away, then disappearing beyond our sight lines.

We were all beginning to tire, and to make matters worse, we were now hiking directly into the wind as we started up the trail.

Eric kept the pace up, and for the first time, I felt my legs begin to "burn" as we climbed. I was too proud to slow down and worked hard to remain with the first group despite the pain of the ascent. Fortunately, I had moved one of my water bottles to one of my front pockets and was able to frequently re-hydrate as we moved up the slope.

At the top of the ridge we rested again. From that vantage point, we could see way back down the valley to snow-capped peaks in the distance somewhere above where we had started the day before. We still had not gotten any glimpse of Aconcagua.

This rest was the longest yet, as we had to wait for Mike and Jen to make it up the ridge, giving them a rousing hand when they made it to the top. Then we waited another ten minutes for Brian to finally arrive with Brent shrugging his shoulders right behind him.

"That was the worst of it for today," Eric informed us once everyone arrived. "It won't be long now. Make sure you have your cameras ready. You are about to get your first view of Aconcagua."

A few minutes later, we crested a hill and could see the tents of Camp Two, also known as Casa de Piedra, nestled along the right side of the river a few miles ahead. In the brochures I had read back in Atlanta, I knew that just before reaching Camp Two we would be able to see the mountain, up a valley to our left.

As we moved quickly along a gradually descending trail towards the camp, my excitement rose in anticipation.

Suddenly, to our left, a valley opened up and a snow-capped peak appeared high in the sky. I began to lift my camera to capture the sight.

"Not yet, David," Eric said. "That's Ameghino."

"Ameghino?"

"Yeah. It's about 19,000 feet. Just a few hundred yards and you'll see Aconcagua way above it."

We practically race-walked the next two hundred yards until the "Stone Sentinel" came into view. Now I stood still, my jaw dropping senselessly, as I saw Aconcagua for the first time. It soared above and to the left of Ameghino, which itself was about the height of Kilimanjaro. The Polish Glacier, rising diagonally from right to left all the way up to what appeared to be the peak of Aconcagua, shone majestically in the afternoon sun.

For the next ten minutes, we took picture after picture of the mountain as Eric smiled knowingly at the scene. He had obviously watched the excitement of climbers at this spot many times before. But even for him, it was an awesome sight of which he admitted never growing tired.

For us, we could not soak in the picture deep enough. Aconcagua was still thirteen miles of trail away, but it seemed so high and so close. Both incredibly awe-inspiring and frightening at the same time, the vision of the tallest mountain in South America stayed on my mind and surely was the cause of my restless sleep that night.

Day Three started very chilly. We woke up before the sun rose above the tall ridge behind us, so no warmth had reached our little beach campsite. I pulled on two more layers of fleece to get through a light breakfast, the dismantling of tents, and the packing of gear for the mules.

By the time we were done, sunlight was hitting the top of the ridge on the other side of the river. We could see it steadily descend the opposite hills, but we were still in the shadows when Eric told us it was time to wade across the river.

Paul and Al were anxious to head out, as was I. We stripped down to shorts and our Teva sandals for the crossing. Brent joined the three of us, and without waiting for the others, we worked our way across the dry, rocky river bed towards the first of about eight channels of water.

Just as we reached the water, Eric shouted from the camp that one of the caballeros would take us across on mules for a minimal fee. We shrugged our shoulders.

Only pansies ride the mules across.

Al plunged right into the water, declaring that he was "not riding no mule." His balance was only slightly challenged by the fact that he had lost one of his sandals on the trail the afternoon before and now was wearing two "left shoes."

Brent and Paul immediately followed him into the water. Quickly the three crossed the first channel without incident. Brent warned me to keep my body and knees pointed slightly upstream to maintain balance.

I had no idea how cold the water was going to be until I stepped knee-high into the first channel. Now I know how the Swedes must feel when they jump into the fjords on New Year's Day. This water was not frozen only because it was moving so fast. After the initial shock, I took a deep breath and worked diagonally across the water. My feet and legs up to my knees were almost frozen by the time I jumped up on the far bank, but my attitude was positive.

"Invigorating," I said to the others.

The next channel was shallow and easily navigated. I hardly noticed the coldness, probably because my feet were now fully numb. The third channel looked deeper and swifter than either of the first two. Al and Brent conferred over the best route, then Al plunged in first again. This time as he reached the roughest current, his trekking pole slipped and down he went. He barely managed to keep his day pack above the surface as he struggled to regain his footing. Water cascaded off his jacket as he crawled up the far bank, shivering like a dog caught in a cold rainstorm.

I watched as Brent and Paul adjusted the course across the stream to avoid the spot that befell Al. Their route still went through a very swiftly moving, thigh-high current, but they made it upright. I followed exactly along the same line. Miraculously, I made it through with only a bit of water soaking into the bottom of my shorts.

By now, we didn't care about the coldness of the water. We just plowed across channels one after another. Luckily, the rest were not as deep.

Just as we reached the last channel, the sun's rays hit the far "beach," allowing us to warm quickly while watching the others take turns riding mules across the river.

Once dry and warm, my feet felt wonderful, as if they had just been massaged. I did not regret eschewing the mule ride one bit. After all, I came for the whole experience, part of which was river crossing. Plus, I spent forty bucks on the darn sandals and I sure wasn't carrying them for nothing.

The freezing river crossing quickly gave way to a blistering hot, steep climb up very dry and dusty bluffs along the canyon carved out by the Relinchos River, the Vacas River tributary which rushed down the gorge below and to our left. We were now heading directly for

Aconcagua, though for the first two hours, we saw no sign of the mountain.

Eric really moderated the pace on this section of the climb. The path was twice as steep as anything we had encountered the first two days. Frequently we moved along narrow scree ledges above 150 foot drops into the gorge. Every once in a while I looked back and could see how high we had come from the Vacas River. The view back down the canyon was spectacular, but safety required that I keep my focus on the path ahead.

Surprisingly, Brian did a good job of keeping up with the group as we gained elevation. Jen and Mike also seemed to be doing fine. We stayed as a group almost seamlessly until the first break halfway up the gorge. There I stripped off all but a long-sleeve synthetic shirt provided by Alpine Ascents, as the temperature was rising and I did not want to get overheated.

The magnetic draw of seeing Aconcagua up closer was all the incentive I needed to trudge up the rest of the steep canyon. I hardly noticed the magnificent waterfalls and cascades several hundred feet below us, but I did not miss the first glimpse of the Polish Glacier just above the horizon at the top of one bluff. I snapped a picture quickly, but Eric chastised me.

"In just a few minutes, you will see the whole mountain," he said. "Don't waste your film here."

Sure enough about ten minutes later, we reached the crest of the canyon and Aconcagua and Ameghino stood in tandem before us in all their glory.

"Photo op," I cried out.

Paul was already pulling a tripod out of his pack as I took a few shots with one of my three digital disposal cameras. I was trying to minimize weight. Paul on the other hand had a beautiful Canon camera with zoom and panoramic lenses, and a metal tripod. Needless to say, his photos turned out the best. Fortunately, we all shared photos and Paul included all of them on two CD's distributed to the group after we returned home.

Eric did not let us dawdle long. In a flat basin in front and below us, we could see other groups scattered along the river. Another crossing.

"We can take a break after we cross," Eric said. He then took off at a pace none of us could match. We followed, enjoying the rare downhill trail.

This time, wading across the stream, about twenty feet wide, was a breeze. Though deeper in one section than the channels below and probably swifter, our technique was now honed and the water did not seem as cold. The ones that had ridden the mules earlier struggled a bit and Jen and Brian needed a bit of assistance, but soon we were all enjoying a snack on the left side of the water.

That restful snack was abbreviated, however, by the arrival of a massive wave of fully loaded mules heading directly towards us.

Without hesitation, the mules plunged through the water, splashing wildly as they went. They did not slow up even a bit as they raced passed us. Some went around, some went right through us, and some took a treacherous course up the bank to our left. It is a wonder that no climber got trampled in the stampede.

As more mules were coming behind them, we quickly gathered our things and moved to higher and safer ground. The second wave of mules passed us just in time to create the perfect foreground for our next scenic photos of Aconcagua.

Once we crested the hill above the river crossing, the incredible view of Aconcagua was virtually unimpeded. A few minor foothills blocked the lower South side of the mountain, but the rest of the mountain stood clearly before us. I found it hard to take my eyes off it.

Since the trail was now wide and relatively flat, Eric told us that we could take our own pace for the rest of the afternoon. He would lead the front group and Brent would bring up the rear.

At first, all of us stayed together as we hiked along a path surrounded by low green foliage. The area obviously got some rain as some of the terrain off the path was spongy. Small green clumps filled with tiny yellow flowers added a bit of color, but my efforts to get a good picture of the mountain with flowers in the foreground was a miserable failure. The flowers were just too small.

We enjoyed a pleasant lunch next to a brook in a meadow filled with thick, matted grass. This was the greenest spot yet on the trip. And the last. As we crested the next hill, beyond it was nothing but arid brown dust and scree. A cooler wind was also picking up enough that I found it more comfortable to hike in a fleece top.

With about two hours left before base camp, we faced steady headwinds of twenty to thirty miles an hour. Every step began to raise dust. I was directly behind Eric at that point, so the dust passed me at knee level. However, I quickly removed my sunglasses and replaced them with goggles to avoid dust from getting into my contact filled eyes.

At first the wind felt good, a nice break from the sweltering heat. But after a while, I realized that hiking at this altitude into a minor gale was no easy task. My thighs began to burn and my calves began to tighten as Eric kept a brisk pace. I'm not sure why, but I was determined to stay up with him—maybe just to prove to him that I belonged on this trip. Plus, Al was right behind me and if he could do it so could I.

I thought I was going to collapse when Eric finally crossed a narrow stream and stopped at a wind-protected levee to our right.

"How much further?" I asked as I reached for some water.

"Not too much," he said. "But I want us all to reach base camp together, so we'll wait here until the rest catch up."

The rest were Mike, Jen and Brian. Al, Stephane, Mitch and I had kept close to Eric. Paul and Tom had chosen to walk together a few hundred yards back and were already approaching our waiting point.

About ten minutes later, Jen came over the hill and crossed the stream with Mike close behind. They looked beat. When Jen arrived, she had a hacking cough that did not sound good at all.

Another twenty-five minutes passed before Brian and Brent arrived, moving at a snail's pace.

Within minutes of their arrival, Eric hopped up and headed around the corner of the levee. Within a few hundred yards we saw the Plaza Argentina sign, marking the entrance to the base camp. We had been less than a quarter of a mile away for the last forty minutes!

My disgust over stopping just short of our destination quickly gave way to the joy of seeing that tents were already set up for us. Better still, we had a nice large permanent mess tent with food and drinks laid out awaiting our arrival. The base camp manager, Ellie, welcomed us warmly, showed us to our tents and invited us down for orientation, along with fruit, cheese and crackers, and other goodies. The base camp would be our "home" for the next four nights.

The next day was a rest day at base camp. After a leisurely breakfast, including fresh eggs that had been carefully packed in cartons carried by the mules, we all took turns trudging over a hill and across about a quarter mile of desert to the water barrel to fill "bladders" for the kitchen. A long hose from the river stretched almost a half mile to a large blue drum, which when filled, probably held over a hundred gallons of fresh water.

One highlight at camp that day was watching a yellow helicopter appear from over the ridge and hover over the camp for about twenty minutes. The helicopters were used to evacuate climbers with urgent medical problems, or, in this instance, to carry away big drums of waste from the outhouses scattered throughout the camp. As quickly as it appeared, the helicopter flew off down the valley and silence returned to the area.

That evening, Jen was examined by one of the emergency medicine doctors from the other group, also named Jen. She was the other blonde in the group, the one who liked to punt the Koosh football. Our Jen's hacking cough was not getting better and we all watched as Dr. Jen asked her questions, listened carefully to her chest, and examined her throat. My initial impression of Dr. Jen being a "valley girl" was quickly proven wrong by the intelligent and careful nature of her medical questions and advice. Luckily, Jen's cough did not appear to be related to the altitude. She simply needed rest and conventional respiratory medicines. Nothing too serious – yet.

After dinner, Eric broke out a deck of cards. I had watched them play Hearts once earlier in the afternoon and quickly recognized that Eric and Paul were the card sharks of the group. I have played a few games of Hearts over the years as well, so I joined in that evening. On the fourth hand, a no-pass hand, I stunned the group by "shooting the moon," taking all the hearts and the queen of spades for the maximum score against the other three players. Thereafter, I became the "hunted." A few hands later I tried to "shoot the moon" again, but was thwarted on the last trick when Eric defied all logic and kept a high club instead of a high heart, enabling him to take the final heart with the last trick. "You mother! " I responded with a smile on my face. But his smile was larger. The game was on.

Day five started just like day four—hot and dry. But this time, after breakfast, we packed up all of our heavy high mountain gear, the crampons, ice axes, heavy Gore-Tex pants and down parkas, along with extra clothing, food, fuel tanks and tents for the "carry" to Camp One, about 2500 vertical feet up the mountain towards the Polish Glacier. With fifty pound packs on our backs and a bit of nervousness, we began the slow slog up the scree-filled hills above base camp. New for me was the requirement that we all wear double plastic boots for all climbing above base camp. I had lobbied to be able to hike in my trail boots which were lighter and more comfortable, but Eric insisted on the double plastics for better support and control in the scree and in case the weather changed.

I had tried to break in the double plastics back in Atlanta, but found them to be pretty awkward on the asphalt street hills at home. However, after a half hour of hiking up scree, the inner lining to the double plastics molded to my feet and I almost forgot I was wearing them.

The bigger problem was the terrain. We were no longer on any gradual slopes. The rocky trail ascended sharply up the side of a huge bank of rock a scree. By the first rest stop, I began peeling off layers to avoid completely overheating. I drank more water than I had consumed in hours of trekking into the base camp. The air was dry and dusty. I could not seem to keep my throat moist.

Shortly after the first rise, we descended slightly down to a narrow stream surrounded by "penitentes," frozen ice formations resembling sails or shark fins created by the winds and snow in the area. Climbing and squeezing through even a few penitentes proved to be a chore, but soon we were back on the dry trail ever ascending higher and higher.

After a few hours, the climb became as mentally demanding as it was physical. Despite the full back packs and the increased steepness of the trail, Eric still planned only one hour stops after the first one. Weary legs were simply not a good excuse to stop. Through sheer perseverance, I was able to keep up with the pace of the leaders, making sure that I got plenty of water on the move.

About one half of the way to Camp One, we were treated to a spectacular view of the bottom of the Polish Glacier. The glacier seemed to hang on the edge of the main peak. The thickness at the edge appeared to be fifty to seventy-five feet thick, but it was hard to judge from a few thousand feet below it. Paul and Tom began talking about their plan to climb the glacier once again. That and Stephane's constant chatter about his favorite rock songs occupied our attention for the next half hour.

As we approached our fifth hour of climbing, a large field of penitentes rose ahead of us, like an impenetrable sea of bumpy sails. Climbers ahead of us almost disappeared once inside them, bobbing up periodically when they stepped up on narrow sections of raised ice.

The last stretch of scree before reaching the ice was particularly steep, so I was very relieved when Eric called for an extended rest and snack break before entering the icy expanse. It was a good thing we rested, because once on the ice, we were faced with constant knee and thigh-high ice shelves, the climbing of which, like deep knee bends, exerts a lot of pressure on the muscles. Soon I was gasping for air. For the first time on the whole trip, I found myself unable to keep up with the leaders, in this case, Eric, Stephane, Al, and Paul. Still, I was able to keep close enough to follow their trail through the maze of ice sails, only occasionally having to look for boot prints to figure out the next step or direction.

Finally, we reached the top of the penitentes and scrambled onto a particularly loose section of scree which required sheer strength of legs and spirit to scale. At the top we reached a level trail over to a rushing brook coming down over the final ledge below Camp One.

Crossing the brook was a balancing act, especially since the rocks were wet and very slippery. I made it without falling, but then faced the steepest climb yet up a very unstable section of rocks and scree to the left of the brook. I scrambled up the embankment only to slide back to square one over and over again until I realized that I could hang onto some boulders to my left as I went up. The only problem was that the boulders were also loose and I did not want to start any cascade of rocks onto climbers below.

Stephane saw me struggling and waited at the top of the ridge until I got very close, giving me much needed encouragement. Finally, I crawled over the top and hit solid ground. The tents of Camp One were just above us. Within minutes we were dropping our heavy packs and Eric was heating up water for hot chocolate. I noticed as soon as we stopped that the temperature at Camp One was at least twenty degrees colder than at base camp. By the time the hot chocolate was ready, I had put on two more layers of clothing. My calves and thighs ached and I was exhausted.

But much of our work was still ahead of us. Tents had to be put up, gear had to be stashed and organized, and we still had to hike back down to base camp before dark.

I remember very little about the trek back down to base camp except that we bypassed the entire field of penitentes on the way down by glissading down a very steep and loose scree slope on the upper side of the brook, digging our heels into the constantly shifting rocks, sinking down to our knees, but descending as if on a magic down escalator. It was tiring, but fun.

I slept especially well that night.

The next day was a well-deserved rest day, starting with a delicious brunch of French toast and fruit. In the morning, I moved gingerly on sore muscles between our tent and the dining tent, but after a longer trip to the water barrel and back, my legs loosened up and felt fine.

The bigger concerns that day were an eye infection which had almost blinded Mitch and Jen's continuing hacking cough which did not seem to be getting any better. As we all looked on, concerned for their welfare, Dr. Jen examined both of them. The cute ER doc put Mitch on some oral antibiotics, coupled with regular rinsing of his eye with purified water. Jen's prescription was merely to rest and drink plenty of fluids.

Brian also looked wiped out from the "carry" up to Camp One. The day before, he had dropped back in the penitentes and had struggled into Camp One almost an hour after the rest of us. He had kept up pretty well on the way back down to base camp, but apparently he had not slept well overnight. Now he was moving very slowly around base camp.

It was not a huge surprise that evening when Eric announced that Brian had decided he had gone as far as he was going. The climb was over for him. Unfortunately, because he had no specific emergency medical condition, Brian would have to ride a mule back to the Vacas Valley trail head. It hurt my butt just to think of that torture.

The highlight of the rest day was an opportunity to talk to my wife for a few seconds on Paul's SAT phone. Kim did not at first realize who was calling, as I had told her that I probably would not have any way of reaching her once on the mountain. She was checking the cybercasts from Alpine Ascents each day, so she knew we had made it to base camp, but that was it. On the phone, I barely had time to let her know our status and tell her I loved her before I lost the connection and the phone went dead. I am sure that must have been comforting for her back in Atlanta!

The next morning we were scheduled to make our move to Camp One with the rest of our gear and food. I was anxious to head up the mountain since, with a rest day after arriving and another rest day after the first "carry" to Camp One, we had now slept four nights in a row at base camp. However, before we could leave for the higher camps where there would be no outhouses, we had to learn proper "wag-bag" techniques. For environmental integrity, each of us would have to collect and bring back off the mountain our own waste. *Wonderful!*

Brent demonstrated. First, a white garbage bag is removed from a green pouch and the green pouch stuffed into a pocket so it won't fly away. Second, the white bag, which has sand and other "chemicals" in the bottom of it, is spread out on the scree and rocks, with at least three, if not four, rocks strategically placed on its perimeter to prevent the wind from blowing it away. Third, using an unsupported squatting technique, the climber dumps into the center of the white bag, that is if he or she has good aim. Otherwise, it is an excremental mess. Once through, the difficult task of wiping with lousy toilet paper in the wind proceeds. Brent suggested several methods for attempting to secure the toilet paper in the bag, but in reality, none of them worked for me. Finally, the perimeter rocks are removed, the white bag is closed with whatever has stayed in it inside it and the bag is "swirled" close, moving all contents into the sand and "chemicals" at the bottom, then re-secured inside the green pouch. Small Handi-wipes are provided in the green pouch, but are easily lost in the whole process.

All I can say is that whoever invented this process is one nasty "sicko."

Even before we could use any "wag-bags," our departure that morning was again delayed by health concerns. Mitch's eye was even worse, noticeably swollen, red, and almost completely closed up. He looked like I did one time when I got a very bad allergic reaction to poison oak and missed a whole week of school with two closed eyes despite several steroid shots. Mitch's fate was no better. After another examination by Dr. Jen, she decided that he needed IV antibiotics on an emergency basis. Ellie, our base camp manager, began the complicated process of arranging for a helicopter to evacuate him. Fortunately, Dr. Jen was able to convince the operators of the urgency of the situation. At least Mitch would not have to ride a mule for thirty miles.

But we were now down to seven climbers, and one of those had a bad cough. Unbeknownst to me at the time, Tom was also developing a bad case of diarrhea, and was not feeling too good either. I continued to happily take my small dose of Cipro prophylactically every morning, to Dr. Jen and Eric's chagrin. There were "two schools of thought" about taking antibiotics as a precaution, and Dr. Jen and my doctor obviously went to different schools. All I know is that I had successfully avoided any bacterial infections or stomach ailments whenever I had taken the Cipro pills. That's all I needed to know, especially after seeing the "wag-bags."

With others getting sick around me, I was determined to stay healthy and diarrhea-free so that I could have the best chance of reaching the summit, which still was at least a week or more away.

The "move" to Camp One seemed easy compared to our "carry" two days earlier. This time, due to acclimatization and a bit cooler day, I moved much easier up the scree slopes. Even the penitentes at the top did not phase me. Our team cut at least an hour off our time, so everyone was in good spirits when we arrived. The only snafu was that a few spots we had designated for our last two tents had been taken by another group of climbers, so Tom, Paul and Stephane had to set up their tents on the other side of a ridge near the ER doctors' camp. This split us up a bit, but we all gathered for dinner and lingered about the camp drinking hot chocolate and coffee until it got too cold to stay outside.

I kept looking up the mountain to try to determine where we would go the next day. Eric pointed in the general direction of a ridge or col about 1500 feet further up. The ridge ran between Aconcagua and Ameghino at about 17, 800 feet, and was rumored to be a quite windy spot. But from Camp One it looked peaceful and dry.

Apparently, the night was not so peaceful in our guide's tent that evening. When we awoke, we couldn't help but notice that Brent was gone. Eric provided only the barest explanation, alluding to "differences of opinion." The bottom line was that Brent had decided to leave the team and Ellie and the "powers that be" at Alpine Ascents would be working on getting us a replacement for our second guide. Meanwhile, we would go ahead with our "carry" to the next camp and hopefully by the time we returned the situation would be resolved.

It took us less than three hours to reach Camp Two, on what Eric referred to as Burrieza Col. The climb was gradual along a curving upwards semi-circle trail up the scree slopes, followed by a few long switchbacks near the top of the ridge. We rested briefly in a windy spot at the top of a pass where the trail split to the left for our "false Polish" route and continued straight ahead to a lower, more circuitous route to the top. From this vantage point, we could see dozens of lower peaks in the Andes range, but the view was obstructed to our left by a large hill of rocky scree. Apparently, the ER doctors would be taking the lower route, so the two teams which had been climbing almost in tandem up to that point would be split up for a few days.

While we rested at the windy pass for the final climb to the Burrieza Col, Eric hiked quickly down the straight path to a cache spot and returned with a plastic bottle of white gas, which he added to his load. I later learned that Alpine Ascents caches all the extra unused fuel from the higher camps there to reduce the burden of lugging fuel up and down all the way from base camp.

The final push to the col was a bit of a strain as we encountered a head wind, but I knew we only had a few hundred vertical feet to go, so I kept up the pace right behind Eric until we were standing next to a series of windbreaks big enough for three tents right in the middle of the ridge.

At Eric's direction, we dumped all of our backpacks into garbage bags and placed them in three piles where tents would eventually be erected. Then we covered the piles with rocks, which were abundant in the area. This would "reserve" the three tent spaces for when we returned with the rest of our gear the next day.

After the caches were established, Eric led us up the slight hill behind the windbreaks. At the crest we were treated to a stunning view of the jagged peaks of the Andes to the north of Aconcagua. There must have been twenty peaks in the 15,000-17,000 range, all snowcapped and glistening in front of us. But where we were was completely free of snow, still a perfectly dry desert of rocks and scree in almost every direction.

We did not stay long. Eric was anxious to get us back to Camp One for additional rest as we had no scheduled rest day before our "move" to Camp Two on the col the next day.

This time, rather than re-trace our steps down to the pass and along the switch backs, Eric led us straight down the mountain in a beeline for Camp One. In moments he was several hundred yards ahead of us, virtually skiing down the scree slopes, with Stephane and Paul close behind. Al, Tom and I tried to keep up, but clearly, none of us had made the Olympic downhill team. We pushed ourselves, moving at a good clip, but took time for a few drink stops. Meanwhile, I could see Eric and our two teammates almost flying down the hill, already almost back at Camp One.

They made the trip in only eighteen minutes according to Stephane. Al made it in twenty minutes and I followed, thighs weary from the descent, in a mere twenty-five minutes.

"That was fun," I exclaimed breathlessly. "Too bad we can't go up that fast."

Our euphoria from the rapid descent did not last long. Within an hour after we arrived, a front of dark clouds started moving in and the wind picked up. We hustled to get dinner concluded, as the temperature was also dropping rapidly. This time we did not linger over any hot drinks.

"Let's hope it blows over by the morning," Eric said after the pots were cleaned up. "Hopefully, we will be up at Camp Two tomorrow night."

That evening, in our tent, Al and I tried to figure out exactly what had happened between Eric and Brent that led to Brent leaving the mountain. Stephane had managed to find out that the dispute was over Eric overruling Brent on a couple of minor decisions in front of the group.

"You're kidding me," I said. "Eric is the lead guide. What he says goes."

"Well, something tells me there might be something more to it," Al replied, "but it's over and there's nothing we can do about it."

"Yeah, but I wondered what really happened."

My wondering did not last long. The storm hit us with a vengeance. First, the winds started flapping the tent sides uncontrollably, making constant whap-whap sounds which made sleeping almost impossible. Then the thunder and lightning rolled in, crashing and striking all around us.

I lay there on my back listening to the racket, hoping that our tent lines were securely fastened.

"Now we know why Eric spent so much time teaching us the proper tent line techniques," I said.

All night long the winds kept pounding the tent and the thunder kept rolling, though it sounded like it was moving up the mountain. At some point, probably from the monotony of the flapping of the tent sides, I fell asleep, only to wake up at 2:00 A.M. to the sound of snow or sleet particles hitting the top of the tent. I had to pee, so I slipped on my boots and slid outside. There was already 2-3 inches of snow on the ground and it was still coming down. Even in the dark, the whole mountainside was now shining white up to the col.

Okay, now we are going to have some real alpine climbing!

We did no climbing the next day. The snow kept coming. Near whiteout conditions prevented any activity besides sleeping, eating and playing cards inside the tents. We were socked in until the snow let up. No one was going anywhere.

Except Eric, our guide. Sometime that day and definitely that evening, he and Dr. Jen became an item. All I know is that Stephane, who had moved into the tent with Eric to help with the cooking after Brent departed, made the mistake of excusing himself to give Eric and Dr. Jen some privacy. Stephane later told me he nearly froze himself to death waiting outside the tent before he finally interrupted the rendezvous.

Rather obvious hugs and embraces between the two the following morning before the ER doctor's group headed up the mountain the following morning confirmed Stephane's story. Alas, because the doctors' group was going a separate route once beyond the Col, the fledgling couple would be apart until about thirty vertical feet below the summit four days later.

With the snowstorm over for the time being, we packed up, loaded up, and headed up the mountain to Camp Two, this time for a "move." The storm had dropped about eighteen inches of snow. Drifts had been formed several feet deep, but the actual trail was very exposed to the wind and was almost clear in spots. Nevertheless, we were now hiking with crampons attached to our double plastics. We would do so for the rest of the climb to the summit.

Once again, the climb was considerably easier than the first "carry" to Camp Two. Two more days of acclimatization almost assured that. Once again, the entire way up, Stephane carried the conversation, describing in extreme detail all of his favorite recipes for various gourmet meals. Back at base camp, he had volunteered to cook the pasta dish for dinner and had spiced the taste up with some grated orange rinds which turned a bland meal into a zesty one. Such a simple addition to the meal, but one I would never have imagined. Instantly, he gained the credibility of a mountainside sous chef and was called on again and again to help with meals while the rest of us took turns washing dishes and cleaning up.

So for hours at a time, we were treated with Stephane's descriptions of mixing various herbs, spices, and sauce ingredients for the magical flavor he liked to create. Salads, entrees, appetizers, desserts, he had a million of 'em, and if we hadn't run out of trail, we probably would have heard every one.

As for me, I was dying for Double Whopper with cheese, with lots of ketchup, lettuce and tomato and some salty french fries, with no fancy herbs or sauces!

At the top of the ridge, still below the Burrieza Col where the trail split, the snow and winds started again in earnest. The temperature dropped like a rock. I tightened the hood of my Gore-Tex shell jacket and buried my chin inside the front flap, but snow was still finding its way onto my face and down my neck. Unfortunately, I had not anticipated the need for a neck fleece or balaclava yet. I did, however, manage to find a pair of Gore-Tex lined gloves to keep my hands dry and warm.

The last thirty minutes up to the col were miserable. My legs were still relatively strong, but the wind kept blowing me back or off course and into deeper snow, making my progress much slower. With visibility decreasing and no second guide pulling up the rear, Eric modified his pace to make sure the team stayed together. Still, the few times I looked back, I could not see all the way back to the last climber in the group.

We finally made it to our caches in the windbreaks of Camp Two. The rocky piles were completely covered in snow. On the other side of the windbreak, two tents of some Australian climbers had already been set up and were flapping in the wind. At least we would have the prime spots on the down wind side of the rock walls. As if that would do any good at all.

Setting up tents in the wind and snow after clearing the rocks and items cached beneath them was a tiring, breath-depleting and chilling experience. However, under Eric's watchful eyes, we made sure to securely fasten all the tent lines carefully with the heaviest rocks we could find in the windswept portion of the col. By the time we managed to set up three tents, we were completely exhausted.

This time, with only three tents, Al was moved over to Mike and Jen's tent and I smushed in with Paul and Tom. Stephane and Eric, along with most of the food and cooking gear, occupied the third tent.

At this point, no water sources were available, so Eric and Paul gathered snow from drifts beyond the tents for melting in the large stew pot. It was a time-consuming chore, but we had made it to the camp just after two o'clock in the afternoon, so we had all afternoon and evening to do nothing but melt snow and drink hot chocolate.

It was too cold and windy, and, at times, too snowy to stay outside the tents for much longer than as necessary to pee. I made the mistake of trying to go number two onto a wag bag in the snow drifts to the side of the tents, simultaneously freezing my butt off and losing countless sheets of toilet paper in the wind. But I had to go.

I wondered whether it would be even worse higher up on the mountain.

That night was the worst yet. Sixty to eighty mile an hour winds pummeled the tents and the thunder and lightning was back, this time frighteningly close. Plus, we were now trying to sleep three to a tent, meaning that we were practically on top of each other.

Tom and I wondered if the tent was going to blow away several times. The flapping of the fly above the main tent body was violent and relentless. Somehow, Paul had managed to go to sleep amid the racket, but I basically stared at the ceiling most of the night. At one break in the storm, I managed to go outside to pee and was treated to a partially clear sky with incredible stars peeking out from behind the clouds. However, within minutes after I returned to the tent, the storm started up again.

Sometime after three o'clock A.M. I finally fell asleep out of sheer exhaustion, only to wake up at five o'clock to the distinct smell of urine. Pee bottles inside the tent are even nastier than the "wag-bags." And both Tom and Paul were using them. At dawn, I took another Cipro pill.

Everyone seemed pretty wasted the next morning, even after breakfast and hot chocolate/coffee served by Eric in our tents. The winds, lightning and thunder had kept most of us awake. We were ready to get off this col. I will never know why that exposed spot was chosen for a camp in the first place.

The great thing about that morning was that we were joined by our replacement assistant guide, Sherpa Lakpa. We had met Lakpa down at Pampa de Lenas on our first night out from the trail head when he came down from base camp with the two climbers from the prior expedition. But now Lakpa had been assigned to help us reach the summit. It was a nice trade-up. Instead of Brent, who had never himself been above 14,500 feet before, we got Lakpa, who had merely climbed to the top of Everest nine times and who clearly was the best climber on the entire mountain. He was a helluva nice guy, modest, unassuming and incredibly diligent. It was an honor for us to climb with him.

Eric and Lakpa huddled for about five minutes after breakfast, plotting and planning our next steps. The wind had substantially subsided by about 9:00 A.M., so they decided we would push up to Camp Three and not take a rest day at the col. The bigger decision was whether we would make a "carry" to Camp Three and return for another night on the col, or try to "move" to Camp Three and leave the col behind.

One of the benefits of having an incredible climber like Lakpa on the team was that it provided flexibility for decisions like this. The hybrid solution made sense to everyone. This day we would "move" almost everything up to Camp Three. Lakpa and any others who felt strong would come back to Camp Two to bring up the rest of the gear we couldn't carry on the move the next day. Those who were tired would have a complete rest day at Camp Three and would not have to return to the col and re-climb the traverse to Camp Three. I certainly hoped that I was one of the ones who would get the rest day.

I can only describe the move to Camp Three as a slow and steady trudge. We were carrying heavy packs in order to move as much as possible and make it easier for the guys making the trip back down the next day. The ascent was not particularly steep, but it was relentlessly uphill in fresh snow conditions, meaning that our boots were sinking into and below the surface, making progress much harder. I had settled into the fourth or fifth position in the line and tried always to step in the footprints made by Eric and/or Lakpa as they broke the trail above me. However, being heavier, I found myself post-holing fairly frequently. Needless to say it was tough going.

But I, and the rest of the team endured. Now that we were approaching the high camps and were only a few days away from a summit try, our focus intensified. We had a job to do and there was nothing to stop us except our own foibles. Frankly, I do not remember much about the climb to Camp Three except following the footprints ahead of me and trying to keep hydrated with water. Once or twice we took a good break and I vaguely remember the peaks of the Andes to the north shining in the morning sun when it managed to peak out of the clouds. The scenery was absolutely stunning, as evident from photos taken by Paul and Al which I saw later. However, I was too tired to really notice and take it all in that day.

It did not seem very steep and the climb was not that long, but at more than 18,000 feet, any vertical climbing is taxing, especially in soft snow conditions.

Approximately four hours after leaving the col, we worked our way around a rocky outcropping and staggered into Camp Three, situated on a wide ledge looking back over at Ameghino. We were now at 19,200 feet and almost directly at the level of Ameghino's summit. Even more spectacular was the Polish Glacier, slanted straight up from Camp Three almost to the summit. For the first five minutes after we arrived, we stood staring at the glacier and imagining ourselves scaling it to the top.

There were dozens of tents set up all across the ledge and up the slope towards the glacier. Each tent was surrounded by six foot high windbreaks. I immediately wondered if it would be even more windy here than it had been at the col the night before. I certainly hoped not.

After setting up tents and getting a late lunch, we worked to replenish our water supply. The problem here was that everything was frozen solid. Camp Three had three ponds scattered around the ledge, but each was covered with a foot of ice. The one immediately behind our three tents, however, had a soft spot in the middle, where climbers had dug through the ice with their ice axes to create something akin to an ice fishing hole. Paul and Tom took turns hacking away at the spot until, voila, water appeared. Then we took turns filling all our water bottles and containers. The ice hole would have to be reopened each morning.

I did not have a temperature gauge with me on the trip, so I never knew how cold it was at any of the camps. All I know is that once we reached Camp Three we had substantial sub-freezing temperatures at all times. At night it was best to be inside the tent in a minus 20 degree down sleeping bag with four layers, including a down parka, to stay warm. Even though I kept my water bottles inside the tent and wrapped them in extra socks and clothing, they still iced up by morning. I would have to sleep with the water bottles in my down sleeping bag the rest of the way.

The next morning, Lakpa, Paul, and Al were selected to go back down to Camp Two to bring up the rest of the gear. Our third guide, Dave, whose responsibilities included the high camps, was climbing up from base camp and would meet them at the col and help carry the gear back up to Camp Three. I was quite relieved to be omitted from the retrieval team, as was Tom, who at this point was really beginning to suffer from stomach and diarrhea problems. He had already decided that he would not try the Polish Glacier as initially planned. He told me that at this point he would be more than satisfied to make it to the summit whatever easiest way he could. I fully agreed with that approach.

Fortunately, the rest day at Camp Three turned out to be a beautiful sunny day, with only moderate winds. It was still too bone-chillingly cold to stay outside for more than fifteen to twenty minutes at a time, but at least we were not completely hunkered down in our tents. Remarkably, by midday, I felt great. I had no soreness from the trudging climb up from the col. I had gotten a good night sleep despite still being crammed in three to a tent and continued seventy to eighty mile per hour winds through the night. My spirits were completely rejuvenated.

Later that afternoon, after the small group returned from Camp Two, I was able to make my second call to my wife on Paul's SAT phone. Once again, I lost the signal after about thirty seconds, but later my wife said I really sounded excited and ready to go for the summit. It is amazing how much a good night's sleep and a rest day can change the outlook at over 19,000 feet. The next day we would be at 20,600, the "high" Camp Four, an altitude above that of the summit of Mt. McKinley.

From Camp Three, the trail moves straight up through scattered rocks towards the Polish Glacier for about a quarter mile, then veers to the right diagonally up a fairly steep traverse. We had heavy packs so as to avoid having to send anyone back for more gear from Camp Four. The plan was to take what we needed for three days in case we could not summit the next day. In my pack was an extra day's food bag to feed the entire group, if we got socked in at the high camp. So there would be no "carry" to Camp Four, just a "move."

It was a truly beautiful day. The snow on the traverse had frozen, melted and re-frozen again several times, so it was much firmer under our feet. Postholing was at a minimum. The sky was clear, and though the temperature remained frigid, the winds were comparatively mild. While I had struggled to keep going two days earlier on the climb to Camp Three, I felt great on this climb, even at the higher altitude.

When the team took an extended break two hours into the climb, Lakpa and David moved ahead with all three tent bodies and flies. They moved swiftly up the snowy traverse which was getting steeper by the minute, leaving a nice trail of footprints for us to follow. They would get the tents set up and have a pot of hot water boiling for us for when we arrived. *Nice.*

Nice also described the view from our rest stop on a windswept bit of scree between the sections of snowy traverse. We were now well above any peaks around us and it was at least 10,000 feet down to the valley floors between the peaks to our north and east. From our vantage point we could see the tops of at least fifty snow-capped peaks. If the scree slope on which we were sitting was not at about forty degrees, I would have taken a bunch of pictures, but it was difficult enough just to sit and avoid sliding down.

Once we resumed climbing, the sun seemed to be right in our eyes. For the first time in days, I felt almost too warm. I unzipped my down parka part way and opened up my Gore-Tex shell for a little ventilation. We were working hard as a team as the slope steepened. Eric kept up a reasonable pace and this time the team stayed entirely together. It seemed like all of us were feeling better after a good night's sleep.

As we approached what looked like the ridge below Camp Four, Lakpa appeared from above to let us know we were getting close. We worked our way up towards him and then followed him up the steepest section yet on the entire climb.

"Careful up here. It's a bit icy," Eric warned as he negotiated his way up and across a narrow ledge next to a rock outcropping above us.

I watched as Stephane and Al successfully went up the ledge. As I took my turn, I looked to my right. For the first time on the whole trip, we were on a clearly exposed ledge. I quickly re-focused my attention to the path of ice in front of me. Following precisely in the crampon marks made by my partners ahead of me, I stepped surely up and across the slick ledge and to the safety of the hard-packed snow beyond and above it.

No problema!

I kept moving to clear the way for the rest of the team, all of whom maneuvered their way up and over the ice. Soon we were within sight distance of the yellow North Face tents, smartly set up and flapping in the wind of Camp Four.

The hot chocolate tasted very good once we got settled in. Though the sun was still beating down on us after we stopped hiking, the heat from our bodies escaped and the cold air at 20,600 feet started to seep in. I had only a few minutes to look around before having to retreat to the tent and the warm sleeping bag.

This camp was very small, situated on a ledge perhaps thirty feet wide. The windbreaks were closely bunched and huddled together. This worked to our advantage later as we passed food between the tents without going outside. I wondered how Lakpa and David had managed to get the tents so well anchored, but was glad that we had not had to set them up at this altitude.

Behind the tents, a steep snowfield with some scattered scree and rocks rose up to some craggy ridges. Rock towers lined the snowfield to the left and right. Beyond the tents on the opposite side of where we had arrived, the landscape sloped down to another passage, one that would be used by Dr. Jen's team, who presumably by then had circled around from the east.

The tent for Tom, Paul and me was the closest to the edge of the ledge, with about ten to twelve feet of rocks before a long drop off. I would have to remember that when I got up at night to pee! Just to be on the safe side, I decided not to take my contact lenses out that night. It would be a big mistake to walk around blind with such little room for error.

Cooking anything decent was out of the question that night, as by 4:00 P.M. the winds had come back in with a vengeance. Snow was whipping across the ledge, causing spindrift to filter in on top of us inside the tent. Eric managed to get us some hot water to fill our bottles and soup bowls before retreating to his tent, then packages of ramen noodle soup and oatmeal were thrown across the gaps between the tents for distribution among the occupants.

Stephane successfully connected on two of three packages of the ramen, but the third got caught in a particular wicked gust of wind and took a right turn off the mountain a few inches before it could reach my outstretched hands.

An offering of noodles to the Gods.

Tom and I shared a noodle soup package, then tried to stomach the pasty oatmeal. I hate oatmeal. I considered bypassing it in favor of some Snickers bars and the rest of my private bag of almonds. However, I needed to save them for summit day sustenance. So I concentrated on the grey mash in my bowl.

Either we had too much oatmeal or too little water, I don't know. But it was almost impossible to get down. I finally resorted to dumping some M&M's into it to give it some taste. The candy melted in it and gave it a little chocolate moisture as well, but even then I thought I was going to throw up as I tried to force a few more spoonfuls into my system. The blue M&M's bled into the goo and created a ghoulish mess. God it was awful. But it was the only warm meal we would have before going for the summit, so I suppressed my urge to vomit and ate three quarters of the bowl before finally surrendering the residue to the elements.

That night seemed to last forever. The wind blew so hard I could not tell whether it was snowing or if all the snow hitting our tent was just being blown in by the wind. I was thankful that Lakpa and David had buried the tent lines under such large rocks, because several times it felt like we were about to be picked up and thrown off the mountain. Snow filtered down on our heads, the tent flies flapped like jack-hammers on a driveway, and my stomach periodically heaved causing me to burp disgusting oatmeal tastes through the night.

At six o'clock in the morning, I felt the wind subside for a few minutes and slipped out to pee. Being careful not to move too far from the tent opening, I relieved myself beyond a rock. Then I looked up to see the dawn on the horizon. The sun was not yet visible, but an orange/yellow wedge of bright light crossed from a point on the left to the wider part of the wedge on the right where it collided with one of the rock towers just beyond the tents. Above the wedge of light the darkness was interrupted only by stars in the clear sky and by particles of snow spinning across my vision in the wind.

I remembered that I had put the last of my three digital disposable cameras in my down parka to keep it from freezing as I tried to sleep. Now I'm glad I thought about having it, as the photo I took of the summit day dawn turned out to be a piece of art. The twinkle of stars and sparkling snowdrift superimposed on the contrasting colors of the dawn and darkness of the night sky made for a stunning photograph, even with a crappy throwaway camera.

Summit day always brings a huge burst of excitement, coupled with a healthy dose of anxiety.

Will my legs hold up on the final ascent? How thin will the air get? Will I be able to breathe and keep going? Can I keep up with the others and not be a drag on the whole group? Will the weather hold up, and if not, will we push on or turn back?

On Aconcagua, summit day did not start quite as soon as we expected. The original plan was to wake up at 6:30 A.M. and be hiking by 7:00. However, when we woke up, the winds were particularly vicious, blasting us at about eighty to ninety miles an hour. With no word from Eric, we stayed warmly snuggled in our sleeping bags, patiently waiting for directions.

At about eight o'clock, Eric shouted out across the wind that it did not look good for a summit attempt that day, but he would re-evaluate periodically. About a half hour later, Eric fought the winds and brought us hot water for coffee and hot chocolate and a few breakfast bars.

"Go ahead and eat in case the winds let up," he yelled. To me, he did not look optimistic.

The granola bars went down with hot chocolate a lot better than the disgusting oatmeal from the night before. I tried to munch into a Snickers bar as well, but it was frozen solid. I moved my zip-lock of goodies into my sleeping bag, hoping the bars would soften. I did not want to break my teeth on the way to the summit. That is, if we were ever going to leave for the summit. The winds were still fierce at 8:45 and 9:00 A.M.

Nevertheless, I went ahead and dug out my double plastics, gaiters and crampons from the drift of snow that had covered them in the vestibule of the tent. I had wisely covered the top of the boots with the gaiters so the insides of the boots were still dry. My inner insulation booties for the double plastics always remained dry and warm in the tent, ready to slip on at a moment's notice. If the winds broke, I would be that much closer to being prepared to go.

Just as we resigned ourselves to be hunkered down for the rest of the day, the winds subsided to a mere fifty to sixty miles an hour. Eric shouted to get dressed.

"We're leaving for the summit in fifteen minutes."

The scurrying which occurred in our tent over the next fifteen minutes is hard to describe. Usually, with three in the tent, we took turns getting dressed to avoid getting in each other's way. But with only fifteen minutes to add layers, adjust our clothing, load our packs, and get our double plastics, crampons and gaiters on, there was no time to wait. Gloves and goggles had to be found under sleeping bags and gear. Water bottles had to be packed for access. Cameras had to be readied. Food for the climb had to be organized and packed so as to be accessible and warm enough not to freeze. In short, chaos ensued following Eric's go ahead.

However, at 9:30 A.M., we all shouldered our packs, adjusted our ski poles and ice axes, took a sip of water, and began the ascent.

Ahead of us, just barely visible in the windy, snowy conditions were two other climbing groups. One was the ER doctors' team, which had already worked its way up from a lower camp just below and beyond our Camp Four. I did not recognize the other team, but really didn't care, as I was already huffing and puffing, trying to get my breathing pattern down on the first steps of the climb.

From the tents, we worked our way diagonally to our right for about four hundred yards. The trail was mostly hard snow with gaps of scree where the wind had swept it clean. I was "sucking wind" by the time we reached the end of the switchback and started back to our left. I took a few deep breaths and blew out through pursed lips to expel the carbon dioxide and maximize the flow of oxygen to my system. I would have liked to rest and catch my breath, but Eric was already into the program to which we had become accustomed. We would rest only after an hour of climbing. Because of the late start, we could not afford any more frequent breaks. Jen, Mike and Tom appeared to be having difficulty as well, as they fell back a bit on the very first slope. I stayed with the lead group of Eric, Al, Stephane and Paul.

Finally, about one half way up the steep snow slope above Camp Four, my breathing calmed and I caught my stride. It seemed like only minutes later that we reached the top of the slope and sat down next to the Refugio Indepencia, a dilapidated hut the size of a large tent with a collapsed roof. Not exactly a useful shelter, but apparently a regular stop on the summit climb. There we took our first rest. Eric reminded us to drink plenty of water and get something to eat as it would be a long day and we had to keep up our energy. I managed to find a Snickers bar soft enough to eat, took a few bites, and washed them down with a few healthy swigs from my first of four water bottles. The others arrived at the Refugio just as we were leaving.

The next section of the climb was another even steeper field of snow, this time with five and six foot drifts—a quite spectacular climb in a "winter wonderland" way. The temperature felt like it was warming and the winds appeared to be subsiding. My only discomfort was when we worked our way through some deep drifts. The wind blew snow across at eye level, instantly filling my face with fresh snow and ice particles. I shook most of it out, then pulled the cord to my Gore-Tex hood a bit tighter while still leaving enough room for ventilation.

Just when I thought this climb might not be too bad, we reached the top of the deep snow slope and stepped onto an exposed ridge overlooking a long steady drop off to our right. Straight ahead and another thousand feet up we could see the bottom of the Caneleta, the almost vertical gorge to the summit. It did not look that far away.

Looks can be deceiving.

One glance at the Caneleta was all I could make before having to turn my back as a blast of wind hit us. Eric estimated the gust to be eighty miles per hour. The wind was accelerating all the way up the slope below, whipping across the top of the crescent shaped ridge. For the next forty-five minutes, we shuffled sideways with our backs to the wind, just trying to stay on our feet. Only by carefully balancing with a ski pole and an ice axe and plodding steadily sideways with firm crampon assisted steps were we able to stay erect on the narrow trail.

There was no way to rest or get any water on this section. The gusts were simply too stiff and the wind chill too severe to stop or worry about access to any bottles. We crouched further down and tried to minimize the surface for the wind to hit and just kept going, one side step next to the other.

At the end of the crescent shaped ridge, a sharp rock tower, yellowish in color, provided a windbreak. One climber from the unidentified group ahead of us was resting there, blocking the way. The guy looked out of it. Eric spoke to him in very sharp tones, trying to determine his alertness, then helped him access his water supply. We huddled behind the rock while getting some water of our own.

Once Eric determined the other climber was okay to continue the climb, he turned his attention to each of us. He noticed that Al's nose was exposed and was beginning to get some frost nip.

"Where's your balaclava?" he asked sharply.

Al sort of shrugged and then pulled his bandanna over his nose to try to warm it. I realized that I did not have a balaclava on either, but luckily, my goggles covered ninety percent of my nose. Only my nostrils and underside of the nose were exposed.

Beyond the sharp rock tower was a long traverse up a wide expanse of snow and rocks up to the base of the Caneleta. At times the trail was moderate in steepness. At other times it was steep enough that we had to implant our ice axes in the snow banks to secure our progress. At all times the deep snow and increasingly thin air was slowly taxing my strength. I could feel my legs and my whole system slowing down with almost each step forward. We were rapidly approaching 22,000 feet in elevation, almost three thousand feet higher than the top of Kilimanjaro.

Sometime shortly before we reached the bottom of the Caneleta, I started falling behind the others. We had passed the second group ahead of us and dropped off the laggard who had followed us from the sharp rock tower. Now I was the laggard for our lead group, barely staggering into a sheltered spot beneath a large overhanging section of rock at the base of the Caneleta. I was only about forty feet behind the other guys but it seemed like a mile. They reached the rest stop a good five minutes before me, leaving me with much less time to rest and recuperate for the toughest and final section of the climb. I found half a meat stick and downed another Snickers bar in an attempt to re-boost my energy.

The Caneleta rises only eight hundred vertical feet to the summit, but Eric warned us that it would probably take three hours. We had covered the two steep snowfields, the windy ridge, and the wide expansive traverse up to the Caneleta in only four hours, so I struggled to understand how it would take three more hours to reach the summit. Usually in even tough conditions, I could make five hundred to seven hundred fifty vertical feet an hour. But about ten steps into the Caneleta, I realized that it would take everything I had to make it to the top.

The difficulty was the steepness, the loose footing, and the increasingly thin air. Because the Caneleta was exposed to the sun and sheltered from the wind, the snow was soft and loose, on top of even softer and looser scree and rocks. As a result, every step was a step forward and a half step back. Some steps just sunk in and slipped back to the prior step. My ski pole and ice axe were only slightly helpful in maintaining balance, and almost useless as supports for upward climbing.

At times I felt like I was crawling up sections of rocks on all fours, just to keep my momentum going up.

One of the dangers of the Caneleta is the risk of rock slides or boulders tumbling down from above. As a result, Eric led us up the very right side of the Caneleta, close to the cliffs of rock separating us from the South Face of the mountain. Though the safest route, it was also the steepest. Here we did not have the luxury of moderated switchbacks. Rather we were climbing straight up, clawing and scrambling as we went, trying to avoid sliding back down with each step. In the grueling effort, I completely lost track of time or progress. I just focused straight ahead, trying to stay in contact with the others.

Despite my best efforts, I fell fifty vertical feet or so behind by the next rest stop. I arrived breathlessly and exhausted only moments before Eric stood and said we had to keep moving.

Shit! I just got here! Gimme a break!

This time I had to rest, get a snack and some water or I knew I would never make it. I begged for three minutes and Eric reluctantly gave me two. Then they were off again, working their way into a few diagonal switchbacks which looked a bit easier than the trail behind. I managed to down some almonds, drained my third water bottle, and followed about fifty feet behind them.

Soon they turned back to their right on the next switchback as I continued across to my left. As I turned back to the right, they reached the next switchback and started out to the left again, directly above me by some forty vertical feet. I put my head down and vowed to pick up the pace to close the gap.

"ROCK!!!!" I heard Eric yell above me. "WATCH OUT BELOW!!!!"

I instantly turned and looked upwards. A boulder several times larger than a bowling ball was hurtling down the mountain above me. Either Stephane or Al had slid and loosened the rock. Now it was heading in my general direction, but it looked like it would go about ten feet behind me on its current course. I planted my ski pole and ice axe and waited for the rock to pass. But about twenty feet above me it collided with another rock and veered right towards me like a heat seeking missile. I quickly jumped three steps forward as the rock careened past me, missing me by three or four feet. I watched it roll down below finally slowing to a stop maybe two hundred feet below.

My exact words at that moment violate the second of the ten commandments, so I won't repeat them here. Suffice it to say that I thanked God vociferously after repeatedly taking his name in vain.

Somehow the close call with the runaway boulder energized me again. For the next thirty minutes, I steadily closed the gap on the others. Though I never caught up with them completely, I was close enough that I was only five minutes from the top when I saw Paul standing up on the edge of the summit outcropping loudly announcing his summit success. At the same time, climbers were descending from the summit and passing me on their way down as I stood there gasping for breath. I didn't realize it was the doctors' group until I recognized the smiles of Dr. Jen and the girl from Montreal as they passed. They gave me encouragement and announced, "You're almost there. Just keep going."

Up ahead I saw that Eric was waiting for me just below the summit. He had apparently stopped there to talk to Dr. Jen as she descended from the top. Since I was just a few yards down the trail, Eric decided to escort me up the last few rocks.

With the others already at the top, I wanted to make a final burst up the rocks to the summit, but the best I could do was a slow plod, one step at a time, stopping for air every five or six steps. I was wasted.

But my focus remained on one thing. Making it to the top of South America.

Al, Stephane and Paul gave me a whoop as I took the last step up onto the summit, atop a pile of rocks about the size of a large swimming pool, with a stake holding a row of colored flags in the middle. Looking to my right, I saw the awesome sight of the South Face of Aconcagua, a steep, snow-covered cliff descending 9000 feet to the valleys below.

This time I cried with tears of joy and relief to be there, at the top of the western and southern hemispheres. It was 4:30 P.M. It had been a seven hour climb, not long by high altitude summit standards, but a tough one under very difficult conditions. Eric later said that it was the hardest summit of Aconcagua that he had experienced in twelve expeditions he had led.

After bear hugs and high fives all around, I suddenly realized that I had reached the apex of my mountaineering career. This was as high as I planned to go. Denali was almost 3000 feet lower, my wife had vetoed Everest, and most of the other higher mountains, all in the Himalayas, were way more technical than I wanted to tackle.

All of the major climbs I had made up to that point spun through my mind, culminating in the top of the very mountain on which I was standing. What a feeling!

So I raised my ice axe and spun 360 degrees with my arms out, taking in the views in all directions and enjoying every aspect of the moment. Then I collapsed on a flat rock beside Al. I needed water and another Snickers bar to fully celebrate the feat.

After about ten minutes of picture taking, Eric announced the two minute warning to start the descent.

Damn, I just got here. Fourteen days of climbing and only fifteen minutes at the top! What's the deal?

The deal, of course, is getting back down safely. At that moment, I wondered where Tom, Jen and Mike were. I didn't think they had turned back, but the last place we had seen them was back on the long snowy traverse when we started up the Caneleta.

Shortly after stepping off the summit, my question was answered. Tom and Dave, the third guide, were about fifteen minutes below the summit. About a hundred vertical feet further down we could make out Jen's light blue parka, along with Lakpa's red jacket. Mike was with them.

The whole team of seven would successfully summit that day.

It took only a few minutes for us to scramble down to Tom. He was exhausted and looking pretty pale, but he was still moving steadily upwards. Our encouragement helped him along. About ten minutes later we passed Jen and Mike on their way up. They didn't say much, still focusing on what lay ahead. In marathoner terms, they had hit the wall, but they were fighting their way through to the finish line. I was especially proud of Jen, who had been fighting her cough for the whole trip and had just kept going. Mike steadily toughed it out the whole way glued to Jen's side, providing constant support for her climb.

I was a little disappointed that the entire team had not been able to be at the summit together. However, it was getting late in the day, and, understandably, Eric wanted to get back to the camp as quickly as possible. Tom, Jen and Mike would be in good hands with Lakpa and Dave, and we would have hot water and food ready for them when they got back to Camp Four.

Frankly, I remember very little about the descent other than it was a LOT easier. We had unbelievably incredible views of the South Face just after we left the summit. I realize that "unbelievably incredible" is a bit redundant, but "doubly spectacular" doesn't sound as good.

I remember resting once more at the sheltered spot at the bottom of the Caneleta because there Stephane vomited briefly, demonstrating that even the well-acclimatized, strongest climbers can be affected by the altitude. I remember waltzing across the crescent shaped ridge in the warm afternoon sun with almost no wind this time. And I remember resting once more at the ramshackled Refugio, finishing off my last drop of water from my fourth bottle before descending the last snow slope straight down, eshewing the switchbacks.

It was 7:30 P.M. when we arrived back at the tents. Five minutes later, I was fast asleep inside my sleeping bag. I awoke an hour later to the sounds of the remainder of our climbing team arriving safely back at camp. Little did I know then that the summit day was an uneventful breeze compared to what we would encounter the next day in the "viento blanco."

By five o'clock in the afternoon the next day, after eight hours battling sixty to a hundred mile an hour winds coming down from Camp Four and only an hour or two after I had been launched into the air twice, Al and I sat on our packs trying to muster the strength to descend the final 2500 feet down from Camp One to base camp. The winds at Camp One were still strong enough to knock us over, but we were at least in a partially sheltered spot between two ridges.

Eric gave us a long break there while he went to check in with the Willie Prittie, the renowned, long-bearded guide for the next Alpine Ascents team. They had reached Camp One, but were hunkered down in tents, waiting for the winds to subside. I found a meat stick in the bottom of my food stash—my last one. Boy did it taste good after the tasteless fare we had suffered through for the last three or four days. A few almonds, a section of a dark chocolate Toblerone from Eric, and a lot of water helped revive my energy and spirits. After the constant blasting and two involuntary flights and crash landings I had experienced during the last eight hours, I needed all the help I could get to keep going.

Once we crossed over the ridge, slid down next to the brook, and took the plunging "escalator" walk down the loose scree just below Camp One, the winds finally weakened to a manageable roar. Now Eric, Stephane, Al, Tom and I kept together, a seriously fatigued but happy bunch of mountain warriors nearing the end of the road.

But before we could reach base camp, Al's heavily loaded back pack took its toll. Al had climbed relentlessly throughout the trip and had never faltered even a bit up to that point. We were all amazed by his strength and endurance. He was a "horse," according to Eric.

He also had made the mistake of carrying more than his fair share of the load down from Camp Four. Somewhere in the constant battering and falling to the ground in the winds, his pack had gotten out of balance, causing undue stress on his back and legs. At the same time, Al had run out of water and didn't tell anyone. So he was becoming dehydrated and his leg strength was evaporating before my eyes.

"Are you okay?" I asked him after he seemed to teeter sideways a few times, almost falling.

"Just need to get to base camp," he answered evasively.

I moved directly behind him and continued to observe him closely for the next five minutes.

About a quarter of a mile later, Al's left leg gave out and he went down on a knee.

"Stop!" I yelled at Eric, who was about ten yards ahead. "Al's down."

Al struggled to get back up. I asked if I could get him some water.

"All out," he replied sheepishly.

I gave him a half full bottle. That left me with only a third of a bottle for myself.

The water seemed to revive Al, at least for awhile, but soon he started teetering again on a particularly steep scree section where a fall could result in a bad avalanche and possible injury.

"Wait up Eric," I shouted, "Al's about to go down again."

"We've got to keep going guys," Eric responded. "Al, you okay?"

"Yeah," Al lied.

We pressed on. Less than two minutes later, at the bottom of a scree slope just above a set of penitentes, Al tumbled forward, landing on both knees, then fell forward all the way to the ground.

"Alright, guys, we have to stop and let him rest," I said, this time not as a request.

We helped Al up, and for the first time he mentioned that his pack was off kilter. He was already out of water again. He had finished off the partially full bottle I gave him in only a few minutes. This time Eric pulled out a spare bottle, refilled Al's supply, and worked to adjust Al's pack. After about a five minute unscheduled break, Eric gave the two minute warning and off we went down the trail.

Soon we could see base camp below us and we knew we were getting close. But the last series of switchbacks seemed to last forever. Al managed to keep on his feet, but still teetered right and left as he went. I thought he was going down again at any moment. But he endured.

It was close to 7:30 P.M. by the time we reached our tents at base camp and collapsed, our legs simply giving out.

It would be another hour before Jen, Mike, Lakpa, Paul and David arrived. Paul and David had stayed up at Camp Three that morning with the intent still of trying to climb the Polish Glacier the next day. But when the winds did not break by midday, they had packed up and hurried down through the winds as well, catching up with Mike and Jen just before arriving at base camp. On arrival, Jen went directly to her tent and did not come out.

Remarkably, as wiped out as I had been all day long until Camp One, I felt good back at base camp after a short rest. I walked down to the mess tent, enjoyed some juice and snacks and wondered when the party was going to start.

Later that evening we all gathered for some dinner. Eric broke out a few beers that had come in with the mules two weeks earlier. In truth, we were all too tired to celebrate.

However, some other climbers who had made the summit a day before us and had enjoyed a day's rest while we were coming down through the wind, partied all night in some nearby tents. Music was blaring from their direction. Obnoxious laughing and singing could be heard into the wee hours of the morning. I just wanted to sleep. And sleep I did, until about noon the next day.

After a day's rest, we loaded the mules and headed out. This time we virtually sprinted down the mountain, bypassing the camp by the river and making it all the way to Pampa de Lenas, the first camp on the way up, in one day. We expected another feast of caballeros-grilled carne, but mysteriously, the meat could not be found. Instead, Eric arranged for us to have a pasta meal served by a local mule company group, complete with boxed wine.

Not the same.

We all decided to forego the tents that night. As darkness approached, a rosy, yellow twilight fell over the entire camp, making the mood surreal. Then as the sunset disappeared into pitch black darkness, we were treated to the most amazing star show I had ever seen since early on my summit day on Orizaba years before. This time, however, we were looking up at a different set of stars, including the Southern Cross. For hours we lay on our backs enjoying the view before lapsing into a deep coma until the morning sun began to warm the valley.

Breakfast that day was worth the wait. The gauchos had found the missing carne, and since we were not in a hurry, we had dinner for breakfast. The succulent chunks of steak and cucumber and tomato salad hit the spot! I only partially resisted the temptation to gorge myself to the max, knowing that we still had a five hour hike out to the trail head.

That night, back in Mendoza, we celebrated at Frances Mallman's 1848, a fine restaurant located in a historical building on the other side of town. I thought we were mightily under-dressed in t-shirts and shorts, but once inside, I realized that this was a favorite spot for climbers after expeditions on Aconcagua. There were several other groups equally as casual.

I remember drinking some wine and having a hard time reading the fine print on the fancy menus in the dimly lit setting. But I can recall very little else about the meal itself, except that it tasted bland compared to the carne and salad at Pampa de Lenas on the trail or the incredible steaks at Don Pablo's before the trek.

Much more interesting than the food was the budding romance between Eric and Dr. Jen unveiling itself before our eyes. Their attraction for each other was obvious, but with so many people around, they seemed reluctant to get too close. Stephane thought they were made for each other and, not so subtly, tried to push their romance along. But Eric seemed to be playing it cool. Or maybe he was just a bit overwhelmed, I'm not sure. We were all rooting for him, as Dr. Jen was quite a catch, especially for a mountaineer. Six months after the climb, Eric confirmed in an email that they were still dating, but I've since heard the relationship did not last. A mountain guide's life is just too nomadic.

Halfway through the meal, another guide came inside from a courtyard and began speaking to Lakpa at the end of the table. I recognized him as Wally Berg, my law partner's guide. He had successfully reached and guided climbers to the summit of Everest several times, and I knew he was guiding the Tennessee couple I had met in the fall on a "two-fer" of the highest mountain in Chile and then Aconcagua. Eric joined the conversation. I watched as they de-briefed on each others' expeditions.

When the guides' conversation was breaking up, I approached Wally, re-introduced myself, and quickly learned that his whole group was eating out in the courtyard beyond the windows behind us. Some of his group had reached the top of the Chilean mountain, but they had been forced to turn around on Aconcagua due to the winds, as they were a day or two behind us. Wally told me that Martin, my law partner's Australian tent mate on an expedition to Antarctica was in his group, along with the couple from Tennessee.

I followed Wally back to his group and spoke with Martin the Aussie, who true to my partner's word had lost a thumb to frostbite in Antarctica. He had successfully reached the top in Chile, but was mightily disappointed to have been turned back on Aconcagua. The couple from Tennessee were even more disheartened. Apparently, she had gotten ill on the Chilean mountain and he had chosen to stay with her rather than try for the summit. Then the weather on Aconcagua did not cooperate and they did not have time left to wait out the storms. It was heart-breaking to see the looks on their faces when they realized that we had made it to the top only one or two days before their scheduled summit attempt.

I knew the feeling. It was exactly how I had felt a few years before when we had been turned back on Elbrus in the white out. Although one can experience a mountain and gain a lot of pleasure from a climb without reaching the summit, when so much time has been put into training to make it to the top, anything less can be a complete bummer, at least for me.

The final night in Mendoza involved a lot of beer drinking and another trip to Don Pablo's. With thirty-six ounce beers costing only two dollars at the Nutibara Hotel, the whole group was pretty toasted before we jumped in taxis for the trip to the restaurant. To our surprise, the taxi driver took us across town to another, more modern version of Don Pablo's at a shopping mall. Apparently it is a chain. The atmosphere was not the same, but the steaks were just as big. This time I ordered the larger filet mignon and after about twenty minutes of carving I finally managed to eat the whole thing, leaving absolutely no room for dessert.

However, there was plenty of room for Malbec wine, compliments of a climber who had been with the next Alpine Ascents group, but had broken some ribs coughing too hard, requiring him to hike back out with us. We all toasted each other until there was nothing more to say.

I secretly paid the entire tab for the group before anyone could object, then thanked each of them for helping make my last high altitude mountain a success. At that time, I fully expected Aconcagua to be my last of the Seven Summits.

But just to make sure I kept my options open, the next day on my trip home, I carefully retraced my steps to the shop in the Santiago Airport and purchased a beautiful lapis necklace, bracelet and earrings for my wife. I wanted her to know how much I appreciated her allowing me to go off for almost a month, chasing my mountain dreams.

ADDENDUM:
REAL TIME CYBERCASTS FOR ACONCAGUA TRIP

The perspective of the trip from the guides on a day-to-day basis is slightly different than a regular guy's impressions. Here is the series of cybercasts from our guides and the guide for Alpine Ascents' fourth team regarding the days we were on Aconcagua.

1/7/2007—Expedition 3 Begins
Hello this is Eric with Alpine Ascents, Expedition 3, Aconcagua. We are at the ski resort town of Los Penitentes, elevation around 8500 feet. We just finished some nice beef for dinner and are going to bed for an early rise as we head up the Vacas Valley for our first camp. Tomorrow our trek will take about 5-7 hours and the distance we'll cover is about 8 miles.

Everyone is doing really well and is very anxious to get to the mountain, and we will give you an update probably three days from now because cell reception isn't so good in the valley and we'll let you know when we get to base camp...

1/11/2007 Team 3 Rests in Base Camp
Hello family and friends. This is Alpine Ascents Team 3 on Aconcagua, from this point forward known as team "Carne Plus One" (for our vegetarian team member). We are at base camp at Plaza Argentina, 13,800 feet and today is our rest day. So far we've had some complications with the computer so our cybercast has been spotty, but in the future we expect it will be easier going in that department. The weather here is great: it's about 60 degrees, mostly sunny, with a light breeze. Again, today is a full rest day, so we are all hanging out and eating well. Tomorrow will be a big day as we push to Camp 1 at 16,200 feet...

1/13/2007 Carne Plus One Carries to Camp 1
Hello everyone checking in on Team Carne Plus One. We are here at base camp taking a rest day after a very successful but long carry

yesterday to Camp 1 at elevation 16,200 feet. For our carry we left base camp at 9:30 A.M. and arrived at Camp 1 about 4:00 P.M. We were able to set up three tents, which will make our move tomorrow that much easier. Everyone did really well. We're acclimating to the thin air. We then made our descent back down to base camp, which took about 2 to 2 1/2 hours. Our evening in base camp consisted of Stephane taking charge of cooking up his famous pasta and red sauce, which was very tasty. We finished up the night with some of us playing a game of hearts…Our plan tomorrow is to move up to Camp 1…

1/14/2007 Move to Camp 1

Hello family and friends. Thanks once again for tuning in to Team Carne Plus One. Today we moved up from base camp to Camp 1, a move of roughly 2,700 feet, which we did for the first time two days previously. Today we chopped off at least an hour of our time, which shows that the group is acclimating properly. Everyone is feeling strong, tonight we are well rested and enjoying a dinner of tortellini and pesto with sun-dried tomatoes. We're looking forward to carrying some gear up to Camp 2 tomorrow. We're going ahead and do that push up before returning to Camp 1 to sleep another night. We're right on schedule and everybody's feeling good.

1/15/2007 Carry to Camp 2

Hello everyone. Thanks for checking the Alpine Ascents Aconcagua cybercast. This is team 3, known as Carne Plus One. Tonight we are located at Camp 1 at 16,200 feet on the flank of Aconcagua. Today we moved some food, fuel, and equipment that we won't need until higher up to 17,800 feet, which is our Camp 2. We started off the morning in full sunshine with a leisurely breakfast of eggs and bacon. Then it took us about four hours to move our supplies on up to Camp 2. Now we're back down to Camp 1 where we're starting a dinner of burritos and quesadillas. The team looks really strong and we're excited to be acclimatizing well.

We are also sad to report that we have lost two of our team members. Mitch came down with an eye infection that just wasn't getting better at this altitude. He is now safely back in Mendoza and hopefully recovering quickly. Also, Brian decided that riding a mule out 30 miles to the trail head was less work than climbing the mountain, so hopefully he is drinking a tall cold one for the rest of the team as he relaxes in Mendoza. So thanks for checking in. The group would like me to express to everyone that we are all ok and that we miss our loved ones...

1/17/2007 Team Carne Plus One Takes a Weather Day

Greetings in cyberland. Well, the clouds have settled in and given us some snow, so team Carne Plus One settled into their tents yesterday to wait it out. The snow flurries came and went throughout the day, accompanied by a little thunder, but all was well in the cozy team tents. Activities included reading, card games, jokes and I'm sure a few tall tales and lies were told. This morning the weather was slightly improved with sun in the morning and snow flurries not settling in until afternoon. So the team decided to push on up to Camp 2, where they will set up their tents and spend the night. Camp 2 at Burrieza Col tends to be a bit breezy with the wind funneling through the pass, but hopefully the team won't have the full Aconcagua wind experience. The plan for tomorrow will be to cache gear up at camp 3 (19,200 feet) and then return to Camp 2 for another night.

1/19/2007 Team Carne Plus One at Camp 3

Hello everyone out there checking in with Alpine Ascents Team Carne Plus One. We are at 19,200 feet, our Camp 3 on Aconcagua, where we spent last night. Everyone slept really well, minus the wind and constant spindrift. Now we're looking forward to a nice leisurely rest day today. Giving you a breakdown of the last few days, on January 17 we were finally able to move up from Camp 1 at 16,200 feet to Camp 2 at 17,800 feet at Burrieza Col. The move went really well. We were able to set up tents, climb in and get set up and have hot drinks just in time before round two of the wind and snow storm. The next morning was still pretty breezy but we were able to do our move up to Camp 3 at 19,200 feet. We took only our essential gear and everyone made it up in about 3 1/2 hours. We had some really deep snow coming up; some spots in the trail had about two foot drifts. Luckily there were a lot of people ahead of us making the trail. We set up tents and moved right in just before round three of wind and snow. Everyone was fed and in bed by 7:00 and then there was a constant 50-60 mph wind all night, with gusts up to 70-80 mph. There's only so much you can do to live with the spindrift—we have to keep the tents zipped up tight, but then that creates condensation on the top of the tent, which then melts later and rains on everything.

This morning Lakpa and I broke out some bacon quesadillas for breakfast. Everyone had a good appetite. Our plan for today is to relax. Paul and Al, the two pillars of our expedition, will be heading down with Lakpa to meet Dave at Burrieza Col to pick up the rest of our gear and bring it up to Camp 3.

1/20/2007 Team Carne Plus One Moves To High Camp

Hello everyone out there checking in with Team Carne Plus One. We are up here at Camp 4 at 20,600 feet on Aconcagua. We made the move up today from Camp 3. Everyone did an excellent job moving up here today by moving slow and steady. We contribute a lot of our success today to Dave K. and Lakpa—both of them pulled up here in record time. By the time the rest of the team got there they had the tent platforms dug out, the tents set up, and hot water going. So kudos to those guys for their assistance. Everyone is doing well and we're keeping our fingers crossed for tomorrow. Keep us in your prayers and hopefully we'll be able to pull it off. Everyone sends their love to their friends and family and we'll hopefully be calling in from the summit tomorrow afternoon.

1/21/2007 Team Carne Plus One To The Summit!

It's been a long and challenging day for Team Carne Plus One, but they pulled it off. They had planned to leave Camp 4 this morning at about 7:00 but cold and high winds delayed their start until about 9:00. They battled the wind throughout the day, but by 4:00 P.M. Eric was standing on top of Aconcagua with Paul Z., Al B., Stephane S., and Dave Schaeffer. Lakpa and Dave K. brought up the rear with Jennifer and Mike G. and Tom L. Eric says it was the hardest summit he's ever had on this mountain. All were safely back to Camp 4 by about 8:30 P.M. Lakpa, Dave K. and Paul then packed up and headed down to Camp 3 to spend the night. Dave and Paul will rest there tomorrow before starting early the next morning (Tuesday) for an attempt on the technical Polish Direct route. Everyone else will pack up tomorrow morning and head for the warmth and thick air of base camp. So congratulations to Team Carne Plus One for a job well done.

1/23/2007 Team Carne Plus One Blows Into Base Camp

This is Eric with Team Carne Plus One calling in from Aconcagua Base Camp. Here we are. We all made it back down safely yesterday evening. We had a nice dinner prepared by Ellie, Lakpa, Dave and myself. We had spaghetti, which was delicious. Our day yesterday began with a wake up about 8:30 in the morning at Camp 4 at 20,600 feet. The wind had not stopped all night, so we were pretty buried with a lot of spindrift and had to spend the morning digging the tents out and dealing with wind gusts up to 60-80 mph. The whole team worked really well together to get the tents down, and it took us about an hour and a half to move from our Camp 4 down to Camp 3 at 19,200 feet. We were able to pick up our cache and then continue on down to Camp 2. The winds had increased to maybe 100 mph gusts. I've never experienced descending in a storm like that—I've been stuck in it, but actually coming down with the pack weights we had, we had our crampons on, but still these gusts would take us off our feet and throw us immediately to the ground. So it was a pretty big challenge to get back down, and that continued all the way down to Camp 1. A lot of teams have been stuck at Camp 1 and have not been able to get up to the higher camps because of these winds. As a side note, Paul and Dave had to abort their attempt on the Polish Direct. It was really a big bummer for both of them because Dave had been able to climb it himself earlier in this expedition and Paul had trained a lot for this climb and was physically ready for it. They ended up leaving Camp 3 after the rest of the group started down just because the winds were getting that much more desperate. The phenomenon we were experiencing up there is called "viento blanco", which translates as "white wind," which is when the whole mountain becomes encapsulated in a lenticular cloud. This morning the winds were still really high, but hopefully things will mellow out in the next few days.

1/23/2007 Team Mas Alto (Alpine Ascents Team 4) Stops At Camp 1 – Willie Pritt's Report, same day

Well good morning out there; at least it's a good morning for us here at our Camp 2. This is all going to be a bit confusing because we are actually in the upper part of traditional Camp 1. We attempted to do a move to Camp 2 yesterday to Ameghino Col, the low spot in the ridge between Ameghino and Aconcagua at 17,200 feet, but we got nuked pretty good. We had what is called a "viento blanco" going on here. People on the upper mountain were pretty much fighting for their lives. We had a tremendous amount of wind, whiteout, snow, and lenticular clouds all over the sky. Even at 16,200 feet here we were dealing with 40-70 mph continuous winds with higher gusts. So after about three hours of struggling against that we called it quits and carefully, with a lot of teamwork, set up our tents here at 16,200 feet. Today it is clear but the wind is still blowing probably 30-50 mph with higher gusts, so we're still trying to decide what we'll be doing today. Willie Prittie for Team Mas Alto★

★ I just hope my wife got our team's 1/23/07 message that we made it to base camp before she read Willie Prittie's account the same day about people on the upper mountain "pretty much fighting for their lives." I wouldn't take it that far, but the description of being "nuked" by the "viento blanco" is quite apt. I'll never forget that day and the full experience of the Aconcagua winds.

MOUNT VINSON—ANTARCTICA

"WEATHER PERMITTING"

When I returned to Atlanta from climbing Aconcagua, my wife described me as a zombie. Physically, I was back in the ATL. But for about a week, my head and my soul were still blowing in the winds high up in the Andes. She kept asking me when her husband was coming home. I certainly knew I was tired, but apparently she felt my personality and spiritual being were still buried on the mountain.

Maybe they were.

Physically, I felt okay, except for some nagging crustiness around the tip of my nose and nostrils and a bit of temporary numbness at the ends of my middle and fourth fingers. Plus, three and a half weeks of strain on my legs and very little good sleep had taken their toll on my body. With time I knew I would recover.

However, the most annoying after-effect of the climb was my taste buds not working. Even the spiciest foods barely registered. Ice cubes in drinks felt like plastic. Everything tasted bland and metallic. I found myself eating pickles, jalapeno peppers, hot buffalo wings, anything spicy or sour, trying to stimulate any sense of flavor. For almost six weeks, nothing worked. I began to wonder if I would ever enjoy eating again.

I never did figure out exactly what caused the loss of taste, but it probably was a combination of repeatedly burning my tongue on the hot chocolate at high altitudes and drinking iodinized water for almost a month. Who knows!

After a month and a half, flavors finally started to return. As was my usual custom after returning from a mountain expedition, I began munching on everything in sight, mostly junk food, candy, and ice cream, regaining some of my lost weight.

Then, for a few months after returning from Argentina, I focused on work, other projects, and my children's high school soccer seasons, all of which dominated most of my waking hours. It is amazing how far behind one can get when missing almost four weeks at the start of the year. I did not have time to think about mountains.

By June, five months after that trip, my mind slowly turned back to climbing. I began to contemplate another high altitude adventure, at least in theory. The problem was that I had promised my wife that Aconcagua would be as high as I would go. That eliminated a lot of the Himalayas. Several of the guys on Aconcagua had talked about doing Cho Oyu, which is supposedly the easiest of the fourteen 8000 meter peaks in the world. Sherpa Lakpa would be guiding that trip, a definite plus. However, the cost and the risk seemed high, and it is another mile higher than Aconcagua. No good.

As summer arrived in Atlanta, a long hot drought with hundred plus temperatures for seven or eight consecutive days hit us. Despite the heat, I noticed my waistline continually increasing. I had not been training for almost five months and felt like a slug. I had to do something.

What I need is some nice cool weather. What about Antarctica? Mt. Vinson's still on the list and is significantly lower than Aconcagua. No blistering heat there! But am I ready for that much cold?

My law partner had tried Vinson two years earlier in November, at the early part of the southern hemisphere summer. However, the temperatures had been so cold and the weather so volatile that his group had not been able to attempt the summit before having to turn around for their safety. His tent mate had cut his thumb and lost part of it to frostbite. My partner had described the trip as "instant survival mode."

So I already knew that the sub-freezing conditions in Antarctica could, by itself, make a successful summit impossible. Plus, when I looked up Vinson on the Alpine Ascents website, the price tag of $29,500 hit me like the sticker on a new Jaguar.

So I let the idea ride.

In July, out of the blue, I received an email from Alpine Ascents indicating that they still had a few openings left for their fifth planned expedition to climb Vinson in January 2008.

Damn. Why didn't I think of that!

Properly prompted, I couldn't stop dreaming about it. Some good financial news helped ameliorate the cost concerns. My constant snack food binging and the lack of anything to train for was taking its toll. The solution was easy. I just needed another mountain to climb.

A chance meeting with my lawyer friend Jim, who had made both trips to Elbrus with me, led to a lunch to discuss the idea of Antarctica and climbing Mt. Vinson. Jim was "totally stoked" about making the trip.

Just like that, a decision was made that we would both go.

Now all I had to do was to convince my wife. This time I knew I better have a good quid pro quo in hand.

That night at dinner I took the plunge.

"So here's the plan," I began. "Jim and I have decided to go to Antarctica in January to climb Mt. Vinson together. It's only 16,000 feet, not much higher than Whitney or Long's Peak. Much lower than Aconcagua. But that will get me my fourth of the Seven Summits."

My wife, Kim, looked at me glassy-eyed, as if in disbelief.

"Then, the following year for our twenty-fifth anniversary, you and I will go to New Zealand for ten days," I continued, "tacking on two or three days in Australia at the end so I can get the fifth summit there...and you can celebrate with me at the top of that one because you can drive to all but three hundred yards from the top."

I waited for the protest, but none came.

I think the only thing Kim heard was New Zealand, a destination that she has dreamed of visiting for years. Amazingly, she did not veto any of the rest of the plan. But she did mention that she thought she may be due a "girl's trip" to Tuscany, just to even it out. Later when she realized how much the Vinson trip cost, she said the Tuscany trip would be upgraded to "first class." But that was fine with me. I was going to Antarctica!

I immediately started training. Within days, I felt on top of the world. I had a renewed energy and a focus that had been missing for six months. With only five months to train and get all the logistics together, I could not waste any time.

A few days after submitting my deposit for the trip, Alpine Ascents sent me the package of forms and equipment list for Vinson. The first thing I noticed was that medical evacuation, trip cancellation, and flight insurance for the private flights to Antarctica and up to the base camp were mandatory and expensive. Then there were five pages of questions about my medical history and more detailed questions about my climbing experience than ever before. Although Vinson is still considered a moderate "walk-up" mountain, some prior technical mountain experience or training is required. Fortunately, my Orizaba, Elbrus and Aconcagua experiences, including the rope team and self arrest training we received from Sasha on Elbrus sufficed.

The equipment list was daunting to say the least. A sleeping bag and down parka and pants, graded to forty-below zero degrees, were required. Overboots to go over my double plastic boots, also graded to forty below, were mandatory. Insulated nose guards, water bottle parkas, and down booties were all highly recommended. None of this equipment is stocked at the traditional REI outlets or at High Country. All of it had to be specially ordered.

And it was expensive. I shelled out $600 for a Mountain Hardwear "Ghost" sleeping bag, another $1000 for a Mountain Hardware "Absolute Zero" down parka and pants, and added a North Face equipment bag for $120. Then I ordered "FortyBelow" overboots that had to be specially sized and fitted for my Koflach double plastics for another $125. It seemed like overkill, but after seeing the frostbitten thumb of my law partner's tent mate on his Vinson expedition, I was determined to have absolutely all the best equipment and warmest clothing possible.

A few telephone calls and faxes, including to an insurance outfit out of Denmark, secured me the requisite insurance coverage and a round trip ticket to Punta Arenas, the departure point at the southern tip of Chile. With all my tickets and the key equipment purchased or ordered, I sent in the balance of trip cost and locked myself in.

My friend Jim paid his deposit and we met at a local bagel place on the last Saturday in August so I could brief him on all the logistics. He was fully gungho for the trip and took careful notes on the gear and insurance needs.

The next Monday, Jim called me with sorrow and regret melting from his voice. His father had suffered a crippling stroke and Jim could no longer go on the trip. He would have to spend the next few months arranging for round-the-clock care or a nursing home placement for his father, as well as arranging for all the financial aspects of that devastating malady.

Now I was back on my own for the trip, just like Aconcagua. Oh well, while climbing mountains like this is done in teams, it really is an individual challenge with internal focus, fear, and perseverance. Reaching the top is a group celebration, but it is also a personal achievement for each individual on the team. It is comforting and usually more fun to share the experience with a friend, but making new acquaintances on a climb can be equally rewarding.

Mt. Vinson, at 16,094 feet, has been finally declared the tallest in Antarctica, after several inaccurate geological surveys had another peak listed as the highest. Vinson, named after a famous Georgia U.S. Senator who I'm sure did something outstanding to deserve the name recognition (regular guys don't really care who the mountain is named after), rests at the center of the Ellsworth Mountain range on the interior of Antarctica. We would not be seeing any penguins on the ice either on the "march" or with "happy feet," unless of course those movies were playing on the flight down to Chile.

Historically, the most difficult part of making this climb has been getting there. Obviously commercial airlines do not have any routes to Antarctica, so private or military aircraft must be arranged. Fortunately, with the rise of the Seven Summits as a goal for many mountaineers, more frequent flights on C-130 Hercules military cargo planes, or the Russian-made equivalent, are available for climbers with the primary guide groups. But the steep cost still deters most climbers who don't have thirty grand to spare. I am very fortunate to be able to afford such an extravagant adventure.

From Punta Arenas to a frozen ice runway at a place called Patriot Hills on Antarctica is a five hour flight by military transport, followed by another hour flight on a Twin Otter propeller aircraft up to the base camp for Vinson at the foot of the Ellsworth Mountain range. Once there, over a thousand miles inland, the expedition is isolated with no immediate ability to retreat anywhere. The challenge of Vinson is not only the steep climb and the seriously frigid conditions, but the sheer remoteness of the locale. According to the literature, only eight hundred climbers have ever climbed to the summit, and only a few at a time.

Perhaps it is that statistic which drew me to this adventure. The final frontier on earth; the pristine frozen wasteland; the almost untouched environment; they all called my name. I answered affirmatively.

Getting in shape seems harder as each year goes by. To force myself to train and to accelerate the process, I emailed Al, my tent mate from Aconcagua, who lives in Denver, and arranged for the two of us to climb Mt. Elbert, the tallest mountain in Colorado. Al indicated that he was booked the first weeks months of September, but that as long as we climbed before the first of October, he predicted we would avoid much snow on the mountain. We settled on the weekend of September 22-23, 2007.

I managed four or five weeks of evening hill work and a few long runs on the weekends in preparation for the Elbert climb. However, with the extreme heat in Atlanta, which held throughout August and well into September, I was only able to master ten and fifteen hills at a time. Just before I left for Colorado, I managed to run twenty hills once on a cooler night, but was exhausted when I finished. Still, I felt that climbing a 14,000'er should be a relatively easy task, given my other high altitude successes.

Elbert turned out to be anything but easy. As usual, the acclimatization hike the day before the big climb was under clear blue skies and was beautiful and pleasant. Al and I strolled up a moderate trail, passed a large lake where a couple of local yokels were fishing in wader/ innertube devices and orange jackets, and then free-climbed up a steep mountain flank as far as we could go without causing a rock avalanche. The top of the climb was tough and steep, but my legs felt fine and the views were gorgeous. I felt great and fully energized for the real climb the next day.

However, that night, on the weather channel, we noticed a huge cold front heading our way. Light rains and snow flurries were predicted. The weather guy focused most of his attention on the Denver Broncos— Jacksonville Jaguars NFL game the following afternoon, and little note was made about what the storm might be like at 14,433 feet at the top of Elbert.

We found out the next day. We began our hike in a light drizzle at about 6:30 a.m. Temperatures were not too bad at first. I was able to stay warm with two light layers on top and trekking pants below. But by 8:30 a.m., as we reached the tree line and moved into the more exposed section of the climb, the wind and rain picked up, requiring me to add my Gore-Tex shell jacket and some light gloves.

Snow flurries began to hit us as we worked our way up toward the first "false" summit, a monumental mound of mountain almost straight above us which was already streaked in snow. I began to have my doubts about the wisdom of ascending further, but Al kept the pace up, moving further and further up the slope. At the bottom of the steepest section of the first "false" summit, I seriously considered turning back, just because it was cold and wet and didn't feel like climbing anymore. But Al was like the "Ever Ready Bunny." He never stopped, and damn it, I was not going to let him out-do me. So I kept going.

By the time we circled up and around the steep right side of the first "false" summit, probably seventy percent of the path was covered in snow. The rest was wet, loose scree, a rather treacherous combination. But my trekking boots seemed secure and my ski pole gave me balance. At the top of that section, Al waited patiently while I added more layers, double insulated gloves, a pair of Gore-Tex pants, and goggles. I was cold and tired of getting wet. So, if we were going higher into what looked like almost complete blizzard conditions, I was going to be fully geared up for the assault. Looking up at the snow-filled slope, I wished I had my double plastic boots. And maybe some crampons.

The next hour was a constant battle, working our way up through snow drifts with stiff winds sweeping the snow across our path or straight down the mountain into our faces. Al pushed ahead by fifty, then hundred feet, leaving footprints for me to follow. The regular path was completely obliterated by the snow. For awhile I had no problem following his trail, but once we crested a second "false" summit and started up the third, the winds were so strong that Al's prints were almost gone by the time I reached them.

While focusing on the snow ahead, I did not realize that two climbers were steadily approaching me from behind. As they passed me, I noticed one of the young guys was still in shorts. Apparently, he had not expected to be caught in the first major snowstorm of the Colorado fall either. But he kept on going with his friend, both of whom soon caught up and passed Al as well.

At that point, visibility in the snowstorm was down to about fifty to seventy-five feet. I saw the two guys stop briefly at the top of what appeared to be the third summit, then begin hiking further up to their left.

Where the hell is the summit? I've about had all I can take of this garbage.

Al pointed at a high mound crested with rocks up to the left as if to indicate the true summit, and sure enough the two guys ahead of us quickly reached that apex.

Finally! We're almost there!

Not yet. After pausing on that mound, the two climbers moved further up and beyond to their left.

I blew out some air in disgust, put my head down, and forced my tired legs up the slope to where Al was waiting for me at the top of the third apparent summit. There I tried to peer over through the thick snow and clouds to find the true summit. We had to be close. But the guys in the lead had disappeared into the mist on a narrow ridge beyond the next mound.

I took a long swig from one of my water bottles and headed up in that direction. I was now on an exposed crest and the winds threatened to blow me over the edge. But I crouched low and endured, soon standing on the fourth "summit".

Now we could finally see the top!

Ahead of us was a very narrow snow-filled ridge of moderate steepness, leading up to a level spot, beyond which was another small mound with a large pole sticking up in the wind. The other climbers had already reached the summit and were heading back in our direction. As they walked, they hunched over in an effort to stay on their feet in what was now gale force winds.

Al and I inched our way up the sharp ridge, bracing ourselves against the wind blasting us from our left. We crossed paths with the other climbers and Al quickly zoomed ahead. Moments later, I watched him wave his arms at the summit. I decided to take my time, closing the final twenty feet at a snail's pace.

This time there was almost no joy at reaching the summit, just a vague awareness that I had made it despite awful weather conditions. Looking back, it was quite an accomplishment, given the limited training I had devoted up to that time and the incredibly difficult and unexpected conditions we faced. But at the time, when I finally reached the summit, I simply took a knee and tried to get out of the wind and snow. I looked around to be sure that this fifth summit, a small circle of rocks with a pole on the far side, was really the true summit. A cylinder tied to the rock wall to our right containing a log book confirmed we had in fact reached the top.

Al and I managed to sign the paper inside the cylinder without it getting too wet, then took turns trying to get a few summit photos of each other. Of course, the clouds were enveloping us so that visibility was reduced to about thirty feet. There was no background of view to give the shots any perspective. For all the pictures show, we could have been in someone's backyard on a mound of rocks holding our ski poles vertically upward in triumph!

Five hours later, after what seemed like an interminable descent, followed by an awesome shower back at the hotel, Al and I enjoyed filet mignon, baked potatoes and one helluva tasty caramel and nut-topped cheesecake at Quincy's Restaurant in Leadville, the historic mining town near the base of the Elbert and Massive peaks.

It would hurt me to walk for three days, and the snow, rain and wind had left me with one heck of a chest cold, cough, and sore throat. But I had lost five pounds and my leg strength was well on its way to the level needed for Antarctica.

And I had earned the right to wear a really obnoxious T-shirt declaring that I had climbed Elbert, ELEVATION 14,433 FEET, the highest point in Colorado!

On January 7, 2008, I followed almost the same flight schedule for the trip to Aconcagua the year before. Atlanta to Miami on American Airlines, then the overnight flight from Miami to Santiago on LAN Chile. Aconcagua was stunning in the early morning light as we passed it shortly before landing in Santiago, though it looked like it had much less snow on it than the year before.

This time the procedures were different at the Santiago airport, as I was continuing on to Punta Arenas on a domestic flight within Chile as compared with the last year when I flew immediately out of Chile to Mendoza, Argentina. Instead of being able to follow the "IN TRANSIT" signs straight to the international terminal, I had to go through passport control and customs, and find my way to the domestic terminal.

The American Airlines ticket agent in Atlanta had told me that my bags were checked all the way through to Punta Arenas. Out of an abundance of caution, I had elected to carry on my down parkas and pants, my double plastic boots, my Gore-Tex shell and my heavy expedition gloves in case the checked bags were lost in transit. Nevertheless, in Santiago, I decided at the last minute to make sure my other bags weren't coming off the baggage conveyor there.

Good decision. Sure enough, as soon as my flight number started flashing about the conveyor belt, my green backpack and my yellow North Face gear bag quickly appeared. Obviously they were not checked all the way through. Had I not double-checked, I would have ended up in Punta Arenas missing most of my gear and clothes.

Not realizing how far it was to go through customs and get to the domestic terminal, I hoisted the heavy green backpack on my back, slipped my blue day pack over my right shoulder and carried the yellow North Face bag and my red Adidas carry-on sports bag in each hand. I must have looked like a colorful pack mule making my way down the concourse, or, more accurately, an idiot who should have used one of the free luggage carts!

An official who was standing near the exit of customs pointed toward an elevator about a hundred yards ahead and said "Third Floor" in responses to my cryptic "Punta Arenas, por favor."

By the time I got to the elevator, I was sweating profusely and the blood had just about run out of my hands from the weight of the bags. Fortunately, when I got off the elevator on the third floor, more luggage carts were available. This time, I snagged one for the trip down to the domestic ticket counters.

LAN Chile had about twenty counters with four or five lines. I had no idea which one to get in, but a helpful, roving ticket agent pointed out the proper line. Soon I rechecked my two larger bags, making sure to still carry on my key boots and cold weather gear.

I arrived at the gate after another trip through security, which is much more lax than in the U.S. It was still before 8:00 a.m. and my connecting flight did not leave until 10:30 a.m., so I had plenty of time to stretch my legs, explore the little shops, and splash some water on my face in the restroom.

When I returned to the scheduled gate for my flight, I noticed a young guy with a North Face shirt sitting in the waiting area.

"Are you by any chance heading for Antarctica?" I asked.

"Yes, I am," he replied.

"Alpine Ascents?"

"Yep."

"You must be Jim," I said, remembering the list of climbers Alpine Ascents had sent the week before I left.

"That's me."

"Excellent. I'm Dave Schaeffer from Atlanta. Looks like we're in for a great adventure."

"Yeah. I'm looking forward to it."

For the next half hour, Jim and I verbally traded climbing resumes and a few stories. We were both excited about the trip to come, wondering out loud how tough the weather and the climb would be. He seemed like a regular guy like me, though much younger.

A young lady from Australia sat down across from us and joined in the conversation. She was a teacher on vacation and was heading for Patagonia and Torres del Paines, a spectacular national park several hours north of Punta Arenas. Between the three of us, the conversation never stopped. Soon our departure time arrived.

Unbenownst to the three of us, the LAN Chile gate person had announced in Spanish that the gate for our flight to Punta Arenas had been changed. I suddenly noticed that half of the people waiting had disappeared. We gathered our bags and got in line with the people remaining. Once in line, we realized that the board above the counter had another flight number listed.

Shit! Our flight leaves in five minutes and we are at the wrong gate!

Someone mentioned another gate number and we quickly took off running. I immediately noticed that Jim was a lot faster than me. I followed him and the young Aussie girl through some glass doors, down the stairs (the escalators were not working), and halfway down the lower concourse to the correct gate, my daypack and carry-on bag bouncing along all the way. Breathlessly, I handed my boarding pass to the man at the gate.

Fortunately, we made it on time. Soon we were settled in our seats on the plane, trying to catch our breath. About two minutes later, the plane began to back out and we were on our way to Punta Arenas.

The flight south to the tip of Chile took about three hours. I managed to catch a few minutes sleep, read some, then tried to see the scenery from the window seat. Sadly, it was almost completely overcast with miles of clouds in all directions. On the west horizon, however, an occasional snow-capped peak peeked through the clouds, leaving me to wonder what the rest of the southern third of Chile looked like.

As we approached Punta Arenas, the clouds cleared, revealing much more level terrain. I could not tell if the land was solid or a boggy swamp. To the west I could see a large section of water (which I later identified as the Otway Sound), and soon the plane was descending towards the coastline.

Immediately after crossing the shore, the plane slowed and banked into a steep right hand turn. I found myself looking almost straight down at the water of the Straits of Magellan. For a moment, I thought that the plane was going too slow to stay in the air. I took a deep breath as I imagined us going down into the frigid water. I checked under my seat for a life vest just in case.

But the plane stayed in the air just long enough to cross back above dry earth, go over a two-lane paved road and land on a short runway.

As we taxied in, my eyes immediately honed in on an enormous, silver cargo plane parked at the north end of the small terminal, its tail looming up into the sky like a huge whale tail. It was the Russian Illyushin, which would take us to Antarctica. Next to it was an American Hercules, another cargo plane, a mere midget compared to the Russian behemoth.

"Did you see the Illyushin?" I asked Jim as we walked into the terminal.

"Yeah, amazing, isn't it?" he replied. "I can't wait to fly over to the ice on it."

But we would have to wait—six days in fact. The subtitle of this chapter on Vinson is "weather permitting." This quickly became the story line for the entire trip.

Weather had not permitted the prior Alpine Ascents group of sixteen climbers to leave Vinson Base Camp, so the guide for my group of three climbers had not made it back to Punta Arenas to greet us. Neither had the guide for the other Alpine Ascents group of four climbers who would be climbing alongside us. Instead, another young-looking Alpine Ascents guide, who was between trips on Aconcagua, met us and arranged for transport to the Tierra de Fuego Hotel in downtown Punta Arenas. There we were told that crosswinds at Patriot Hills were too harsh for the Illyushin to land and that we would be "on call" periodically for the next few days. We would have an orientation meeting with ALE, the Antarctica Logistics and Expeditions company which ran the Illyushin and all operations at Patriot Hills and Vinson Base Camp, in the morning. We would get more details on the weather forecasts then.

Meanwhile, we had our gear check. We had to pack all of our heavy gear and most of our clothes in bags to be put on the Illyushin immediately, so that when good weather came, they would already have all our luggage stowed on the plane. We were to keep a few town clothes for one or two days in Punta Arenas and enough cold weather gear to get from the landing area at Patriot Hills to the tents once we landed.

Jim and I were assigned to the same room. Immediately upon arriving, we began pulling every bit of clothing and gear from our bags and laying them out on our beds for the gear check. When we went down the list of necessary items, I quickly discovered that my glacier glasses with nose guard had disappeared from my backpack. To this day, I have no idea what happened to them. Otherwise, my gear passed inspection. Our Alpine Ascents host insisted that I go out with him to a mountain gear shop up the road to replace the glasses. Fortunately, I found an identical pair of Julbo's for a reasonable price. However, I would have to do without a nose guard to block the wind and sun from my schnozz.

That night both sets of climbers and Garret met for dinner at a smoky pub-like restaurant in the basement of an ancient Chilean palace near the town square. It gave us all a chance to get acquainted.

The third member of my climbing group was Johan, a 34 year old "professional adventurer" from Sweden. He was outgoing and gregarious, full of stories about kayaking from Sweden to Africa, hiking in Mongolia, and a plethora of other wild trips. Vinson would be his seventh of the Seven Summits, having already reached the summit of all other continental high points, including Everest. I was duly impressed, especially after he explained how many sponsors he had paying his way for this trip and that he intended to do specials on both of his TV shows in France and Sweden after the trip.

The Alpine Ascents fellow also chimed in that he had conquered Everest the year before.

Okay. I'm completely out of my league!

Fortunately, the other group of four climbers were regular guys more like me.

Two were lawyers from Portland, Oregon. Mark, a thin, gnarly looking guy in his mid-forties, was a devoted climber, mountaineer, and Boy Scout troop leader who lived to push his limits. As it turned out, he like me, was an alumna of the University of Virginia Law School, but had found his way out West to practice, while I stayed in the East. He had successfully climbed Mt. McKinley, but had been badly injured in a rock slide that took the life of another member of his rope team on the

McKinley descent. Amazingly, even after such a disaster, he was climbing again.

The other attorney, named Steve, was older, taller and less experienced. He had climbed Kilimanjaro, but had no other high altitude mountains on his resume. I learned later that he was contemplating a run for State Representative in Oregon and, like me, coached high school mock trial teams. He was, by far, the most cerebral of the group, with a broad range of intellectual pursuits, and an unsurpassed chess game. He also was constantly optimistic about everything. Regular guys just hate those positive attitude types!

Even taller, and the Paul Bunyon of the group, was Craig, who turned out to be a former NFL player — a defensive end for the Patriots and the Steelers. Even at age 59, the man had a vice grip for a hand shake. Fully six foot five inches tall, his lengthy gait left everyone in his dust. He and Mark were close friends and they told stories about getting up early on a Saturday morning, driving to Mt. Hood, climbing to the top and back down in less than eight hours, and returning home for a late lunch. Again, I felt like a rank amateur. Craig was the quietest of the group for the first few days, but slowly I realized that he had a competitive but laid back personality and was probably the strongest climber in either group.

The final member of the four man team, a forty year old guy named Dave from San Francisco, looked vaguely familiar. It did not take long for Dave to figure out that we had been at Elbrus at the same time. When my friends Jim and Ken had been under the weather after our successful summit, Dave and his group had invited me to have beers with them outside our little hotel at the Cheget Village near Mt. Elbrus. We had fun reliving some of the trials and triumphs of that Russian peak.

The pub fare was passable at best. My "scallops au gratin" entree (my French translation for the Chilean menu name that I can't recall), though supposedly a house specialty, was tough and chewy, though the melted cheese across the top was quite tasty. The mixed salad was just a bunch of tomatoes and onions with no dressing on them. However, the local cerveza was quite good. Each of us partook of at least three bottles before the waiter finally brought us the check. That is, except for Steve, who chose the sober route with a few cans of ginger ale.

After the meal, Johan quickly offered to pay for the whole table, and despite protests left and right, put the entire tab on his credit card. This, of course, started a pattern of each of us taking turns paying the tabs. Little did we know that we would be eating a lot of dinners in Punta Arenas while waiting for the proper weather conditions to fly over to the "ice".

The next morning, we had our "orientation" with the folks from ALE, the logistics company who handled all flights and supply functions to and from Antarctica. The meeting took place on the third floor of an older building called the Croatia Club a few blocks from our hotel.

The main guy, an Aussie with an attitude who I nicknamed McKnowitall, commanded our attention with some harrowing stories and pictures of frostbite victims, due to climbers not following the basic safety rules or doing stupid things like failing to attach their gloves onto their parkas and losing them on summit day. The frostbitten thumb of my law partner's tent mate on his trip to Vinson two years earlier was among the anecdotes. His failure to timely bring to his guide's attention a cut on his thumb was held up as an example of exactly what not to do.

Next, we sat through about an hour of rules and regulations, the history of ALE, of which McKnowitall was very proud, followed by a discourse on weather and the infamous Katabatic winds which constantly whip down from the South Pole in the direction of Patriot Hills, rendering landings very "iffy". The gruff Aussie constantly assured us that he wanted us to get to the "ice" as soon as possible, but safety considerations had to come first. Any crosswinds over 20 knots at the blue ice runway at Patriot Hills would prevent any landing. ALE's staff would not send the Illyushin out from Punta Arenas unless and until they could predict at least an eight to ten hour window of calmer conditions.

During a cookie and juice break, I noticed that the other groups waiting to fly over to Antarctica were quite diverse. There was a couple from Calgary, Canada, who planned to climb without a guide; four fairly young guys from Poland, all of whom looked pretty rugged; three young Koreans and their guide; an older Japanese gentleman; and a Dane who intended to climb all seven of the continental summits in a row in just 120 days, with the help of his Swedish guide.

After the snack, we were treated to a photo display of the trip to Vinson and the expected camps on the climb. Most of the show was devoted to the plane trips to Patriot Hills and to Vinson Base Camp. At the end of the session, I still felt like I had no real idea about route from Vinson Base Camp to the summit. I had still not seen any map of the route of any sort, let alone a nice topographical map with distances and altitudes.

We were told that the normal route up what was referred to as the "headwall" had become too unstable, with falling cyracs and possible avalanches making it a safety hazard. In lieu of that route, a few of the top guides had installed a fixed rope up a steeper ridge just to the east of the "headwall." The fixed rope would be used to ascend the 3000 feet to the upper slopes and high camp. This would require the use of ascenders, a clever metal gadget which slides up a rope, but grabs onto the rope to prevent sliding down. I, of course, had never climbed a fixed rope or used an ascender before, but Jim assured me it was a "piece of cake."

Before we left, McKnowitall told us that the earliest we could possibly leave for the "ice" would be evening on the next day, so we had at least a day and a half to "cool our heels."

Shit. The delays are already starting.

The next few days followed a similar pattern. We would meet in the lobby hotel at 10:00 a.m. in the morning for a weather briefing and news on whether a flight would be possible that day. We would show up excited to go, only to learn that the weather did not permit any flights and to check in the next day at 10:00 a.m. or 6 p.m.

Meanwhile, on the first delay, we hopped into some taxis and headed out of town to see, you guessed it, some penguins.

And I had told everyone I knew that I would not be seeing any penguins!

Around Punta Arenas, there are two major penguin colonies. The first and largest is on an island in the Straits of Magellan just north east of the city, but it takes a ferry to get there. On the day in question the ferries were not running. So we opted for the second choice, a smaller colony on the Otway Sound, almost directly north of town.

The taxi driver took the first left past the airport onto a dirt/gravel road in the middle of what looked like endless pastures. For the next thirty-five kilometers the scenery did not change, except for a few glimpses of snow-capped mountains in the distance to the west. I actually fell asleep for about twenty minutes despite the rough ride across the peninsula to the Otway Sound.

The sun glistened across the water as we approached our destination. Mountains on the far side of the sound gave a magnificent background to the scene. The taxi pulled into a small parking area next to a low lying building with lavatories, a ticket booth and an enclosed eating area. Apparently, the penguins were beyond the structure.

By about a half mile. No problem. I could use the exercise. Maybe it would wake me up.

Jim and I paid our entrance fee and turned toward the trail. It did not take us long to realize that the half mile hike was directly into the teeth of a thirty mile an hour wind. I zipped up my windbreaker, lowered a shoulder and stepped in behind Jim. It felt good to be hiking, but I figured he could set the pace.

My legs were actually starting to "burn" a bit by the time we reached a sign that showed a circular boardwalk through the penguin colony. We were still in the marshes several hundred yards from the beach, but we headed counter-clockwise towards a lookout structure visible near the shore. Suddenly, penguins appeared to our right and left, huddled among the bushes and reeds along the path. Some were nestled in burrowed holes. Some had baby penguins alongside, their new brown fuzz contrasting with the black and white colors of their mothers.

These penguins were only about eighteen inches high, but were still cute enough to keep my attention for an hour or more. The only prior time I had seen penguins outside of a zoo was on a beach near the Cape of Good Hope south of Capetown, South Africa, so it was a thrill of sorts. However, these little creatures were nothing like the swimming and sliding emperor penguins of "The March of The Penguins" movie fame.

The next day, we were greeted by another delay of at least thirty-six hours. Now I was getting annoyed. There was not that much to do in Punta Arenas. I was not about to go see more miniature penguins. The whole group of Alpine Ascents climbers milled around, trying to find something worthwhile to do.

The Aussie girl at the Santiago airport had talked about Torres des Paines, and I had seen photos of the spectacular rock spires and waterfalls at that national park on the Alpine Ascents website. An earlier Antarctica group had been given a three day delay and had taken the time to hike the entire park. But we had only thirty-six hours and the park was about a four hour drive north. My compadres quickly nixed the idea of driving that far and possibly not making it back in time for the next check-in time.

However, I overheard the Danish climber, named Henrik, and his guide, Soren, talking to the hotel concierge about flying up to Torres des Paines. So I listened in.

Apparently, a small airline company had just started flights from Punta Arenas to Puerto de Natales, which was the closest town to the park—almost three hours north. But to get tickets, one had to go to a ticket office about six blocks away and hope for room on the flight. The concierge speculated that there might be some flights that day, but could not get any information over the phone. So Henrik, Soren, and I hustled over to storefront ticket office, only to find a long line of people moving nowhere. After about a forty-five minute wait with almost no progress, Soren pushed up to the front to try to get a flight schedule. Somehow he learned that the new schedule had flights only two times a week and there were no planes going to or from Puerto de Natales in the next two days.

I had seen a Hertz car rental place a few blocks to the south on one of my early morning runs, so I volunteered to go over and see if I could find a suitable rental for us to drive to Torres des Paines. We would have to leave immediately, try to reach the park before dark, get a few hours sleep, then begin our hike up to the spires by 4 a.m. and drive back in the afternoon to make it back by 6 p.m. the next day. Not an easy or casual trip.

But what else are we going to do?

Since we were taking some gear with us, I selected an SUV, and, despite an astronomical rental rate, signed on the dotted line as the Chilean man smiled. I opted for some local insurance as well, as I understood we would be taking some unpaved and curvy mountain roads along the way. The man advised me in broken English that, despite the insurance, the deductible on any damage to the car was US $950.

"Well, I'll be sure not to get in a wreck," I said cavalierly.

"Not a wreck, senor...it is de flying rocks you watch out for," he responded.

He then left to get the car ready.

Thirty minutes later, the car was still being washed and tidied up. I kept looking at my watch. It was already three-thirty in the afternoon and we had to get to the park by night fall.

"Just bring it out," I pleaded. "It's going to get dirty again anyway."

Another fifteen minutes later, I drove the SUV out of the Hertz building, having been careful to walk around the car several times and note all the scrapes, windshield cracks, and paint chips along the sides of the cars. There were so many blemishes, I wondered what we were getting ourselves into.

Thankfully, Soren managed to find a place for us to stay the night, if we could ever get to the park. The main hotel was booked solid, but there was something that sounded like a hostel with a bunk room available. We were only going to be there for a few hours sleep anyway.

The next problem was that we only had very rudimentary maps to get us to our destination. The concierge drew a rough map on a napkin and told us to follow the signs to Central Torres.

Great.

Three hours later, we passed the airport at Puerto de Natales after some awesome views of a huge lake and snow-capped peaks beyond near the town center. As soon as we were beyond the fenced runway, the paved road ended. The signs said Torres des Paines was still over 100 kilometers away.

Needless to say, with a $950 deductible, I was reluctant to fly down the gravel road at a fast pace. But after realizing that we would never make our destination before dark if I plodded along, I had no choice. For the next hour, we bounced, shook, and skidded between potholes and ruts, leaving a huge cloud of dust as we zoomed down the road. Several times we were sure we had gone the wrong way and almost doubled back only to find that we were on the right route. Then we got close enough to see the Torres des Paines towers and spires....and the aqua colored lakes with pink flamingo-like birds on the shore....and the llamas (actually relatives of the llama called guanacos) on the side of the road. Every single time, we had to stop for Soren to take five or ten pictures. Or twenty. Sometimes with a tripod.

I thought we would never get there. Even after we stopped at the park entrance and paid our fee, there was another seven kilometers to go, but only after squeezing the SUV through the narrowest suspension bridge I have ever driven over. We actually had to push the rear view mirrors in flat against the car body on both sides to make it through, with about one or two inches on each side to spare. The damned insurance deductible was totally at risk, but I made it through without a scratch. The rest of the road to the hostel was so filled with potholes and ruts that it was almost impassable, but we just kept going. Soren got another twenty or thirty shots of the mountains and spires as the night descended on us. It was pitch black by the time we finally checked in to our bunk room at 8 p.m.

Fortunately, we still were in time for the second seating of the evening meal, which came with the price of the room. We had a pleasant but rather bland meal with a couple med students from the U.S. who had just completed a twelve hour hike in a remote part of the park. Exhausted, we went straight to bed. I set the alarm on my watch for 3:30 a.m., as we planned to be on the trail by 4 a.m. The path to the towers was said to be at least a seven hour round trip and we needed to be back on the road to Punta Arenas by noon.

It seemed like I had just put my head on my pillow when the alarm went off.

"Let's go boys," I said, jumping out of the bunk.

I don't know where I got the energy, but I was ready to go in less than ten minutes. It was another thirty minutes before Soren had all of his camera and climbing gear together.

These guys are going to climb all seven summits in 120 days? Not at this rate.

In the dark, it was hard to figure out where the trail started. We had been told the trail head was just behind the nearby hotel. But there were no other climbers up yet and there were about five possible trails behind the hotel. I guessed wrong and wasted at least twenty minutes going up the wrong path before Soren scouted out a cross–country path to the real trail. After fording a few streams and working our way through a few marshes, we found the main trail heading up toward a pass.

Of course, the weather did not cooperate. Within minutes of hitting the trail, a light rain began. Soren and Henrik immediately stopped to put on Gore-Tex jackets and pants. I slipped on my Gore-Tex shell jacket, but continued to climb in a pair of trekking pants, which soon became very wet. Just as I was about to change, the sun filtered through. I stripped off my jacket and my pant legs began to dry.

For about an hour, we ascended a well worn path up along traverse leading up to a canyon between two peaks. The sun and rain were intermittent, so I never did put on my Gore-Tex pants. Once we reached the shoulder and headed into the canyon, the path crossed long, dark scree sections paralleling a rushing stream below. Now the path was completely dry and the warm sun almost massaged our shoulders. About a half hour later, we dropped down to a ranger hut and camp, complete with a new-age, white propeller windmill. Alternative energy sources suited this environment. Apparently, hikers can reserve campsites or rooms in that hut on longer trips around the park.

But we had no time to dawdle. We kept going without a break.

The next hour was spent working our way up muddy, slick paths through trees in a light drizzle. Miserable to say the least. Though we had come so far to see the spires, I worried that unless the weather changed we would not be able to see anything.

After crossing an open area with beautiful views of the rest of the canyon, we began a steep climb up a ridge of exposed rocks. At first the sun came out and I had to strip down again to avoid overheating. I hoped for full visibility by the time we reached the spires.

However, moments later the clouds swooped in again. The rest of the way, we climbed in a bitterly cold rainstorm.

I wanted to put on gloves, but at this point we were scrambling up rocks on all fours. Getting a solid grip on the boulders was more important than comfort.

Soren kept up a fast pace despite the increasingly steep climb and soon was fifty or sixty feet ahead. Henrik was somewhere behind or to the left of me. I climbed alone, working my way up along the orange painted bullet/target marks on the rocks ahead of me. Every time I thought I was approaching the crest of the rock ridge, another hundred vertical feet of boulders lurked above and beyond.

Shit. Why didn't I just stay in Punta Arenas with the rest of the guys. They're probably laying around relaxing—and dry right now!

Finally, I saw Soren standing erect high up on a ridge above me, taking more pictures. I knew then that I was approaching the apex of our climb. My thighs burned as I pressed up the rest of the way, ignoring the frigid rain and wind in my face. At the top, I collapsed onto a rock and reached in my pack for some water and my gloves. My hands were numb with cold.

On clear days, I can imagine the view must be awesome from that point. In front of us was an amphitheatre of rock above a dull, but amazingly beautiful, light green lake with sheer walls on the far side leading up to the base of the Torres des Paines towers. The spires at the top of the towers were completely shrouded in the clouds. When the wind shifted, we could see the lower portions of them, like shadows in the mist. But the sun never came out again to melt away the cloudy view, or our disappointment.

As it was already after nine o'clock, we did not have much time to rest at the top. Still, I intentionally dawdled, not only so that I could warm up my hands and get something to eat, but just in case the sun would reappear and give us one quick glimpse of the magnificent formations.

Alas, after fifteen minutes, the view was not improved and we had to start our descent.

We made great time on the way out, arriving back at the trail head by 11:15 a.m., having passed several hundred climbers heading up the mountain as we headed out. By the time we reached the car, the sun was blazing down on us. I speculated that those scumbag climbers who had the luxury of sleeping in and reaching the spires in the early afternoon probably got perfect views!

Nobody ever said life is fair!

After a couple of Cokes and an ice cream bar revived my spirits, we headed back down the gravel road towards Puerto de Natales. I made it almost all the way through the narrow bridge before scraping the crap out of the right rear view mirror and passenger side door handle on the next to last bridge support when Henrik failed to warn me I was getting too close.

Oh well, it's not like $950 is even a grand!

Henrik took the wheel after we filled up with gas in Puerto de Natales. Moments later, we found out that, in his spare time, he likes to race cars. This SUV was not very aerodynamic or stable, but Henrik decided to test its limits. Soon we were careening around curves at 140 kilometers per hour and hitting 160 and 170 kilometers on the straightaways.

Soren must have been used to it, as he calmly sat back typing away at his tiny laptop computer, updating their website. I held on for dear life, quite often reminding Henrik that we only have to get there by 5 p.m. to return the car. Henrik ignored caution, pressed harder on the accelerator, and soon we were on the outskirts of Punta Arenas. He cut a good hour off the time I had taken to drive the same distance the day before.

My heart was pumping when the Hertz man inspected the car when I turned it back in. There had been some minor scrapes on the same rear view mirror when I picked the car up the day before, but not half as bad. He asked if we had any problems and for just a second, I thought about saying no. But then my conscience kicked in and I showed him the scratches from the bridge.

He laughed. "No problem, Senor…these are just scratches. We have to repaint every few months anyway. Have a good day!"

"Gracias, Senor," I said and practically skipped back to the hotel.

At 6 p.m., we got the call from ALE.

"Check back tomorrow at 10:00 a.m. But it doesn't look good for the next three days," our Alpine Ascents representative announced.

Great frustration set in among the group. Our walking around clothes, which we hoped to last two or three days, were now quite rancid. I had only kept two clean pair of socks for the stay in Punta Arenas. Jim began to complain about the stench in our room, primarily from my socks, shoes, and jogging outfit. On the fourth day after we arrived, I had to buy two more pairs of socks and an extra pair of jogging shorts just to make it through.

With so much spare time, I finished off two books, at least one of which I had planned to take over to the "ice" to pass time there. Spanish language TV was not too satisfying either, though plenty of American TV re-runs were playing with Spanish subtitles.

Out of sheer boredom, one night our Alpine Ascents leader convinced Jim, Dave and me to meet him at a somewhat seedy looking nightclub called Kamikaze. A lot of very young looking locals were crammed into a tunnel off the sidewalk trying to get in. Despite a $10 cover charge, we joined the line and soon were inside. I felt completely out of place, given the fact that I was probably at least twenty-five years older than most of the people inside and hardly any of them spoke English. But the beers were cold and there were plenty of sights to see, if you get my drift.

By 2 a.m., the place was really hopping. The large dance floor was overflowing, mostly with girls dancing with each other. Jim had been cajoled onto the dance floor by an aggressive blonde in a zebra stripe shirt, but he seemed to be enjoying himself. I had nursed two beers and was hanging out with Dave when our leader dragged me over to talk to two girls he had met. On the way over, he told me that to get two girlfriends onto the dance floor, you have to provide them both with dance partners. So I assumed that he intended to dance with the good-looking one and wanted me to bump and grind with the plumper one. Not exactly what I had in mind, but I felt obliged to help him out.

However, after introducing me, he immediately excused himself and headed across the room. Left alone, I tried to converse with the girls. The pretty one spoke some broken English, but with the loud music and my complete lack of fluency in Spanish, the communication was hopeless. Instead, I asked if the girls wanted to dance, but without another guy with me, dancing was apparently taboo. Rather, the prettier girl grabbed my arm as if I had come with her and asked me to stay close because she saw someone she knew but didn't want to talk to him. At least that's what I think she said. I wondered what I had gotten into.

For the next half hour, the girl had me in almost a vice grip. While keeping my free hand on my wallet, I kept looking around for a rescue party. But Dave had apparently left the nightclub completely, Jim was still gyrating on the dance floor. Our Alpine Ascents host was huddled with some other girls on the far side of the room.

No help anywhere in sight.

Finally, I saw Jim waving in my direction, looking like he needed rescuing as well. I used the opportunity to escape, motioning to my captor as if I would be right back.

"Time to get going?" I asked Jim hopefully.

"Yeah, but you have to help me ditch this girl," he said, referring to clingy zebra lady.

"Alright, I'll round up the others and then we will come back and tell you we are leaving; then let's get the hell outta here."

After working my way around the dance floor, I passed on the message to the Alpine Ascents guy that we needed to leave and that Jim needed rescuing. He immediately agreed and headed in Jim's direction, spoke to him, then met me at the exit.

"Where's Jim?" I asked.

"He's staying. That chick in the zebra outfit is hot for his body."

"Okay, but I thought he wanted to get out of here."

"Apparently not."

A few minutes later, I was walking quickly along the six blocks to the hotel. At 4:30 a.m., the streets did not look quite as safe as during the day. I felt relieved when I plopped down on my bed in the hotel and slipped under the cool sheets in my newly purchased running shorts.

About fifteen minutes later, Jim arrived alone.

"I thought you were going to rescue me," he said in an accusatory tone.

"I told our fearless leader to get you out of there."

"Well, he just said you were leaving, but that I should feel free to stay as long as I wanted. He didn't give me any out. I finally had to just pull her off me and run for it."

"Sorry," I replied.

He shrugged and then a shrewd grin came across his face.

"Did anyone tell you the story on the chick you were hanging out with?" he asked me.

"No, what story?"

"She's bad news. Married. Everyone was waiting for her husband to show up and beat the shit out of anyone trying to pick up his wife."

"No way!"

"Yeah, why do you think they led you in and then disappeared? They were making sure their butts weren't near her when her husband showed up."

"Thanks a lot. What about my butt?"

At that point, I did not know what to believe. At least I was out of the club in one piece and Jim had not brought anyone back to the hotel.

All I know is that I am getting way too old to hang out with young Chilean ladies at bars called Kamikazi!

On the sixth day after our arrival in Punta Arenas, the check-ins moved to two hour intervals. Excitement was clearly in the air. The weather reports from Patriot Hills were improving and predicted times of departure were loosely bandied around. We even started packing up and optimistically told the hotel concierge to extend our check out time because we didn't want to pay for an extra night.

Finally, at 2:00 p.m. we were told to be ready to go to the airport by 4:00 p.m. They expected to be able to fly out early in the evening. After exchanging high-fives all around, we quickly retreated to our rooms to finish packing. Two of my smaller bags, the small day pack and the red sports bag would be left at the hotel. Everything else was crammed into my large backpack or pockets. We were told to wear our double plastic boots, even from the hotel to the airport, as we would have to hike a half mile to the Patriot Hills camp once we landed. Parkas, fleeces and gloves were to be kept handy, so that they could be put on when we landed.

Jim and I were ready by three o'clock and went ahead and checked out of the hotel. The bus showed up about thirty minutes early, but it seemed like an interminable wait before the ALE representative motioned us to load our bags. Once everyone was aboard and all the bags stowed, we realized that we had several more stops on the way to the airport. We quickly picked up the Canadian couple who were quite ready to go. Then the driver circled around for about fifteen minutes trying to find the private residence where the four Polish climbers were staying.

Why didn't they just stay at a hotel downtown?

After another fifteen minutes, the Polish guys finally strolled out to the bus, their gear hanging out all over the place. Apparently, they had not gotten the word we were leaving until a few minutes before we arrived.

My patience was wearing thin by the time the bus got rolling again, but soon we were pulling up to the terminal and the ALE rep was giving us strict instructions about going through military customs, as we would be flying a military cargo plane.

We were all business once inside. A quick walk up to the second floor led us to the security screening machines. I noticed a nice souvenir shop to the left with maps and T-shirts of Antarctica, but did not have time to stop. Just beyond the security machines on the left was an impressive glass box of scissors, toe nail clippers, knives and other small metal items confiscated from fliers. Some in our group snapped photos, I suppose just to prove that other countries also take security seriously.

We could see the Illyushin aircraft out the windows of the waiting room and I assumed that we would shortly walk down the steps to the tarmac and across the fifty or so yards to the plane. However, after another twenty minute wait, we were led down the stairs and had to re-board the bus in order to drive the last leg to the plane.

What are we—invalids?

A few minutes later, we hopped off the bus, grabbed our backpacks at gawked at the enormous cargo plane before us. Everyone scurried to take pictures, but the ALE folks restricted our movements and the sun was shining in the wrong direction to get any decent photos. With my disposable digital camera, I knew I would be wasting a shot, so I moved quickly to the narrow ladder and climbed up into the fuselage.

Once on board, I realized just how big the plane was. One could park about four Greyhound buses inside the cargo deck. Instead, however, the deck of the plane was covered almost from end to end with large black fuel tanks covered with boxes and crates of supplies and other gear. Our climbing gear, which we had not seen in six days was stowed in the rear of the plane and smartly secured with net-like straps.

Along both sides of the plane were jump seats which could be pulled down from walls. They were unpadded seats with no backs and almost no leg room, as the cargo was piled up almost to the seats. I pushed my way across to the far side and worked my way towards the rear of the plane to the last jump seat which was situated about ten feet from one of the only four port windows in the entire plane. Coincidentally, I found myself standing right in front of my yellow North Face gear bag.

Most of the Alpine Ascent climbers must have dawdled outside trying to get pictures. By the time they boarded, the jump seats on my side of the plane were pretty occupied, so they ended up on the oppo-site side. Fortunately, as we were the last groups to fly over in the three month season, we only took up about half the seats and there was plenty of room to stretch out and walk about.

My stomach acids started building up as the mammoth aircraft taxied toward the runway. The Russian flight assistants had handed out ear plugs as we entered the plane and we quickly found out why. The roar of the jets on take off was deafening. I held the plugs to my ears and dug my feet into the stored bags in front of me as the Illyushin gradually accelerated.

The plane used every bit of the Punta Arenas runway to finally get off the ground, creeping into the sky amid a chorus of cheers from within. About five minutes after take off, we were told we could move around. I was surprised to look out the porthole and see that we were still above land. I had thought that we would zip above and beyond the Straits of Magellan and quickly be over the ocean. However, for about forty-five minutes, we continued to fly south over a myriad of peninsulas and islands that make up the southern tip of Chile. Punta Arenas is actually nowhere close to the most southern tip of the country.

The next two hours were nothing to write home about. There was little to look at but endless clouds or water below – mostly clouds. Boring to say the least.

On the bright side, we were treated to some fairly dry sandwiches and chips, a very rich chocolate bar, and some soda. Given the fact that we had not eaten since noon and it was already approaching 9 p.m., anything edible was appreciated. I supplemented the meal with a few almonds I had stashed in my carry-on backpack.

Things got exciting when we approached the Antarctic Peninsula, which is the closest point of the continent. At first we noticed scattered ice bergs in the water below, then the mountains on the peninsula appeared from out of the clouds. Finally, we got close enough to see some of the large cruise ships moored off shore between the larger ice bergs.

Soon, everyone on the plane was taking turns pressing their faces to the porthole windows to see the first amazing sights of the frozen continent or to try to take photos of it through the glass.

As ready as we were to be there, I knew that the flight was expected to be almost five hours long. We had only been airborne for a few hours, so we were actually only halfway to Patriot Hills. It was another hour before the plane crossed over the border of ice and water at the south end of the peninsula. We still had another 1000 miles to fly inland.

Once above the mainland, most of the surface below us consisted of flat oceans of thick ice above the underlying land. But as we moved further toward the South Pole, which is situated about 500 miles beyond Patriot Hills, craggy, rocky hills and mountains appeared to pierce through the icy ocean, creating wonderful shadows and contrasts in the otherwise pure white landscape. The scenery was mesmerizing. I found myself almost glued to the window, marveling at the sights below.

Shortly before 11:30 p.m., we were told to return to our seats and prepare for landing. We had to not only put our seat belts on, but were instructed to dress warmly for expected icy conditions on landing.

Despite the late hour, the sun was still shining brightly. It looked like noon outside. However, once seated and belted in, we could no longer see anything through the portholes and just had to imagine the plane swooping down onto the "blue ice" runway.

I sat nervously as the plane descended. Landing a huge cargo plane filled with hundreds of barrels of fuel on a slick ice runway with no control towers or air traffic control just did not seem safe or wise. The tension mounted as the landing gear was dropped into place. The plane groaned and felt like it was going to completely fall apart as we approached the landing. We had no idea how close we were to the ground when suddenly we received a huge jolt as the wheels touched down.

Holy shit! That's one rough landing!

The plane lurched and slid as the wheels sought traction on the ice. The high-pitched screech coming from every side hardly helped my anxiety. I immediately envisioned the plane careening off the runway, crashing into the ice, and the whole works going up in a fuel tank fed explosion like in a James Bond movie.

But the Russian pilots kept the plane on line. Soon we felt the reassuring reverse thrusts of the jet engines and the plane slowing down. I'm sure there must have been wild applause at some point in the landing, but in my excitement, I don't recall it.

Just as I was about to relax, the entire rear cargo ramp slammed down leaving a gaping wide hole in the back of the plane. The ramp appeared to drag along the ice, also helping to slow down and stabilize the plane's movement. Along with it came a blast of cold air which made me thankful that I was wearing my forty degree below parka.

The plane taxied to the end of the four mile runway and spun its wheels as it tried to turn around. Additional forward thrusts of the jets were required to get the plane moving again.

Finally, the Illyushin came to a stop near several snowmobiles with luggage sleds behind them.

One by one we worked our way up to the front of the plane. They apparently no longer deplane passengers on the rear ramp because several people had recently slipped and bruised their rear ends on the ramp, ruining their trips.

I felt like Neil Armstrong stepping down on the moon as I descended the narrow stepladder to the ice runway. I gingerly planted both feet on the ground, took about twenty steps over to the snowy edge of the runway, turned and marveled at the sight around us.

The long range of the Patriot Hills loomed fifteen hundred feet above and beyond the "blue ice" runway. To my left was an ocean of ice with what looked like several prominent islands sticking out on the horizon. To my right, probably ten or more miles away were pointed peaks at the far end of the Patriot Hills range. Behind me, a half mile away, were the multiple red, white and blue tents and minor structures of the Patriot Hills camp.

Holy crap! I'm in Antarctica…and in the middle of nowhere!

The first person to greet us was Todd Passey, the guide for the other four climbers. He had been on the ice with other climbers for over a month. His leathery, tanned face and scratchy looking beard showed it. As I watched him interact with the group, my immediate impression of Todd was that he was a grisly veteran with a bit of bravado in him. A good guy who had been around the block a few times. I was not far off the mark.

Todd waited patiently while we all took turns getting awesome photos of the Illyushin on the "blue ice" runway, while trying not to slip and bust our butts. The ALE folks were scurrying around, getting bags off the plane and zooming off on snowmobiles pulling sleds of baggage. It was a pretty amazing operation.

After a few minutes, Todd called us together for a few ground rules to get us to the camp. He emphasized that we should not underestimate the low temperatures and pointed out that the first job when we got to the camp was to get the tents up.

"Safety and warmth first."

I asked where our guide, Vern Tejas, was. Todd quickly informed us that he was still at Vinson Base Camp and we would just meet him there—"weather permitting." Then he pointed in the direction of the camp.

"Let's get moving."

Shortly after we started our short trek to the camp area at Patriot Hills, I realized that distances are deceiving. I was all excited and started out at a brisk pace, thinking I could cover the distance in a few minutes. Fifteen minutes later it looked like we were just as far away as when we started. I was already starting to sweat inside my forty below parka.

The going was really not that tough. The landscape was almost completely flat, though when I looked back at the Illyushin after about twenty minutes, I realized that we were working up a very mild incline. With a fairly full backpack and double plastic boots walking on shifting snow and sometimes bare ice, the little hike to the only "civilization" in sight eventually became a bit of a chore before we got there.

By the time we reached the camp and set our packs down, my inner layers were completely soaked and my face seemed like it was frozen.

Nice start, David!

The tents and our mountain gear bags were already piled in a heap next to some other tents on the left side of the encampment. The ALE crew had done a good job of sorting and delivering the gear. We watched Todd demonstrate the proper tent building technique, then followed the leader. Fortunately, the wind was not blowing and the sun stayed clear of clouds, so we had no problem setting up four tents to form our mini-camp.

There was little to do except go to bed. After all, it was almost 1:30 A.M. Not that you could tell from the sunny blue skies. At this time of the year in Antarctica, the sun simply never gets below about thirty degrees above the horizon. It rotates around the sky like the end of the small hand on a clock—except counterclockwise!

That night, I was snoring loudly almost before my head hit my makeshift pillow—just ask Jim!

Our breakfast was served at Patriot Hills in a community tent near our individual tents. Not the big community tent with full time cooks, beverage service, wine and fruits galore which was reserved for climbers contracting directly with ALE. Not the medium size community tent used by the cross-country skiers who were in Antarctica for the sole purpose of being dropped off sixty to six hundred miles from the South Pole with the intent of working their way face first into the Katabatic winds to the South Pole in ten, twenty, thirty, or sixty days. But rather, we were assigned the smallest community tent on the compound, with a stove, a sink, a snow melting water container at one end and a few folding "church" tables crunched together at the other end.

Home.

I was the second one up, besides Todd of course. Dave was sitting at one of the tables reading a book and Todd was scrounging through some bags looking for something to cook. As usual, I had overdressed and was cooking inside my jacket within minutes. For some reason, perhaps because of the stories my law partner told about his trip to Antarctica, I had expected to be freezing constantly, whether outside or in tents.

However, the temperature inside our dining tent was quite comfortable and even too warm when the stove was going full blast.

After breakfast, all seven of the Alpine Ascents climbers gathered around as Todd showed us how to prepare our ascenders for the climb up the fixed rope. His fingers nimbly bent and twisted the rope into figure eight knots and other loops as we watched. Most of the other guys were very familiar with the ropes and knots and quickly imitated Todd's work. I, on the other hand, suddenly remembered why I had flunked the Boy Scout knot tying test when trying to become a tenderfoot.

David, try not to look too much like an idiot.

Rather than ask Todd to demonstrate again, I saw that Craig seemed to have a good hang of the knots and got him to "show me the ropes."

Okay, bad pun.

Then Todd started on the next part with another set of knots that was even more complicated. I was hopelessly lost.

Fortunately, I was not the only one who needed help. Everyone pitched in and soon I was tying perfect figure eight knots and had an ascender tied snugly on a three foot line with a loop for a carabiner and another loop to attach to my harness. We had fun burning off and twisting the cut ends of the rope with a cigarette lighter while trying not to scorch our fingers. A similar but faster process was used to create safety ropes to attach to our backpacks and ice axes. Everyone and everything would be attached in some way or the other when we went up the fixed rope to high camp at Vinson. I couldn't wait.

And for once, we did not have to wait too long. The calm weather held up. Early that afternoon, we were instructed to pack up camp and get ready for the one hour flight to Vinson Base Camp.

The red Twin Otter airplanes which were parked about a hundred yards away from our dining tent were quite cool. Propeller driven, they each had three skis attached, two under each wing and one under the cockpit. They were secured by wires to prevent them from sliding away or tipping over in the wind. Each plane held up to ten passengers, with a minimal stowage area for baggage in the rear.

The Twin Otters were piloted by a Russian crew of two, under contract with ALE. At various times the crew could not fly if they had been on duty for more than twelve hours or if it was meal time. However, on the day after we arrived at Patriot Hills, they were ready to go pretty quickly. Soon I was climbing the two step ladder into the fuselage and placing my butt into one of the small, fold down seats inside.

Now it was getting exciting. As remote as we felt at Patriot Hills, we would now be set down on a glacier in the valley below Mt. Vinson over a hundred miles from anything or anyone, with absolutely no way to return unless and until the Twin Otters showed up.

Todd and the seven of us were able to spread out comfortably inside the plane. The other Twin Otter was much more crowded. I watched as the Japanese gentlemen, the Canadian couple, the Koreans, the Poles, and the Dane and his guide disappeared into the other aircraft. It reminded me of colorfully dressed clowns all fitting into a single small VW!

We were all heading for the same place with the same goal in mind—the highest point in Antarctica. So far we were traveling in tandem and we would all be on the mountain at the same time. However, I wondered whether we would stay together once there. The Poles and the Koreans looked incredibly fit and the Canadians seemed raring to go.

Our Twin Otter zoomed down a snow runway for only a few hundred yards before we were airborne. My eyes stayed glued to the windows, taking in the amazing views. Below me was a rough, windblown ocean of snow and ice for as far as I could see in all directions, interrupted from time to time with craggy peaks of jagged rocks poking out of the frozen white sea.

Once we got near Vinson Massif, the peaks forming the Ellsworth Range got higher and higher with glaciers and huge crevasses abounding right and left. Some of the crevasses were at least twenty feet wide and a half mile long, with no discernible bottom. Running along the bottom of the ridges of rock, the crevasses formed a barrier to the mountains. Not that anyone could ever get to these mountains on foot anyway!

After what seemed like an endless series of peaks and valleys, Todd mentioned that we were approaching the Branscomb Glacier on which the Vinson Base Camp was situated. I strained my eyes to try to see Mt. Vinson, but the cloud cover was too low.

The Twin Otter flew past the glacier, then circled sharply to the left as if on a hairpin highway off ramp, only counterclockwise. After making a two hundred seventy degree turn, the plane was lined up perfectly to land on the glacier. We slowly glided down into the pure whiteness. I suppose the propellers were still rotating, but we seemed to be descending in complete silence. I could not tell where the sky ended and where the snow started.

The pilots brought the plane down smoothly onto the surface. There was almost no bump at all. Soon the plane was skimming up a gentle incline towards a few yellow tents dotted on the glacier ahead of us.

Moments later, the door opened and we stepped out onto the Branscomb Glacier. A very tanned man with a big smile, dressed entirely in purple velvet from head to toe, greeted us.

"Welcome to Vinson Base Camp! I've been waiting here for you for seven days."

The man was Vern Tejas, our guide and one of the greatest mountain climbers on the planet, having climbed all of the Seven Summits, including Everest, seven times each. Jim had climbed Aconcagua with Vern a few years before and had told me he was a famous womanizer with a babe in every port, or more accurately, in every country with any high mountains. My first impression on seeing him, though, was that he looked like a gay Hobbit!

First impressions can be deceiving. After setting up our tent and gathering for some hot chocolate in Vern's "Posh" tent, a blue and white nylon tepee of sorts, we learned that Vern had just gotten married—to a voluptuous redheaded attorney from a large law firm in New York. And the nuptials had been performed at the summit of Mt. Vinson on the first climb of the season.

As an attorney myself, I couldn't help asking who performed the ceremony, trying to determine whether the marriage was legit.

"Todd did the honors," he said, referring to the other guide.

"Really. I hate to tell you this, but, unless they have different rules down here, I don't think a mountain guide can perform a marriage ceremony," I said. "Are you planning on making it official back in the States?"

"Oh, but Todd was ordained as a minister early on and still is as far as we know," he came back. "Just in case, my wife is checking out the legalities of it back in New York as we speak. It's not a problem."

"Okay," I said with a healthy dose of skepticism. Vern frowned in my direction.

"What are we having for dinner," Johan asked, changing the subject.

"Oatmeal," said Vern with a straight face.

I looked at Jim, who smiled broadly. Vern was a great kidder and an even greater mountain cook. "Oatmeal" was always his response to any question about meals. But strangely enough, not once did we have oatmeal on this trip. That would have ruined Vern's reputation for culinary excellence.

Indeed, Vern's meals were delicious. Many hours were spent in the "Posh" watching him masterfully cook meats, rice dishes, pasta, french toast, quesadillas, eggs and bacon, and the like on two burners, all the while keeping a large pot of water boiling with fresh melted snow.

The "Posh" tent was set up over a dug out trench in the snow, leaving two hard-packed bench-like seats to the left and right and the kitchen counter of snow in the rear. A slit in the rear allowed the steam from the pots and pans to escape, and a single pole in the middle held the entire "tepee" up. There was no ground cloth, but with several layers of bed pads beneath our butts and down booties on our feet, the "Posh" was usually quite comfortable. In fact, when all of us crammed into the tent while Vern was cooking, it was almost too hot.

After sipping on hot chocolate, telling a few stories, and getting to know Vern a bit, we went outside to explore the environs of Vinson Base Camp.

Other than one small hangar-like tent in the middle of the camp, which was the ALE communications tent, there were no structures larger than the two or three man tents like ours. Todd and Vern had the only "Posh" tents. All in all, there were maybe ten or twelve small tents scattered loosely around the ALE facility. Red flags around the perimeter of the camp marked the outer limits of safe walking without encountering crevasses.

The most important feature of Vinson Base Camp, of course, was the outside lavatory, billed as the "toilet with the most beautiful view in the world." Upon use, I must concur with that description. Nowhere else can you sit on a wide open, uncovered and unsheltered box with a toilet seat on top of it and look out on the stunning Branscomb Glacier and the surroundings hills and valleys of pure white snow and ice with the sun glistening and tinting the distant clouds a pale shade of pinkish grey. Taking a dump on this particular commode was a pleasure hard to fully describe.

Not to be crude (okay it is crude, but if you want to know the full facts from a regular guy you have to include the gross with the beautiful), we were not allowed to pee in the same wonderful throne with a view. Apparently, the pee and the crud don't mix well and make it much harder for ALE to dispose of the waste. So, we were given strict instructions to pee in the designated pee hole first and then go #2 in the commode.

On that note, pee holes were pivotal to the environment and to our personal hygiene protocols. Since nothing melts away in Antarctica, if people liberally urinated wherever they wanted as if in the Appalachian woods, soon the entire Vinson Base Camp and the trail through the snow and crevasses to the summit would be a permanent "yellow brick road." Consequently, a single pee hole is established at each camp and we were strictly prohibited from going anywhere else other than in a pee bottle. Vern told us that there was one pee hole halfway up to the first camp, but otherwise any peeing on the trail would have to be into pee bottles or we would just have to hold it until we got to camp.

The luxury of the Base Camp disappeared higher up the mountain. From that point on, the same type of wag bags we used at Aconcagua were required, as the inner regions of Antartica have no wildlife or even any bacteria, no one wants to wreck its pure and pristine condition. Of course, we were personally responsible for bringing our own crap back down from the higher camps.

Been there, done that.

Halfway through the first afternoon at Vinson Base Camp, I was surprised to see the Canadian couple loaded with full backpacks and pulling sleds behind them as they worked their way up the glacier. It took them about an hour to climb up the slope immediately above the camp and disappear beyond the ridge. Apparently, they planned on establishing a camp higher up on the glacier without taking a night to acclimatize at base camp.

We had no such plans. Alpine Ascents is very conservative when it comes to acclimatization. The year before, we had taken our time on Aconcagua and used more camps than most, but it made for easier climbing days and kept us strong for the summit push. Similarly, our schedule on Vinson called for a full night at Base Camp, which was at approximately 7500 feet, two nights and one rest day at the first camp at the base of the fixed rope at just over 10,000 feet, and two nights with another rest day in between at high camp at 13,500 feet, before attempting to summit.

Apparently, the Canadians planned on moving up much more quickly. Certainly their choice.

Temperatures dropped precipitously when the sun rotated behind some of the surrounding ridges that evening. There was little to do other than to slip into our forty below sleeping bags and try to stay warm. I wore several layers of fleece inside my Mountain Hardwear Ghost bag, and remained snuggled in it the entire night, with the exception of one cold trip to the pee hole. I was still not completely used to going to bed in continuous "daylight," so my actual sleep time was sporadic at best. I was grateful that the next morning, Vern did not seem to be in that much hurry to hit the trail. Every bit of sleep would pay benefits later on.

Around ten thirty the next morning, with the peak of Mt. Vinson clearly visible beyond the steep ridge to our north, we finally strapped all our provisions onto sleds, adjusted our harnesses around our waists, hoisted up our backpacks onto our shoulders, and hooked up into a four man rope team for the trek up to the first camp. Most of the other groups, including the other Alpine Ascents team, had already left.

Vern would lead our rope team, now dubbed the Katabatic Crew by Jim, making sure that we kept clear of any crevasses or unstable snow bridges. I went second with Johan and Jim behind me. Each of us were tied in front and back with our sleds in between. We were just far enough apart that carrying on conversations as we hiked was difficult, if not impossible.

The first few steps are always the toughest for me, as I work to develop a good breathing pattern and my leg muscles adjust. As usual, I dressed too warmly, underestimating the heat generated from the sun and from our efforts in ascending the gradual slope above Base Camp. It is hard to explain how the sun, all that white snow, and the ice work together to exponentially magnify the heat generated inside layers of fleece and down parkas. Within twenty minutes of starting out, I was sweating like a pig. Fortunately, after we reached a small level spot at the top of a ridge, Vern stopped the rope team to remove clothing. He made it clear that there would be no more interim stops to adjust clothing between the planned hourly rest stops the remainder of the day, but he was making an exception this first time. Thereafter, if we needed to adjust clothing or gear between normal one hour rest stops, we would have to do it on the move.

I quickly removed my entire down parka and stuffed it into the top of my backpack, leaving me with just a layer of Capilene and a Patagonia shirt on top. I also had one too many layers on my legs, but was only able to unzip the sides of my Gore-Tex pants for a bit of ventilation before Vern gave us his two minute warning.

For the rest of the day, despite the fact that the air was cold enough to freeze my sweat, I continued to drip profusely as the sun continued to bake us. The only prudent thing to do under such conditions was to keep moving and to keep the breaks short. That is exactly what we did.

I also mimicked Vern as he scooped up snow in his beanie and dumped it on his head to keep from over-heating. The snow felt equally wonderful on my head when I tried the same trick.

Fortunately, the pace was moderate and the slopes we were ascending were gentle. After the first break, I fell into a comfortable rhythm and breathing pattern. I kept my head down, making sure I kept up with Vern while staying far enough behind to avoid the rope slacking too much. The rope needed to slide along the ground most of the way. If I fell back at all, the rope would raise up and get too taut. If I went too fast, the rope would be too slack and get caught up in my crampons. So, I had to almost perfectly match Vern's pace all day long.

And it was a long day.

My biggest struggle that day was when, after about three hours, we reached the top of the main part of the Branscomb Glacier and turned to our left. At that point the fifteen degree slope increased by about five to ten degrees for about a half hour. For the most part, we had been following wands placed in the snow by others and the trail left by the other groups ahead of us. Footing was solid and packed down. But in this section, which apparently held the greatest crevasse risk, Vern chose his own route through virgin snow.

My only thoughts were that if the other groups had gone up on their trail safely, we should stick to that trail, right?

But I said nothing, just following Vern into the "unknown." Several times I felt and heard what seemed like a hollow base below my steps. Over these areas, the sound of my steps was eerie, with a slightly delayed echo. I imagined a wide open crevasse two feet beneath me.

Now I know why we are roped up...

Fortunately, Vern knew what he was doing. We reached the top of the rise without any incident. But at that point, my nerves and legs were sufficiently frazzled that next three hours to the low camp were a slow, tortuous test of my perseverance. I was hot, my legs and shoulders were tired, and I needed to pee.

Tell me again why I voluntarily paid $30,000 to put myself through this!

Six hours into the climb, we finally saw tents set up ahead. On the right beyond the tents, I could also see the steep ridge on which the fixed rope to the upper camp was supposedly anchored. My legs were shot, but I started to relax, thinking we were almost there.

Fifteen minutes later as we passed that set of tents and kept going, my relaxation changed to distress.

"Okay, Vern, I'm a bit confused," I shouted up ahead, "weren't we supposed to camp back there?"

"No, I like it better up near the fixed rope—at Camp 1.2," Vern replied.

"Super..., Camp 1.2, why didn't I think of that," I mumbled to myself as I plodded ahead, my legs and my mind now completely numb.

Just keep going. Ignore the pain. We've got to be getting close.

About a half hour later we finally spied Todd's "Posh" tent in the distance. His group, now designated as the Sustrugi Five (named after the uneven formation of windblown snow on the icy Antarctica plains) had left an hour or more ahead of us that morning and had already set up camp. Craig and Mark greeted us with "well dones" and "good job, guys" as we reached our destination for that day. I was too tired to respond.

I dropped my backpack to the ground and slumped down beside it, still hitched to my sled and the other guys. Vern worked his way back to me, coiling the rope as he went. He smoothly detached the rope from my harness.

"Take a few minutes to snack and get some water, then we need to get the tents up," he advised.

Forget that. I'm not moving an inch from this spot for the next hour.

But my thoughts were not spoken out loud. Vern had a way about him that exuded authority. On the few occasions I had raised any queries that day, he had exhibited a complete aversion to any questioning of his decisions or instructions.

So, five minutes after I slumped down in complete exhaustion after the seven hour trek from Base Camp, I rose, sucked it up, and helped Jim set up our tent. I must admit that Jim handled more of that chore than I did. But I did manage to provide some assistance.

Strangely enough, I had completely forgotten that I needed to pee.

Amazingly, within thirty minutes of arriving at Camp 1.2, and after finally using the designated pee hole, I felt like a new man. I looked around and saw that we were near the end of a long valley of snow surrounded on three sides by high ridges. Above the ridge beyond our camp was the peak of Mt. Shinn, a spectacular 15,000'er, the shape of which reminded me of a huge, white Hershey's Kiss. The stunning view of Shinn, with the sun filtering through the clouds surrounding it, simply mesmerized me and melted away the aches and pains in my shoulders and legs.

One third of the way there, David. Good job. Just keep going.

Rest day at low camp started slowly. With the sun rotating behind the ridge to our north during the night, making temperatures drop to very frigid levels, we stayed in our tents until almost eleven. Vern had it all figured out. At ten 'til eleven, the sun rotated far enough to the west to come out from behind the ridge and begin warming everything. By the time we joined him for hot chocolate and breakfast ten minutes later, its rays were streaming through the steam hole in the tent, providing ample solar heat with no batteries.

After breakfast, we grabbed our ascenders and practiced working our way around a triangular fixed rope Vern had set up for training. He patiently demonstrated, then watched and encouraged us as we climbed up, across, and down the practice rope, maneuvering our carabiners, then our ascenders past each anchor. Once we had mastered going "up", we had to practice going down. This time, the ascenders would be moved across the anchor first, followed by the carabiner. At all times when crossing an anchor, the carabiner had to be on the uphill side of the anchor.

Jim and Johan had used fixed ropes and ascenders several times before, so they had a bit of an advantage on me at first. However, after about forty-five minutes of practice, I felt comfortable enough and was able to more or less keep up as we worked our way around the triangle.

The next step was to practice on the bottom five hundred feet of the actual fixed rope. Vern, always looking out for our safety, roped us up to walk the quarter mile to the bottom of the ridge and the first fixed rope anchor. There he demonstrated the proper technique once again and then we started climbing. We were not the first on the fixed rope. All the other groups except the two Alpine Ascents teams had eschewed a rest day and were steadily working their way up the rope, high above us. We thought we could see the Polish guys and the Canadians about halfway up. At times, it looked like they were in the same place for thirty minutes at a time.

It must be tough going up there.

But at the bottom, without backpacks, it was a breeze. Within minutes we were at the second anchor several hundred vertical feet up the ridge. We all passed the anchor smoothly and kept heading up. The next section was steeper, probably somewhere around thirty five degrees slope. Still, it was not difficult to climb, especially with the ascender to slide up and pull up on as we went. I felt confident despite this being my first fixed rope experience.

Going back down, we took turns passing each other, Vern meticulously instructing us on the proper technique. I paid close attention to his instructions, but also enjoyed the incredible view from up on the

265

ridge. It was a glorious, clear day. We had nowhere to go and nothing on our backs!

This is the life!

As we practiced our fixed rope techniques, I had noticed the Sustrugi Five being led by Todd up the valley towards a lookout point on a col near Camp 1.2. They were carefully roped up, as the area was notorious for hidden crevasses. It only took them about thirty minutes to reach the col. By the time we were almost back to the bottom of the fixed rope, they were returning to camp. I was getting hungry, so I figured we would be joining them.

But we were not going back to the tents. Having seen our Alpine Ascents comrades hike up to the col for a nice view, we decided to do likewise, quickly roping up and working our way across some unstable looking areas until we reached the path taken by Todd and his crew.

The climb up to the col looked a lot easier when we were watching the others do it an hour before. Most of the way was a gentle rise up the valley. But as we got closer, the slope got steeper and steeper. Finally, we were climbing thirty degree switchbacks, this time without any ascenders for balance. My legs were starting to burn by the time we reached the top.

The view was worth every step up the steep slope. The valley spread out before us in its white/blue splendor as far as we could see. In front of us, however, was a perfect pyramid of black rock interrupting the smooth expanse of snow. It was as if the Pharoahs had plunked down a fourth pyramid in the middle of the Antarctic mainland, thousands of miles from any civilization. Of course, this pyramid was not man-made; but for me, its perfectly symmetrical shape did lend credence to the theory of intelligent design.

We took turns negotiating a slick section of "blue" ice to get to the edge of the col for pictures with the perfect pyramid behind us. Vern and Jim stood precariously close to the edge of the ledge. I did not venture that close, but still posed for the same photo (which came out just fine).

I was famished by the time we got back to the tents. Late that afternoon, Vern served very tasty pork chops for dinner and we got to bed early. It was the end of a wonderful relaxing day. I had a feeling that the next day would not be so easy.

Climbing to the bottom of the fixed rope the next morning was a lot tougher with full backpacks. Thankfully, Vern had stashed an extra tent, several canisters of fuel, and surplus food bags up at high camp on prior trips in December. So we were able to leave a sizeable cache of gear and food at the low camp. Whatever we did not need, we did not carry, including Vern's "Posh" tent, which he reluctantly left behind.

At first, Vern actually set a pretty slow pace. However, even with deliberate steps and a manageable load, the climbing was much more difficult than the day before. This time I started out with three light layers on and my heavy down parka available in the top of my pack. Clouds were partially blocking the sun, so the heat did not build up as quickly as on the prior days. Nevertheless, by the time we reached the fixed ropes, the sun shone brighter. Before hitching my ascender to the fixed rope, I followed Vern's example and stripped down to a single layer and zipped open my pants legs to the max.

"Breathe, breathe, breathe and take it slow," Vern advised as we started up the rope.

That sounded good to me.

I felt fine despite the added weight on my back. Soon I matched Vern step for step as he led the way up the line. With Vern holding the fixed rope steady above me, I confidently worked my way up several hundred feet.

As the slope got steeper, I placed more weight on the ascender and used it to pull myself up the next step. On a couple of pulls, my ascender seemed not to fully catch and slipped back a few inches. I figured my technique was a bit off and concentrated on keeping the ascender tight to the rope. Another fifty feet and it was still slipping, just enough to throw off my rhythm. Not wanting to look stupid, I said nothing and just kept working my way up the line, trying to keep within a few yards of Vern's rear end. He was like a never stopping mountain machine, constantly and seemingly effortlessly moving one foot up above the other. I tucked my head down and concentrated on each step and each push and pull on the ascender.

"What the ★★★k!" I shouted as the gadget slipped back almost two feet, nearly sending me into a backwards somersault.

I steadied myself precariously against the rope.

"You okay?" Vern asked, as I straightened back up and caught my breath.

"Yeah, the ascender just slipped," I replied, thinking that I must have held it wrong or something.

About twenty feet further up, the damn ascender slipped again.

"Shit! What am I doing wrong?" I said in Vern's direction.

He stopped, stepped down to my level and tried to maneuver my ascender up and down. It was not catching correctly for him either.

"Okay, David, you take mine and I'll use yours," Vern said.

"Are you sure? I can get by if I don't pull on it as much."

"No, believe me, before we reach the top, you will need all the help you can get. Safety first."

"Okay, you don't have to convince me," I said, as Vern immediately performed the untying and re-tying of knots as needed to change the ascenders.

From that point on, my new ascender worked like a charm. I have no idea how Vern managed with the flawed gadget, but he could climb this slope in his sleep with no fixed rope anyway.

After about two hours on the fixed rope, we had climbed about 1200 vertical feet and began to approach an outcropping of rocks on the ridge just to our left. The Sustrugi Five, who started up the rope ahead of us had taken a break up near those rocks, so I was hoping for a similar rest. At this point, two of our friends in the other group, Craig and Mark, had almost reached what looked like the top of the fixed rope and the other three were about three quarters of the way up.

Don't worry about them, David. Just concentrate on what you are doing and take it one step at a time.

Just then, Vern took off like he had boosters in his boots. Jim pushed by Johan and me to join Vern in the lead. Soon they were several hundred feet ahead of us, plowing upwards at a furious pace. Keeping to our steady, plodding pace, Johan and I were quickly left in the "dust".

"No reason to hurry, David," Johan said. "We take it at our own speed. I'll be right here behind you."

I could have kissed the man, because I was not able to increase the rate of my ascent and I was thankful not to be left completely behind.

In truth, Johan later told me he was also struggling a bit at this point. He was grateful that I was not also racing up to the rocks.

Within minutes, Vern reached the rocks and made a left turn. Soon he was setting up a temporary lunch spot. Jim reached him within moments. Johan and I took our time, finally staggering into the rocks about ten minutes later. Once stopped, I immediately got cold and had to pull out my parka for warmth.

"Get some water and eat, eat, eat," Vern instructed us.

"Halfway there?" I managed to ask.

"Maybe a third," Vern replied.

Shit.

"Well, we've got all day, right?" I said, but instantly regretted opening my mouth.

"Got to pick up the pace," Vern said sternly. "The weather is supposed to be coming in and we want to be off the fixed rope before then. We need to get going in five minutes."

Damn it. You've been here for fifteen minutes. I just got here. Gimme a break!

I didn't dare say anything. I grabbed a Snickers bar and munched as fast as I could, washing it down with healthy swigs of water. Before I even got the remnants of the nuts and chocolate down, Vern gave us the two minute warning and lifted his pack onto his shoulders. I rushed to stuff my parka back into the pack and reluctantly hoisted my pack up and onto my back. I knew the rest of the afternoon was going to be a tough physical and mental battle.

Come on, David. We're only climbing 3000 feet today. You did almost 5000 on Elbert and back down with almost no training. Just suck it up and climb!

I stepped back into line behind Vern as he resumed the ascent. The slope kept getting steeper and steeper the higher we went. Amazingly, the short rest gave my tired muscles enough of a break that I kept up with Vern for the first thirty minutes.

As we settled into a tempo, now with two deep breaths per step, Vern spontaneously began singing "Ol' Man River."

"Tote dat barge, lift dat bale..." He actually had a very good voice, and the sound of the steady melody took my mind off the pains and aches crying out from my thighs and calves.

Only occasionally looking back, Vern was in his element, leading a team up the steep Antarctic ridge, singing his heart out and enjoying every minute of it.

My spirits were strangely lifted by the music. When he stopped after a few songs, I asked him if he knew any more tunes. That was all it took. He had plenty more folk songs in him and kept the concert up for another hour.

By now the Sustrugi Five were long gone. We were alone on the fixed rope.

Just as we reached a high point at the top of a particularly steep section, Vern told us all to move our carabiners and ascenders above an anchor and sit in place. There on a forty-five degree slope, we took just our second rest in almost five hours.

Ahead of us the fixed rope turned a bit to our right then back to the left up an even steeper, knife edge ridge with steep drop offs on both sides.

"Let's be careful in this next section," Vern warned. "That's the end of the fixed rope at the top of that ridge."

Talk about good news and bad news. He may as well have said, "We're almost there, but look what we have to do to get there!"

One step at a time, David. One step at a time.

The climb to the right went quickly and surprisingly easy after our rest. But then we reached the last narrow ridge.

Fortunately, I have no real fear of heights. If I did, this last section on the fixed rope would have been a nightmare. On the left, the slope dropped off at about fifty degrees. On the right, even steeper – at least sixty-five degrees. The ridge itself was barely two feet wide.

I disregarded the view to my right or left and focused intensely on each step up the ridge. Prior climbers and Vern had left V-shaped steps most of the way up the ridge, making the first part relatively secure. At this point, I was taking three breaths between each step, painstakingly moving up like a snail climbing a sand dune. Behind me, I could feel Jim and Johan's frustration at my plodding pace. But they said nothing. I ignored everything except my breathing and each careful step.

About two-thirds up the final section, Vern turned sideways and worked his way up the rest of the ridge one foot over the other, showing off and completely messing up the nice V-shaped steps I had been following.

Son-of-a-bitch! What are you doing to me?

The rest of the way, I had to dig in my own V-shaped steps. I was not about to try the slick sideways foot over foot technique Vern had just demonstrated. The last thing I wanted to do was to catch a crampon and trip at this point. Once again, I tipped my head down and took it one step at a time.

"Smile," Vern shouted a few minutes later. He snapped a few pictures as I finally reached the top. I gave him a very weak grin and just kept going until I could unhook from the line and collapse in a pile on a flat area to our left. I watched as Johan and Jim posed for the camera with the whole valley back to the base camp behind them, now over 4000 feet below.

I was seriously tired, but happy. We took an extended break, got plenty of water and snacks. The weather seemed to be holding, though some clouds were moving in on the high ridges above us.

Almost there.

"So, where exactly is the high camp?" I asked before we next got started. "How much farther?"

"Just over that hill," Vern replied, pointing up the slope to our right. At only about thirty degrees, the slope did not look that challenging.

My jubilation turned to exasperation when we got to the top of the hill and it just kept going...going...and going. Worse yet, after a full day of sun, the snow was softer on the hill, making footing unstable. Every few steps, I post-holed up to my calve or knee, expending extra energy just to keep moving. Every time I slowed down, Vern jerked on the rope to tell me to pick up the pace.

A half hour passed and the hill seemed just as long. An hour passed and I thought I was going to die.

"How much farther?" I mumbled in Vern's direction.

No response.

"HOW MUCH FARTHER?" I yelled.

"We'll get there when we get there," Vern replied. "Just breathe harder and keep going."

Damn it, Vern. I'm breathing as hard as I can, but I'm about to dig a snow cave and call it a day!

I didn't dare verbalize my thoughts, but they almost slipped out.

Just when I was truly ready to drop in my tracks, Todd popped over the crest in front of us. Amazingly, I had pushed myself to the limits and the finish line was right in front of me.

"Welcome to High Camp! Well-done guys! We've got hot water ready for you."

I stepped up the last few yards to the top of the crest and took the scene in. Dug into the snow five feet beyond the crest were two rows of tents protected by snow walls on the far side and a few more tents beyond the snow wall, with probably twelve tents in all. To the right was another small wall with a red flag on a stick beyond it. Oh yes, the high camp peehole!

Vern kept walking through a narrow gap between the tents over to the far snow wall and punched his ski poles into the ground.

"All your crampons, ice axes and poles go here on this wall," he said as he started to unclip the rope and reel us in. "Now might be a good time to put on a few more layers and your down parka and pants. The winds are coming in."

Almost instantly, the temperature seemed to drop ten degrees, then another ten, as a stiff wind swept across the high camp. I then realized why the tents were so well dug in.

By the time I added fleece layers and pulled on my down pants and parka, I was freezing. Momentarily, while sitting down on the cold snow and ice, I started to shiver uncontrollably. The only thing I could do to stop it was to get back to work, helping Vern and Jim clear a spot in which to put two tents side by side beyond the crampon/ice axe wall.

We had two shovels to work with, but the ground we were trying to level up for the tents was almost pure ice—too hard to dig out. Instead, Vern instructed us to dig up fresh snow from around the site and create a new, more level floor.

For the next hour, we shoveled and dug snow, borrowed chunks of snow from stray snow walls, stomped and leveled – never to Vern's satisfaction. He demonstrated what he wanted and we went back to work. Johan seemed a bit out of it, but helped us toward the end. Finally, the snow was packed and leveled enough to meet Vern's approval and we were permitted to erect the tents. This time the tents were snugged right up to each other so that the front vestibules were only about four feet apart. That way, food could be transferred between the tents without going outside.

Something told me it was about to get very cold if Vern wants to be able to pass food without exiting the tents.

Sometime that evening as we finished setting up camp, one of the Polish guys appeared from the direction of Mt. Vinson. He had safely returned from the summit, only three days after landing at Vinson Base Camp. Later, after I was sound asleep in the tent, I understand the other three Polish climbers also returned to high camp after successful summits. None of them had taken any rest days to acclimatize. I later learned that two of them were nauseous and sick most of the climb but just gutted it out.

Crazy bastards!

That night the sun rotated behind the ridges across the valley to our left. With no direct sun on the camp, everything began to freeze in seconds. Vern waited until just before we went to bed to fill our water bottles with hot water. The bottles went inside insulated covers and then were pushed to the bottom of our sleeping bags, providing an almost pulsating source of heat. At first it was almost too hot inside the sleeping bag, but after an hour or so, I was happy to have the warm bottles inside, as the temperatures were clearly dropping.

I always like to have some fresh cold water available in the tent in case I get thirsty as I sleep. On this night, I had an extra half bottle of lukewarm water, which I placed inside the insulated inner boot of my double plastics. When I reached for that bottle barely two hours after hitting the hay, it was frozen solid, inside an insulated boot inside the tent. Don't ask me how cold it was outside. I am just glad that I was buried in a forty-below down sleeping bag with plenty of fleece layers on inside and hot water bottles keeping me warm.

We essentially stayed hunkered down inside our sleeping bags for the next two days. The first day was a scheduled rest day and the weather was pretty clear, but it was too cold outside to linger or visit, except in Todd's "posh" tent, or if we had to use the pee hole or utilize our wag bags.

Views of Mt. Shinn that first day at high camp were stunning and Jim, Mark and Craig talked constantly about the prospect of climbing it the day after climbing Vinson.

The next day, our first possible summit day, Mt. Shinn was completely obscured by some of the nastiest looking venticular clouds I've ever seen. The winds at the top of that mountain were probably 80–120 miles per hour according to the guides. Similar venticular clouds blanketed the ridges to our north and the higher peaks in the direction of Vinson to the east.

Shortly before breakfast, Vern announced that no one would be going to the summit that day.

The Canadian couple apparently did not get that message, as shortly after breakfast, they began climbing up the valley towards Vinson. The valley looked clear enough from the camp, but winds were swirling along the ridges and Vern said, "They'll be back."

Surely enough, about two hours later, the Calgary duo trudged back into camp, confirming that the valley beyond our sight line was completely shrouded in clouds and the winds were "nasty".

There was nothing to do but catch up on our sleep or shoot the shit with the other guys in Todd's "Posh" tent – all day long. That afternoon, I stayed in the "posh" tent for about three hours to give Jim a chance to get some good sleep. My snoring had really gotten bad in the thin air of high camp and I knew he had gotten no sleep the night before. I felt great with two days rest and wanted to give him the same opportunity. Now we just had to wait for an opening.

Weather permitting! Hope it clears tomorrow.

A mixture of excitement, anticipation and trepidation, summit day is always a total rush. Vinson was no exception. We awoke to clear skies.

The venticular clouds around Mt. Shinn and the surrounding ridges were gone. The sun was shining and the winds were minimal.

Time to go!

Knowing that it would take about at least ten hours to the top and back, I made two trips to the pee-hole and enjoyed a "pregame" deposit into my third wag bag. Whenever I'm nervous, a good dump relaxes me. Plus, I did not want to have to stop on the way to the summit.

Vern was all business, quickly preparing breakfast and giving us final instructions. He said it would be seven to seven and a half hours to the top and we had to take advantage of the good weather, which could turn bad in a matter of a few hours. He said he also wanted to be the first group out of camp, as several other teams would likely be moving faster than us once on the trail. He told us to travel light, clipping everything onto our harnesses and carabiners rather than carrying a back pack. This was a change of plan I had not anticipated, but I embraced it. The lesser the load, the easier the climb.

Promptly at 9 A.M., we roped up and set out from high camp. I had two layers of Patagonia "Capilene" shirts under my down parka, a "Capilene" layer and thin trekking pants under my down pants, a warm Mountain Hardwear beanie, high altitude goggles which covered most of my nose, three sets of gloves, and two one liter bottles of water, all hooked on somehow to my harness or stuffed into pockets of my down parka. Also hanging from my harness was my ice axe, as I would be using ski poles for the first few hours. The only other weight was a Ziploc bag full of Snickers bars and almonds, a small first aid kit, a pocket knife, and my final disposable digital camera, with twenty-seven shots on it.

As usual, after thirty minutes with the sun beating down on us, we had to strip down to avoid over-heating. This time, however, Vern did not stop. We had to zip our parkas down and get our sleeves off on the move. I struggled with my gloves, my sleeves, the ski poles, the ice axe and the water bottles, but finally rearranged my parka so it was hanging in an organized fashion, without dropping anything. I began to wonder if it would have been better to have a pack after all.

The initial slope was not at all extreme and the snow was very firm from overnight temperatures, so we made good time. Soon we crested a hill and could see the ridge and peak of Mt. Vinson in front of us. It was crystal clear and looked to be only a few hours away. At first I thought Vern's estimate of seven or more hours to the summit must be wrong, but after climbing for another hour, the mountain looked just as far away. Each time we crested an incline, new inclines appeared between us and where the ridge really started to rise towards the peak. The distances were so deceiving that after a while I relied solely on my watch to determine how much progress we had made.

By late morning, the sun was in full blaze, making the entire wide valley almost mirror-like—bright, glaring and white. Even my light Windstopper gloves were too warm. My hands were moist and my hair was sweating profusely under my beanie. Off the gloves and beanie came, as I stuffed them into the space between my parka and my waist without stopping. It was too much trouble to zip them in and I knew better to ask Vern for any unscheduled stop. Not even for a minute. Amazingly, as it turned out, even at over 14,000 feet in the middle of Antarctica, I was able to climb for the next almost three hours without any gloves or anything on my head.

We took a good water and snack break after two hours. I felt great. The weather was perfect, my legs were strong, and once my parka was organized around my waist, climbing without a pack was wonderful. I munched on a handful of almonds and digested a half of a Snickers bar to keep my energy up.

Alas, fifteen minutes after we started climbing again, I felt awful. My stomach heaved and I had to go #2. I took a swig of water, trying to ease through the discomfort without stopping. Vern was moving steadily in front of me, encouraging us to breathe deep and keep up the pace. I suppressed the pain for about five minutes, but knew it wasn't going away.

"Vern, I hate to say this, but I think I have to take a dump," I finally said.

"Can't it wait until our next break?" he replied.

"Not unless I want to scrape it out of my pants."

"Didn't you go before we left the camp?"

"Yeah, practically filled the wag bag. I'm sorry. I've got to go."

The next ten minutes was one of the most embarrassing moments of my climbing career. Rather than describe the ordeal in gory detail, suffice it to say that trying to go #2 on a thirty degree slope with an alpine harness, down pants and several layers underneath, with three nearby team mates chuckling at my predicament, is not how I envisioned the majesty and triumph of climbing the highest mountain in Antarctica. Luckily, I had a few scraps of TP in one of my parka pockets and Vern was generous enough to provide an extra unused wag bag for the occasion.

I could have killed Jim when I saw him sneak a picture of me squatting on the hillside doing my business.

Unfortunately, struggling with clothing and harness and wag bag and trying to balance, etc., takes up a lot of energy at this altitude. Though I felt relieved when I finally re-tightened my harness and straightened up, I was breathing hard and my legs were tired from squatting. I had lost my edge, physically and mentally. We still had forty-five minutes until the next hourly stop and I was drained. Of course, Vern quickly made it clear that he intended to make up the time by picking up the pace.

What had been an enjoyable jaunt for me up to this point became a miserable existence. Over the next half hour, my legs felt like they were giving out. I could not keep up with Vern's pace and the rope between us constantly lifted off the ground, becoming taut.

Worse yet, to our right, the young studs from the Korean national Mountain Climbing Team and their guide, threatened to overtake us.

"You must breathe harder, cheeks out, blow harder, three breaths every step," Vern warned. "Keep the pace up."

"I'm going as fast as I can. I just need a break."

"No break. We are already behind because of your unscheduled stop. You must keep going." He turned and pushed up the hill.

Damn it! This guy is going to kill me!

Following in Vern's steps, I increased the speed and intensity of my breathing until I felt like my lungs would explode. I was not about to let him beat me or leave me while the rest went to the summit.

But after ten more minutes, the rope in front of me began rising and becoming taut again. I was gasping for breath, desperately trying to keep up the pace. The Korean team slowly edged ahead of us on the slope to our right.

Vern stopped, turned, and strode down the slope until he was right in front of me.

"David, you must breathe harder and faster, or you are not going to make it."

"I can't breathe any harder. I'm doing the best I can."

"Can't? Can't?" Vern roared.

I instantly knew I made a mistake using that word.

"David, I do not pace my rope team to the slowest man on the team. We go at the pace of the second slowest. You have to pick it up. We are falling behind schedule."

"THIS IS NOT A ****IN' RACE!!" I said defiantly.

I looked around at Johan and Jim for support, but they kept silent.

I continued my retort.

"I will make it to the top. You said seven and a half hours. We're right on schedule. We've gone four hours. Looks like at most three more hours to the top. If you want to go ahead, fine, but I will be coming up behind and I assure you I will make it to the summit today. I just need a five minute break."

Vern shook his head slowly.

"David, I'm not calling you a lollygagger, or suggesting that you did not train hard enough for this climb, but..."

"Fine," I interrupted, "and I'm not calling you a mother****er, so we're even. Now let's just get going. I'll be right behind you."

"Okay, but I'll decide when we take the breaks," Vern replied. "Just keep breathing – hard!"

All out of expletives, I hung on for dear life for the next fifteen minutes before Vern finally called for a rest stop. I could have kissed him.

Lest there be any misunderstanding, despite the verbal sparring, I know that Vern was just doing his job and looking out for the safety of the entire team. When we had our "discussion", the weather was still perfect. To the less well informed, it appeared to be a day when we could take our time and pleasantly stroll along. But Vern knew from experience how quickly the conditions could change. If I was holding the team back, it was totally appropriate for him to push me to work harder. And truth be told, he was right about my conditioning for this climb. I had cut corners on my hill work, at times only running hills once a week, and I had lost only eight pounds instead of fifteen during my training. A few junk food binges that fall had left me with a bit more of a tire around my waist than I should have carried up a mountain. Now I was paying the price.

Thankfully, the ten minute rest helped me immeasurably. We were about to tackle the steepest part of the climb and I felt a sense of rejuvenation and purpose. Perhaps my pride was pushing me to greater heights. Perhaps Vern moderated the pace a bit once he saw the Koreans taking an extended break just ahead of us. Whatever the motivation or reason, I resolved to never again give Vern any excuse to berate me about my pace.

For the next forty-five to fifty minutes, we veered slightly to our left towards a series of scattered rocks. We headed straight towards a narrow pass on the north side of the Vinson ridge which loomed approximately 1500 feet above us to the right. The peak of Vinson was now behind us, but we would be making a wide u-turn up a very steep snowbank to reach the summit ridge. Then we would traverse the final summit ridge southward to the top.

Still roped up, I successfully managed to make it to the last set of rocks without incurring the wrath of our guide. To my surprise, as soon as we stopped, Vern unclipped and announced that we would go the rest of the way unroped.

"We're on solid ground now. No more crevasses," he explained. "Just stay close and follow me up the rest of the way. Use your ice axes now. No more ski poles."

In fact, at that point we cached every ounce of unnecessary gear or extra food—even surplus water. Out of any abundance of caution, I kept a bit more water than I needed. But I left all but one Snickers and a few almonds behind, lightening my load as much as possible.

Soon it was as if we were back on Mt. Elbrus, an unroped, four man line in closed ranks, heading up the steep snow bank. I stayed right behind Vern, matching him step for step, never allowing any gap to appear between us. The going was tough and my leg muscles were working hard, but I had caught my second wind.

About halfway up the steep incline, Vern stopped and mentioned that we might want to take some pictures. Looking back, I saw one of the most incredible views ever. Way down below us, just to the right of where we came from high camp, the whole cluster of five or six mountain peaks surrounding Mt. Shinn shone majestically in the sunlight. It was almost as if they had placed the Grand Tetons in the middle of the Antarctic range, almost two thousand vertical feet below us. Jim rushed up the hill to take some photos of each of us with that view in the background.

From that point on, we were all truly inspired. I focused on a red wand at the crest above and disregarded all else until I reached it, then kept going over to a rock wall near where the Koreans were taking their last break before the summit.

Up above us to the right was a treacherous looking peak which reminded my of a huge Dr. Seuss ice cream sundae, with lots of lumps and bulges culminating in a narrow pointed peak on top. While we took our final rest, we watched as the Koreans gingerly worked their way up between the rocks, making tight right and left turns as they went. Soon they were standing atop this sub-peak at the north end of the final narrow ridge to the true summit.

As soon as they disappeared beyond the peak, we followed in their footsteps. Vern admonished me to stay right behind him and to keep my ice axe firmly planted.

No shit Sherlock!

For the first time on the climb of Vinson, we were climbing on exposed ledges without any ropes to secure the way. At several places two feet to our right, the edge dropped off 1500 feet. Any misstep could be fatal. It did not help that the footing was slick and uneven. I took it slow and steady, focusing on each step, making sure to hold onto rocks beside me as much as possible while steadying my balance with my ice axe.

Actually, despite the exposure, this short climb to the sub-peak was not that tough. Within ten minutes, Vern and I reached the pinnacle and admired the view. Jim took pictures of us posing atop the peak with the sun as a backdrop, then hurried up to pose himself. Vern dropped back down to get the "Jim, Emperor of the World" photos, later displayed on Jim's website.

Seeing the footprints of the Koreans ahead of me, I decided to push ahead towards the summit, which was now just barely visible at the other end of the narrow ridge.

At this point, the top of the ridge varied from ten to fifteen feet wide, with a deathly drop off of over 1500 feet barely three or four feet to my right. I stayed cautiously clear of the edge and followed squarely within the path left by the Koreans.

Within minutes, Vern caught up and passed me on the right, walking so close to the edge that I found myself holding my breath. A little further ahead, Vern turned and posed, pointing out that the Koreans had reached the summit.

Indeed, three little dots were visible on the far bump at the end of the summit ridge. I snapped a photo of the final summit ridge, with Vern in the foreground and the Koreans atop Vinson in the distance.

The tough climb was over. Now we could fully enjoy ourselves. But not without having to traverse one more foot wide, thirty feet long ledge above a sixty foot drop, with very few places to punch in with our ice axes.

Piece of cake. Just don't look down and don't lean back!

Once through that final hurdle, Jim picked up the pace, leading the way along an even narrower ridge to the summit. I was close behind with my head down carefully focusing on each step when he stepped up onto a snowy bump in front of us, turned, threw his arms up, and let loose with a yell.

For some reason, I was surprised. From our side, the snowy bump was just the top of a narrow but gentle rise and didn't look like a peak.

"That's it?" I asked.

I didn't need an answer. As I took the last five steps, I saw that the other side of the bump dropped off sharply to a level area where the Koreans were sitting. To our right was an absolutely sheer cliff. There was certainly nothing higher than it in any direction.

I raised my ice axe and gave it my best yahooooo and shared a high five with Jim.

We've made it. We're there—at the top of Antarctica. The top of the bottom of the world!

Before I could even think, seemingly out of nowhere, Craig and Mark appeared on the other side of the Koreans. Unbenownst to me, the Sustrugi Five had taken another route to the top, bearing right and coming up the steeper south side of the summit ridge. It was a shorter but more treacherous route, requiring considerably more advanced rope skills. Moments later, Todd, Dave and Steve also appeared over the far ledge. Amazingly, we all reached the summit together – even more to celebrate.

Things got emotional when Johan stepped up onto the summit. It was his seventh of the Seven Summits and his tears flowed freely. I found myself bawling as I gave him a bear hug. My tears were initially triggered by sheer joy for his accomplishment. But then I couldn't stop crying. I had overcome a tough day with an exacting guide. Both external and self-imposed pressure had pushed me to the top. Suddenly I realized this was probably my last big mountain climb. My goggles fogged up with the moisture, so I'm not sure anyone else realized how emotional I had become.

Regular guys don't cry, right?

Wrong. But sometimes, we'd rather keep it to ourselves.

It really didn't matter. Overwhelming joy, a glorious day, a wonderful summit, how can I describe it any other way? There is no better feeling.

Vern was the last to stand on the summit, his twenty-second time atop Vinson.

As he stood there, I was tempted to yell "I told you I was going to make it, you son-of-a-gun." But I held my tongue. On top of this mountain, there was no room for negativity. There was too much to celebrate and too many people with whom to share congratulations. And besides, Vern's "encouragement" had helped me get there when I needed a kick in the ass.

After twenty minutes of watching Johan pose for pictures with placards bearing the names of his eighteen sponsors and the Koreans hold up flag after colorful flag with language we could not decipher, the Katabatic Crew climbed up for a final group photo. Vern and I flanked Jim on each side, holding our ice axes high while Johan squatted in front of us. It was a perfect picture on a perfect day.

With a half hour rest at the summit, the fatigue of the ascent was gone and I was ready to get back to high camp. The other Alpine Ascents group, the Sustrugi Five, decided to go back down the route we had come up, so they joined us as we strolled down the summit ridge, retracing our steps around the narrow ledge and back down the lower peak at the other end of the ridge.

Going down the steep snow bank was a piece of cake. The sun was still shining brightly, the views were still stunning below us, and the camraderie and smiles were ubiquitous. I marched either beside or in front of Vern, making sure he knew that I was not going to slow anyone down on the descent.

We reached our cache point in less than thirty minutes, took a short break, then roped up for the long slog down to high camp. I was surprised when Vern asked me to lead us on the way down – first on the rope line.

Shortly after we set off, I noticed that the bright sun was gone. Clouds had moved in above the north ridge to our right, partially blocking the sun's rays. The view of the peaks surrounding Mt. Shinn in front of us was also becoming shrouded. Within minutes, the temperatures started to steadily drop.

Subconsciously, I picked up the pace, lengthening my stride and plunging one foot after the other down the slope.

By the time we reached the point where I had made the unscheduled "potty" break on the way up, the weather was really closing in on us. Though we still had hundreds of yards of visibility around us, only a few patches of blue sky were visible above us. The rest was a steadily enveloping, icy mist.

I kept pushing the pace gradually faster and faster, hoping that I would not catch a crampon and make a fool of myself. I chugged water on move, adjusted my layers and gloves without stopping, and focused intensively on the trail of steps in front of me. At several places the trail seemed to split in two forks with no obvious choice of which to take. But Vern was last in the rope line and not close enough to make the choice for me. So I just plunged forward, taking what seemed to be the most direct route towards the high camp.

We took only one very short break, just long enough to munch on half a Snickers bar and to zip up our down parkas and cover our heads. With the sun gone and the icy mist swirling around us, It was really getting cold.

"Good pace, David," Vern acknowledged. "Looks like you left some energy in reserve."

"Yeah, I feel really good at this point," I responded. "But let's get going. Looks like we may not have much visibility left."

Sure enough, as we started to gradually bear to the left down the final slopes to the high camp, the clouds dropped almost down to our heads. The mist began to cloud my goggles and the footprints in the trail ahead became almost impossible to see. At some points the trail disappeared completely in front of me. But I plowed on, never breaking stride, always rediscovering the footprints just before getting lost.

Every time we reached a new down slope, I thought sure we would be able to see the tents of the high camp in front of us. But each time there was nothing in the distance.

Just keep going, faster and faster, David. You have to be almost there.

At this point, I imagined myself as an Olympic cross country skier, my two ski poles thrusting back and forth in a frenzied rush to the finish. I could feel ice forming on my beard and face, and everything else, but I had one thing in mind – getting back to camp as soon as possible.

Finally, in the distance at a thirty degree angle below us and to the left was the faint outline of the yellow tents, nestled in the snow at high camp.

"YO-HO!" I yelled at the top of my lungs. "There's the tents!"

We were still ten minutes away from the camp, but those minutes went quickly. My legs were starting to tire, but with the finish line in sight, I just kept chugging down the slope, breathing harder and harder until we were standing next to the snow wall besides our tents.

I looked around. All was quiet. We were the first ones down, so no one was there to congratulate us—except ourselves. Anti-climactic to say the least.

Looking at my watch, I realized that we had come all the way from the summit in only two hours and five minutes. The Sustrugi Five, who had been coming down behind us still were nowhere to be seen.

When Jim and Johan unclipped from the rope and came over for high fives, I realized then how cold and fast the descent had been. Jim's face and beard were completely covered in ice. Snot had poured out of his nostrils as we raced down the slopes had completely frozen, forming, using his own word, "snotsicles" almost an inch long. Johan's face was similarly iced over. Somehow I had managed to keep wiping my face as we pressed down into the mist and my goggles covered much of my face, so I did not have to scrape much ice out of my nose or beard.

About five minutes later, we caught our first glimpse of the Sustrugi Five, emerging from the mist and moving down the final slope. Jim took pictures of each of their icy faces as they arrived.

One of them commented on how our team had "just taken off," which I took as a quiet compliment to my position at the front of the rope team.

"Well done, David," Vern said as he finished coiling the rope and started to set up a pot for hot water.

I smiled, mostly to myself. The nagging feeling that I had lost some of Vern's respect on the way up the mountain was now gone. I had led us back down in tough conditions in almost record time and still felt relatively fresh. Whatever small amount of vindication I had recovered gave me a great feeling.

Twenty minutes later, I did not feel so good. Even though I was snuggled inside my sleeping bag, trying to rest, I could not stop shivering. I had pushed myself to the limits, keeping my energy and heat up to lead the team down the mountain through sheer resolve. But as soon as the excitement of making it back down was over and I stopped moving, that heat and energy disappeared. Whether it was from relief, sheer cold conditions, fatigue, or whatever, for the next half hour, I lay in my sleeping bag fighting the shivers, trying to stay still.

Finally, after I sipped on a warm cup of hot chocolate and got some hot water bottles to stuffed into my sleeping bag, the shaking stopped and I fell asleep for a good two hours. I never did see the other teams return from the summit that night.

The weather was not much better the next morning, but Vern had us up early for breakfast, announcing that we would be packing up and trekking back to Vinson Base Camp that day. Jim and a couple of the Sustrugi Five were a bit disappointed that they would not get to attempt a summit of Mt. Shinn, but they did not protest the decision.

In light of my performance on the descent the prior day, I felt confident about being able to climb down the fixed rope and pull sleds back down to base camp without too much trouble. However, I began to have doubts when Vern helped me lift my pack onto my back before setting off. As the last climbers of the season, we had to remove everything from high camp and pack it out. So, on top of all the weight I had in my pack on the way up to high camp, on the way down I also had a full tent, fly and poles, weighing another fifteen pounds, a fuel canister weighing God only knows, some extra food and a couple of metal tent anchors. My pack felt like a concrete refrigerator on my back.

Still, the other guys had equally heavy loads and I figured that I would get used to it on the hike down to the top of the fixed rope.

Suffice it to say, my pace was considerably slower as I led the rope team once again on the first leg down to the fixed rope.

Slow and steady, David. Pace yourself. Damn this pack is heavy. Forget the pack. Just keep moving.

As we approached the top of the fixed rope, I was sure that we would stop for at least a brief rest. However, Vern nixed any rest, telling us to keep our packs on and clip our carabiners and ascenders (now descenders) onto the fixed rope.

Jim and Johan went first and just kept going, quickly moving down the knife edge fifty degree ridge at the top of the fixed rope. I struggled to adjust my left arm around the rope for balance and to get my descender situated. I was already dead tired from the trek down from high camp and really could have used a five or ten minute rest before attacking the most difficult part of the descent. But that was not offered as an option.

Somehow, the rope going down the knife-edge ridge was very slack and had slid over the edge of the ridge by a yard or so. When I had been behind Vern on the way up, he had kept the rope taut, making it much easier for me to balance. Now on the steepest part of the mountain, the rope was neither taut nor on the ridge.

No matter how hard I tried to stay on the top of the narrow ridge, the rope kept pulling me down to the left. About fifty feet down from the top anchor, my left foot went over the left edge and sank into the sixty or seventy degree slope on that side of the knife edge. As I struggled to regain the top of the ridge, my crampons caught together and I went down on a knee.

Still tethered to the fixed rope by the descender and a carabiner, I was in no danger of sliding down the mountain, but now I had to exert extreme effort to get back on my feet with what felt like a refrigerator on my back. On my second try, I regained my footing, but still was not able to get back up to the ridge.

Vern told me to keep going and to try to slowly angle back onto the ridge. I sensed impatience in his voice.

I made it about two thirds down to the next anchor, never quite being able to get back up on the ridge before I went down again, collapsing in a clumsy heap. This time both legs were pinned under me. Now the tethers were really holding me on the mountain. For the first time on the whole trip, I thought I might be in real trouble. I could not get up and there was nothing but a seventy degree drop off in front of me.

Vern rushed down and immediately told me to unclip my back pack. He would take it down to the second anchor down, which was on a less steep spot. Once the pack was off, I was able to stand up, carefully scramble back to the ridge and descend quickly to the next anchor. Then I marched down to the anchor beyond it, where Vern was waiting for me.

The next segment of fixed rope looked reasonably safe, so I assumed that Vern would let me reload my back pack and continue on down the rope. I offered to try again, thinking he would expect me to carry it the rest of the way.

Wrong.

Probably for my own safety, Vern informed me that we would drag my pack down the rest of the way. But first, Vern had to rig up ropes between us similar to those we had for the sleds several days earlier.

While Vern was tying and adjusting the ropes, two of the Sustrugi Five worked their way past us, carefully unclipping their carabiners and descenders one by one from the other side of the rope. I could tell Vern was not too happy about being passed.

Before anyone else could get by, Vern announced that he was ready to go.

"Keep it steady, David," he said. "I'm hooked onto your pack as well as carrying my own pack. So I'll be holding the pack back from sliding down on top of you, but you have to keep moving. Otherwise, all the weight'll be on me."

"Definitely," I replied, somewhat ashamed that he was having to bear part of the weight of my pack, but happy to have it off my shoulders.

For the next two hours, I pulled the pack down the steep slope, working hard to keep it going when it stuck or got halfway buried in softer patches of snow. I hustled down the rope when it began to slide on icier sections. Vern constantly barked out instructions. "Slower... faster...keep up the pace...it's coming down on you, go faster..."

At each anchor, we caught our breaths as we maneuvered our carabiners and descenders across the metal pin holding the rope to the slope. I constantly checked to make sure no one was gaining ground on us from above. I did not want this awkward pack-dragging exercise to slow us down.

I was exhausted to the extent of almost ragdollishness by the time we reached the bottom end of the fixed rope. I could see that Johan and Jim had already reached the lower camp and were starting to reorganize their gear for the next leg down to Base Camp.

Vern rushed ahead to join them without saying anything except: "You can carry it from here, David. Don't keep us waiting."

I took two minutes to munch on a few almonds, swishing them down with a swig of water, and caught my breath. Then I hoisted the damned pack onto my shoulders and began the fifteen minute drudge to the lower camp.

Did I say "drudge"? More like a death march.

Generally, once I'm heading downhill on a reasonably level slope, I can coast along effortlessly, even with a full back pack. But the pack was so heavy and my legs were so wasted that every step was a painful chore.

My only thought was that I had to get there in one piece. I was not about to collapse with the back pack on again.

Somehow, I staggered into camp just before the other three of the Sustrugi Five arrived from behind me.

But there was no time to rest.

The cache we had left while we went up to high camp had to be unburied. Gear had to be shifted from our backpacks to draw-tie bags and tied securely onto the sleds. Vern seemed to be in a huge rush.

What I did not realize was that the first groups back to Base Camp had priority on the flight to Patriot Hills. Everyone on the mountain would be making it back to Base Camp the same day. We and the Sustrugi Five had to get there first to be assured of getting the first plane out. So, the next leg of the descent would be a race to the bottom.

I was not able to be much help with undigging the cache, but after getting a snack and getting a lot more water in me, I was able to unload my backpack about half way and get my sled ready to go. The only problem was that, on inspection, Vern did not approve the way I had tied the load onto my sled, requiring me to start again. In the process, I did not have time to remove my crampons and overboots to make the next few hours of the descent easier.

When every one was roped up and ready to go, Vern noticed that I still had crampons on and suggested that I take them off. Stupidly, I declined, thinking it would take too much time to get them and the overboots (which had slippery soles) off and packed up. I figured that I had come all the way from the summit down to the lower camp with crampons on, so it should not be a big deal to keep them on down to Base Camp.

Mistake #2.

Apparently recognizing that I was in no condition to lead us down at full speed, Vern put Johan in front of the rope line, with me behind him. I would have to keep up with Johan, however fast he decided to go.

It actually felt good to get going again, especially since most of the weight was now on the sleds between us. Johan started out at a good but manageable pace, and soon we passed lower camp 1.0, where the Canadians, Koreans and Polish teams had just arrived.

For now, we were in the lead, with the Sustrugi Five close behind us. The other teams would be hustling down after us.

About half-way down to Base Camp we took a rest for some water and a snack. Todd and the Sustrugi Five zipped by without stopping, led by Craig's long strides.

As they moved past us, Todd reminded us that we had to be the first ones down to get the first plane out. "The Canadians are coming!" he said, gesturing behind us.

Sure enough, I looked back and could see them closing in on us, maybe ten minutes behind us.

"Let's go," we all said at once.

From that point on, we zoomed down the slope, almost race walking. As fast as we went, we could not narrow the gap between us and the Sustrugi Five, who had really kicked it into another gear. Once in awhile I snuck a peek back to see how the Canadians were doing. Every time it seemed like they were narrowing the gap.

About a half hour away from Base Camp, as we were moving at a very quick clip, my right foot landed on a soft spot and postholed about eighteen inches. Instantaneously, I fell forward face first into the snow and slid to a stop.

"WOAH!" I yelled before I even hit the ground.

Luckily, my foot did not stick in the hole and I had no injury. Had I not fallen forward, propelling my foot out of the hole, my ankle probably would have snapped.

My sled was completely turned over behind me.

I scraped and dusted the snow off my pants and jacket as Vern unclipped and righted my sled. Fortunately, everything was tied on well and nothing had fallen out or I would have really heard it from Vern.

"Okay, I'm fine. Let's get going. Nice hole, huh?" I said, not sure if any of my team had seen why I fell.

About ten minutes later, we crested the top of a rise and Base Camp appeared in front of us, resembling a scattered bunch of rocks. The shadows completely washed out any color of the tents and I was not sure that was the camp at first, but as we approached it became clearer.

I watched as the Sustrugi Five finally pulled into Base Camp about ten minutes ahead of us. They headed over to the right where we had cached a lot of gear and seemed to be having a good time.

In retrospect, I should not have been watching them. In that moment of distraction, one of my left crampon spikes caught on the side of my right overboot.

Shit.

I was airborne again, this time falling slightly to my left, head and shoulder first. My sled almost slid over me in the process.

This time it was completely my fault. I had let myself relax before getting to the finish line. Dumb move, but there was nothing I could say.

"That was awesome! You guys should try it," I said lamely.

Five minutes later we arrived at Base Camp, only a few minutes ahead of the Canadians, thereby claiming priority for the flight out.

The Sustrugi Five had already broke out cans of beer which had been hidden in the cache for the celebration of returning from the summit. Mark and Craig seemed especially animated about downing some brews.

Moments later, Vern handed us cans of beer as well. All of the beers were so cold that when we pulled the pop top, the beer oozed out continuously in a slushy, almost frozen spew that would not stop. I found myself sucking the beer down in large gulps to try to avoid spilling it, assuming that the foaming would stop after a few gulps. But it just kept streaming out, until at some point I just let it drain out onto the snow. I did not want to get completely wasted.

Fortunately, I was wise enough to keep my gloves on as I held the beer. We had all avoided any bit of frostbite up to this point and they had warned us not to touch any cold metal with bare hands. One of the Sustrugi Five, in his excitement, failed to heed this warning, holding his beer between his thumb and second finger for a bit too long. By the time we arrived at Patriot Hills, he realized that his thumb and finger were frostbitten, with nasty looking blistering at the tips. It was a costly mistake.

Ironically, our rush back to Base Camp was for naught. The weather did not permit any Twin Otters to fly in from Patriot Hills that evening, so reluctantly we had to set up tents and wait once again for the next flight.

The rest of the trip was an exercise of patience.

Each time the ALE coordinator came to talk to us the next day, the weather did not permit any flights from Patriot Hills. Every two hours, the story was the same. Glimmers of sun peaking out sporadically gave us hope, only to be dashed by the next announcement. We were going nowhere fast.

But, on the evening of the second day back at Vinson Base Camp, after a cloud filled day of sledding nearby slopes and sitting around doing nothing, we finally got news that the Twin Otters were on their way. A two hour window of visibility was predicted, just enough to whisk us off the Branscomb Glacier and back to Patriot Hills.

As soon as the signal was given, the entire camp jumped into frenzied action. Sleeping bags were stuffed, bed rolls rolled, back packs filled and tents dismantled in record time. Everything had to be taken with us.

Within a half hour, everything was loaded on sleds and pulled down to the end of the "runway" where the planes would land.

The cloud cover was still very low in front of us. To me, it was difficult to see how a plane could land in those conditions. But sure enough, the planes were coming.

We heard the Twin Otters before we could see them. Then like a mosquito approaching through the mist, the first plane glided towards us, its skis smoothly shussing onto the snow in front of us. The second plane was only a few minutes behind.

Once again I mostly watched as the Russian pilots and a few of the guides loaded the planes. On the trip to Vinson Camp, the plane had been pretty spacious, with minimal gear stowed. But now, with this being the last flight out for all the guides and climbing teams, our plane would be filled to the brim.

When they finally finished loading and I stepped up the ladder to find a seat, I saw that almost one half of the passenger area was crammed with baggage almost to the ceiling. There were just enough seats for us to sit double to the left side with about eight inches of aisle to squeeze through to get to the seats.

Despite the added weight, the planes seemed to have no problem taking off. Soon we were turning left towards Patriot Hills and waving goodbye to Mt. Vinson.

The next thirty minutes was the most spectacular flight I have ever experienced. Due to the low cloud cover, or maybe just because the Russian pilots wanted to give us a thrill, the plane stayed low, tucked in among the peaks of the Ellsworth Range.

It was as if we were in the middle of an actual IMAX film.

Deep crevasses which looked like tiny cracks on our way over to Vinson now looked like deep craters only a few hundred feet below us. The craggy grey peaks loomed right outside our windows. As the pilots weaved along the valleys between the peaks, we were treated to unbelievably beautiful views so "up close and personal" that photographs through the windows could not do it justice.

Awesome. Awesome. Awesome...even more awesome. Why do I not have a movie camera?

About halfway to Patriot Hills, the clouds disappeared and the sky cleared ahead of us. The planes ascended to more normal flight pattern. Soon we recognized the hills beyond the Patriot Hills camp and shortly after that, the multiple tents came into view.

Landing perpendicular to the "blue ice" runway, I could see that the landing zone was marked with black garbage bags somehow pinned into the snow.

The Twin Otter landed as smoothly as it had taken off. Even though we were still over 2000 miles from civilization, I felt like we had made it home.

That feeling disappeared as soon as the door was opened and the cold wind hit us like a jack hammer. As we steeped off the plane, forty mile an hour winds swept across the camp, battering tents and whipping loose snow in all directions.

"First things first," Vern announced. "Let's get the tents up."

"In this wind?" someone asked.

"In this wind," Vern confirmed.

For the next thirty to forty minutes, we struggled to erect five tents among the two groups. The key was to kick in large metal anchors on the upwind side of the tent, get the smaller pins into the ice and snow, then hang onto the tent fly with all my strength while its ropes were secured.

After we finally got four of the tents up and secured, Vern decided that it would be better for all of the tents to be in a perfect line, to serve as wind blocks to each other.

You've got to be kidding.

I didn't say anything out loud, but couldn't help but wonder why in the hell he had not told us to set them up in a line until after we did the work.

Eventually, we put four tents in a line and Jim and Johan moved their tent over near some other group's tents. Later when it was time to go to bed I figured out why. They had decided that with nine guys in all and five tents, the worst snorer (that being me) would have his own tent. Jim and Johan wanted to get as far away from it as possible. That was okay with me. A tent to myself made the rest of the stay at Patriot Hills quite pleasant as I caught up on much needed sleep, unconcerned about keeping any tent mate up at night.

And sleep we did. And played Hearts we did. And played chess we did. And read books we did. And flew kites we did. And listened to nightly lectures on glaciers melting, global warming, and dogsledding we did. And dug snow in big bins to melt for water we did. And ate everything we could get our hands on we did. And pinched card board boxes of really bad wine from the fancy ALE tent we did – and drank until even Vern, Jim and Dave's guitar playing and singing sounded good!

For three long days and sun-filled nights we waited for the illusive Illyushin to arrive. "Weather permitting" had gotten us again. The cross winds on the "blue ice" runway were too stiff for the huge cargo plane to land. At least that's what they told us. Only, when we hiked down to the runway once or twice each day, there was no wind.

What are they waiting for?

There was nothing we could do but make the most of it. I battled with Craig for Hearts supremacy before getting completely creamed in a game on the third day. I managed to split four games of chess with Todd, who was clearly the better player but left me a few openings for surprise counter attacks. Steve was the chess master, taking seventeen straight games from others. I did not even bother to try to play him. Vern showed off with his parachute driven ski antics and then with some amazing kite flying. These kites were large, like small rectangular parachutes, and very difficult to control in gusty winds. Several times the whole group roared with laughter as Jim or Craig slid hundreds of yards across the ice on their butts, hanging onto the kites for dear life.

Finally, on the third full day after arriving from Vinson at about 11:00 p.m., we got word that the Illyushin was airborne, coming in our direction.

Once again, the whole camp immediately moved into action. With the end of the season and the long delay for the plane, there were fifty-four climbers, guides and South Pole skiers ready to go back to Punta Arenas. Everyone was ready to go and I watched with amazement as the tents were dismantled and packs were packed. Everything in the whole place, except for the group dining tents and staff tents, was marked and piled into heaps for the ALE folks to shuttle down to the runway.

When the Illyushin appeared in the sky, Craig and Mark danced a modified shag on the ice in front of our dining tent, climaxing with Craig executing a nice takedown and falling on top of Mark.

Our trip to Antarctica had come to an end. I was ready to go home.

POSTLOGUE

My Aconcagua guide, Eric, successfully reached the top of Everest from the Tibet side in May 2007. My tent mate on Aconcagua, Al from Colorado, at age 57, climbed Everest from the Nepal side in May, 2008, shortly after the higher sections of the peak were reopened following the Olympic flame being carried to the top by Chinese athletes.

Despite these successes of fellow climbers, I have chosen not to pursue Everest or McKinley. Based on my risk-to-reward ratio scale and in order to live up to my promises to my wife, I will have to celebrate other friends' accomplishments on those two mountains.

However, I have not stopped climbing. In July, 2008 and August 2009, I climbed Mt. Harvard, Grey's Peak and Torrey's Peak in Colorado with my son, adding three more 14,000'ers to my resume. Harvard is not a very tough mountain, but I had a great time with Daniel on a beautiful day. We reached the summits of Grey's and Torrey's Peak on the same afternoon on an equally clear day. In January 2009, I climbed Mt. Koscuiszko in Australia with my wife, Kim, and both children (it is only slightly over 7300 feet high), adding the fifth of the Seven Summits to my list. It was more of a stroll than a climb, but it was fun to see my wife join us at the top. Carstensz Pyramid in Indonesia, considered by some to be the seventh of the summits, is a bit too much of a technical rock climb for my comfort level and skills, so I am happy to go with the traditionalists who count Koscuiszko as the seventh.

I still plan to climb Mt. Rainier, having been turned back twice by weather and avalanche risk in 2009 and 2010. And before I get too old, I expect to talk my brother, Brent, into doing a Nepal trek, possibly up to the Everest base camp or up Island Peak, a nearby 21,000 peak. It is always best to keep the options open.

Despite my successes, I consider myself merely a regular guy who likes to do extraordinary climbs. I am far from a professional mountaineer. Let's face it, Ed Viesters, Wally Berg, David Brashears, Vern Tejas, and many others like them, are not regular guys. Their body fat levels don't even register on the scales. They are super-conditioned humans who have devoted their lives and careers to the art of climbing. Viesters gave up a promising career as a veterinarian to climb all fourteen 8000 meter peaks full-time, without supplemental oxygen, but with plenty of sponsors. Tejas climbs twelve months a year, reaching the summit of each of the Seven Summits once or even twice in the same year. For these alpine stars, it is not only a passion, but a business, a profession. I'm not even remotely in their league.

I have never had my body fat tested and probably would be embarrassed if I did. I love "Whoppers" malted milk balls, M&M's, cashews, potato chips, ice cream, Cokes, cookies, cheesecake....too much to keep the weight off when I'm not training.

I'm a husband, father, and lawyer first, and a mountain climber on the side. Climbing gives me something to look forward to, to train for, and to dream about. Most regular guys see the Everest IMAX movie and think, "Woah, I'd love to climb Everest with that Spanish babe," but they never pull the trigger or explore the possibilities of alpine adventure. Others are content with walking the flat quarter mile to the bottom of Lower Yosemite Falls or strolling among the geysers at Yellowstone, along with everyone else, including two year old children.

That has never been enough for me. Too pedestrian, too ordinary, too touristy. Too easy. Whenever I see a snow-capped mountain, I can't help myself from wondering if I can climb it. Better still if it is in a remote region of the world. I almost died on my family's recent trip to New Zealand when I was that close to Mt. Cook but did not have time to fit a climb into the schedule. I settled for a guided glacier climb with my son and daughter at the Franz Josef Glacier on the other side of the Southern Alps. A nice adventure, but not exactly strenuous.

But I digress. This book was not intended to explore the deep existential reasons for why people climb high altitude mountains. It has not provided any gripping tales of the many triumphs and disasters of various commercial mountain expeditions in the Himalayas. Jon Krakauer, Lincoln Hall and others have already "been there, done that." In any case, regular guys like me don't climb the 8000 meter peaks or journey into the death zones, because regular guys are simply not that crazy. Or more likely, their wives won't let them. Maybe that is why I'm alive to tell these stories, unlike many who have simply pushed the limits a few too many times.

Rather, in writing this book, I hope I have provided potential climbers with a close-up, personal view of how a complete amateur can somehow make his way up mountains much larger than he ever imagined and live to tell about every sordid detail of the experience, day by day and step by step. No glossing over the grime and sweat of climbing. No downplaying of my trepidation, exhaustion, or frustrations. Just the facts as I have experienced and perceived them first hand, with an acquired appreciation for what it takes to climb safely.

I love to climb, but I also love to share the joys and the fears of mountaineering with anyone who will listen. That is part of the glorious journey.

In my old age, I intend to return to Mt. Pisgah in Western, North Carolina. My father continued to climb it until shortly after his eightieth birthday. On that occasion, I stayed close to him all the way up and down, steadying him when he threatened to stumble or lose his balance. A few times, he scraped his arms or legs, but he was game for the challenge and proud to be able to reach the top once again. Better still, he enjoyed picking blueberries for the "Pisgah pie" my mother baked later that evening.

A final bit of advice: Enjoy the air, the climb, the accomplishment, and the return home, regardless of the size or location of the mountain. But in all cases, do your homework, plan the climb carefully, take the right equipment, get an experienced guide, train appropriately, stay safe, and wear strap-on crampons!

And one last thing. If it doesn't feel right or the weather gets too rough, turn around and come back another time. Your life may depend on it.

INDEX